D0072640

Annals of Gullibility

Annals of Gullibility

Why We Get Duped and How to Avoid It

STEPHEN GREENSPAN

Foreword *by Donald S. Connery*

For Carl & Leesa,
Always in my thoughts.
Love,
Steve Greenspan

PRAEGER

Westport, Connecticut
London

Library of Congress Cataloging-in-Publication Data

Greenspan, Stephen.
    Annals of gullibility : why we get duped and how to avoid it / Stephen Greenspan ;
foreword by Donald S. Connery.
        p.   cm.
    Includes bibliographical references and index.
    ISBN 978–0–313–36216–3 (alk. paper)
    1. Deception—Psychological aspects.   I. Title.
    BF637.D42G74   2009
    155.9′2–dc22   2008033231

British Library Cataloguing in Publication Data is available.

Library of Congress Catalog Card Number: 2008033231
ISBN: 978–0–313–36216–3

First published in 2009

Praeger Publishers, 88 Post Road West, Westport, CT 06881
An imprint of Greenwood Publishing Group, Inc.
www.praeger.com

Printed in the United States of America

The paper used in this book complies with the
Permanent Paper Standard issued by the National
Information Standards Organization (Z39.48–1984).

10 9 8 7 6 5 4 3 2 1

This book is dedicated to Richard Lapointe, an innocent man whose gullibility in believing lies told by his interrogators landed him in prison for life and started me on my journey to try and understand the phenomenon of gullibility. Like all of Richard's many friends, I pray that I will live long enough to see this nonviolent but too-trusting man regain his freedom.

Contents

Foreword

Donald S. Connery

Donald S. Connery, an author and former foreign correspondent for *Time* and *Life* magazines, is a long-time investigator of miscarriages of justice. His book *Guilty Until Proven Innocent* described the conviction and rescue of a teenager, Peter Reilly, who was led by police to falsely believe he had killed his mother, whereas *Convicting the Innocent* told of a mentally disabled man, Richard Lapointe, still wrongly imprisoned for murder, who agreed with police that he must have committed the crime he couldn't remember. An advisor to Northwestern Law School's Center on Wrongful Conviction, Connery has been a leading advocate for mandatory recording of all interrogations.

∾

Like a bunko artist, snake-oil salesman, or cult leader, I once gulled the gullible.

It was so easy. Perhaps because we are all too much inclined to believe what we read. Perhaps because World War Two was over and my fellow soldiers, eager to return to civilian life, were giddy and guileless as they headed home from the Pacific.

I was editor of the troopship newspaper. We were sailing from Tokyo to San Francisco. One day I reported that we would soon pass over the international dateline. Those troops wishing to see the fabled dateline in all its glory—a great, glowing, phosphorescent belt on the ocean bottom—should assemble at the stern at precisely 3 A.M. and stare into the sea.

The gathering of the gullible in the salty darkness was far greater than I anticipated. Hundreds of eyes searched the depths in vain. As disappointment turned to anger, I became The Man Most Likely to Be Thrown Overboard.

How I managed to save myself, I know not, but I could have benefited by the knowledge provided by Stephen Greenspan in this remarkable book.

Instead of just pleading for mercy, I could have argued:

> "Look, fellows, I'm not saying that gullibility is good, but it's no disgrace. It only shows you're human. Isn't it better to be a hopeful, trusting person instead of a cynic who expects the worst in everybody? And isn't life all about learning from experience? Actually, I think I did you a favor. You have learned the value of skepticism. From now on, remember the old saying: 'Fool me once, shame on you; fool me twice, shame on me.'"

What amazes me today, more than 60 years later, is that gullibility remains a subject set apart from normal conversation or serious examination. As the author says, it is "a very understudied phenomenon" despite the vital role it plays in human behavior. Is it just too embarrassing to mention?

Call it the part of our being that dares not speak its name.

Ask me about my bank account or my religious beliefs, if you must, but don't make me reveal that I once lost big bucks falling for the pitch of a fleet-footed scam artist who claimed to have seats to a sold-out Broadway musical. Don't remind me of the day in Bombay when I saw a street peddler selling Old Spice shaving lotion. Just what I need, I told myself. I discovered later that I had purchased an Old Spice throwaway recycled with ditch water.

Having read Professor Greenspan's manuscript before publication, I now feel a lot less foolish about such jarring moments of innocence, naïveté, credulity, and trust—or, more correctly—*gullibility*, which is not quite the same thing, as the author takes pains to inform us.

I now know that I am not alone. This book makes it clear that multitudes throughout history have been victimized by trusting the untrustworthy and believing the unbelievable. Great populations have succumbed to the wiles of charlatans. Hitler offers the worst-case scenario, bending the minds of Germany's educated millions to his will. "Professor" Harold Hill of *The Music Man* represents the more common and less harmful rascals who charm us out of our socks.

As a young reporter covering Senator Joe McCarthy, I had an up-close look at the great deceiver whose central role during the "Red scare" of the 1940s and 1950s puts his name on that noxious time in U.S. history.

One night in an American Legion hall in Appleton, Wisconsin (where the crowd roared as he began his speech with, "It's good to be out of Washington and back in America!"), he claimed that his briefcase contained secret documents proving the disloyalty of dozens of State Department traitors who had "lost China" and were now scheming to deliver the nation to the Kremlin.

Afterward, while admirers surrounded the senator, I sneaked a peek at the inside of his unlocked briefcase. It contained nothing but newspapers.

What amazes me is that no one before Steve Greenspan has so thoroughly and energetically opened the Pandora's Box of wonderments about a facet of the human personality that must first have been detected by a cave man con man. It appears to be true that, before this book, no substantial study of gullibility has appeared in the English language, and perhaps not in any language.

The answer may lie in the nature of the beast, making it slippery and mysterious, hard to nail down, even as it plays a significant role in our lives. Growing up, becoming truly adult, means putting aside our childish illusions—about Santa Claus and other fables—and taking care not to take things at face value. Yet we fail repeatedly to question our sources of information, we too often accept falsehoods as truths, and we take Google as gospel.

Gullibility is not generally seen as an affliction yet it can do us terrible harm: losing our life savings to a swindler, falling in love with a sweet-talking scoundrel, or putting our health in the hands of a Dr. Feelgood. We are all at daily risk, although some of us far more than others, for reasons the author diligently explores.

It is no small achievement wrestling this subject to the ground because it encompasses so much as it serves as at least a partial explanation for real and fictional events of amazing global range and variety.

Indeed, what other topic encompasses—just for starters—Rasputin, Machiavelli, lobotomies, *Pinocchio*, UFOs, political spin doctors, the Trojan horse, "refrigerator mothers," multiple personality disorder, William F. Buckley Jr. as a convict's dupe, the Dutch Tulip Bubble, and other all-time great scams, and the invisibility both of "The Emperor's New Clothes" and weapons of mass destruction as an excuse for invading Iraq?

(I choose not to offend the reader or devastate our vast advertising and public relations industries by mentioning gullible gulping on a massive scale—the billions of bottles of expensive water purchased by Americans who enjoy the best free water in the world.)

Professor Greenspan must have felt at times that he was wrestling with not just one octopus but also a whole family of octopi. Where in the world's literature is there not some occasion of gullibility? His reading has been prodigious. The voluminous references suggest an explorer reveling in his quest for revelations and finding, like King Midas, that everything he touches is gold.

At some point, the author surely realized that gullibility, as a subject, was so entertaining, despite the seriousness of it all, that the book he had in mind was in peril of being—perish the thought—readable! What would his fellow PhDs think?

I am reminded of my old professor (later ambassador), John Kenneth Galbraith, who was derided by fellow economists for writing books that dared to be popular as well as weighty. The reader should be warned that the foxy author evades such a fate by claiming that he is simply writing in a "semi-scholarly manner."

As I see it, this is a ruse to give himself license to regale us with innumerable juicy stories about gullibility's victims and victimizers while frequently confessing to the embarrassments of his own lifetime of insufficient skepticism. He feels free to venture into controversial areas, notably religion. Few things in these pages intrigue me more than his description of Jesus Christ, so often portrayed as dreamy and unworldly, as a figure of sharp intellect who was "nobody's fool."

For all the pleasures of these pages, the reader should know that the seed for the idea of this volume was planted during circumstances that demonstrate how a person's gullibility can literally be a matter of life and death.

Before Steve moved to Colorado, the two of us in Connecticut were caught up in a valiant movement by ordinary (yet truly extraordinary) citizens seeking to expose and overturn a horrific miscarriage of justice. He tells here of the plight of the brain-damaged, mentally limited, family man wrongly convicted in 1992 of murdering his wife's grandmother. State prosecutors came close to convincing the jury that he deserved the death penalty.

Lacking actual proof that he did the deed, the police had preyed on his vulnerability to suggestion. Nine hours of psychological battering produced a false confession. He lacked the ability to recognize the lies, ploys, and deceits that detectives everywhere in America are routinely trained to use on suspects in the secrecy of high-pressure interrogation chambers.

Although his gullibility doomed the man to a life behind bars, where he remains today despite all rescue efforts, it is the gullibility of the cops, prosecutors, jurors, and judges—in this case and almost all false confession cases—that is even more striking. Despite a mountain of evidence to the contrary, they believe (or choose to believe) the old myth, convenient for closing cases, that innocent people, unless crazy or tortured, do not confess to crimes.

Thus was Steve, as a psychologist, propelled to probe deeply into the whole business of susceptibility to persuasion. For myself, as a journalist busy investigating our deeply flawed criminal justice system, the experience solidified my sense that far too little was known about why some people are not easily bamboozled and others seem to be sitting ducks for purveyors of baloney.

The findings of this book suggest that every field of endeavor, every profession, every set of human interaction, is replete with examples of people too willing to exploit the gullibility of others, and other people, even if aware of the value of exercising critical judgment, all too ready and even eager to be exploited.

In my own line of work, the picture is too painful to contemplate. A grizzled wire-service editor told me long ago to make sure of my facts. "If your mother tells you she loves you," he growled, "check it out!" Yet one of my childhood heroes, Lincoln Steffens, the great muckraker, was so bedazzled by the promises of the Soviet Union that he famously declared, in the face of rising evidence of vast communist cruelties, "I have seen the future, and it works!"

Even as I dedicated myself to avoiding such folly, I found that the flip side of serious journalism was a wild world of invention (think lurid tabloids sold in supermarkets) aimed at gulling credulous readers. The British "popular press" made it an art form long before I was born.

In 1959, as the New Delhi bureau chief for *Time* and *Life* magazines, I was one of a raucous bunch of competing correspondents waiting on India's northwestern border for the Dalai Lama to emerge from the mists of Tibet. Each of us wanted to be the first to greet the young "god-king" as he escaped the Chinese troops at his heels. Yet the Indian army forbade us from crossing the border by vehicle, elephant, rented aircraft or any other means.

That didn't stop London's multimillion circulation *Daily Mail* from splashing across its front page an utterly fictitious story by its intrepid byliner, Noel Barber, who claimed to have flown over the Dalai Lama's procession deep in Tibet. He told how he looked down on the saffron robes and burning incense of the brave Buddhists trudging toward the free world. Banging away at his typewriter in our tea plantation lodge, Barber knew that his editors knew that it was all make believe. But, as he told me without apology, "our readers must be served."

Nothing remotely so cynical would ever be contemplated by the editors of America's most respected newspapers. Nonetheless, such great dailies as *The New York Times*, *The Washington Post*, and *USA Today* have fallen victim in recent times to fake or colorfully embellished stories, including a Pulitzer prize-winning series of articles, by several of their star reporters. Some of the best editors in the world had allowed themselves to be suckered.

I tell myself: if this stuff happens in the field I know best, what must it be like in business, science, medicine, sports, the arts, and everywhere else? Are we all living in a fool's paradise, being conned at every turn? Are some of us willingly gullible because it is delicious to imagine winning the lottery or greeting space aliens?

What I know for sure is that a deep look at this subject is long overdue. As encyclopedic as this work may seem, the author himself would say that it is by no means the last word on the subject. Okay, fine, but I can't imagine a better beginning.

—Kent, Connecticut,
July 2008

Acknowledgments

If I listed all of the people who have helped me throughout my career, including during my pursuit of the elusive construct of gullibility, I would need many pages. So I will here just limit myself to those who have directly assisted me with this manuscript. I wish, specifically, to express my deep appreciation to the following:

J. David Smith, Robert Shilkret, Robert Schalock, Harvey Switzky, James Patton, Bob Perske, Linda Hickson, Sharon Borthwick-Duffy, Gail Kara, Phillip Guddemi, and Laraine Glidden for their warm encouragement.

Donald S. Connery for early on appreciating the importance of this topic and believing in my ability to produce a worthwhile book about it.

Donald Klingner, for carefully reading and commenting on a much longer orginal draft.

Irma Ned Bailey and Michael Seidel, for answering questions about Swift and Gulliver.

Penny Colman, Alan Taddiken, and Peter Love for generously providing clippings and books.

Valerie Stone, for collaborating on a measure of social vulnerability.

Holly Sumner, for educating me about art gullibility.

My editor at Praeger, Deborah Carvalko, for being both supportive and wise.

My sister, Paula Zitrin, and her husband Roger Zitrin, for helping me secure the leisure to work on this book.

My wife Helen Apthorp, and my sons, Alex and Eli Greenspan, for putting up with my piles of papers and for never doubting that I would eventually pull this off.

CHAPTER 1

Introduction

OVERVIEW OF THE BOOK

The bulk of this book, specifically chapters 2–8, is taken up with stories depicting various forms of gullibility: religious, political, financial, and so on. This accounts for the book's title, *Annals of Gullibility*.

Chapters 1, 9, and 10 deal with theoretical and conceptual issues pertaining to gullibility. This chapter provides an orientation to the topic, including reasons for writing the book, a definition of gullibility, an explanatory model describing four factors that contribute to a gullible outcome, and a discussion of nonhuman gullibility, developmental factors, and the role of gullibility as a form of "foolish action."

Chapter 9 addresses various questions that arise from a consideration of the stories presented in chapters 2–8. These questions include a discussion of the role of affect and self-deception, and an exploration of the extent to which gullible individuals are deserving of some moral blame for their own failings. Finally, in chapter 10, I provide some tips that can possibly reduce one's tendency toward gullibility or at least protect oneself and others from its more serious consequences.

WHY A BOOK ON GULLIBILITY?

This book is the first of several that I hope will contribute to the development of an interdisciplinary field of Gullibility Studies. This book, aimed at a general audience, explores a variety of stories, taken from world literature or from real life. These stories detail the many ways in which overly trusting people (or puppets, in the case of *Pinocchio*) have been duped. My hope is that these stories will contribute to an understanding of a puzzling phenomenon, namely why people, sometimes of high intelligence and education, are duped.

Gullibility is a topic to which most people can relate. Someone whom we trusted has duped all of us on occasion, and we all know people whose extreme gullibility has gotten them into serious difficulty. Yet the small scholarly literature on gullibility exists mostly in professional journals. Attention to gullibility has been mainly by writers of fiction, where a number of great plays (e.g., *Othello*) and novels (e.g., the works of Mark Twain) have taken gullibility as a central theme.

Although my rationale in writing this book is mainly to bring more attention to an overlooked aspect of human behavior, I admit to having some personal reasons as well. One humorous, but largely true, definition of a psychologist is "someone who studies things he is bad at." I was unusually gullible as a child, and still continue to have gullible moments as an adult. Furthermore, I have known people, as in cases of coerced confession to murder, whose lives have been destroyed by their inability to know when to be nontrusting. Thus, this book serves a somewhat therapeutic purpose for me, as it has allowed me to explore a topic that has been occasionally problematic for me, as well as for people whom I care about.

WHAT IS GULLIBILITY?

Gullibility can be defined as an unusual tendency toward being duped or taken advantage of. Obviously, all of us can be duped on occasion. But the term gullibility really refers to a pattern of being duped, which repeats itself in different settings, even in the face of warning signs. This can be seen in a letter to Dear Abby, from a woman who was inclined to marry her philandering ex-husband for the third time, and who constantly falls for his line: "This time, I've changed." As Abby pointed out to the woman, for her to actually believe such a line in the face of her long and painful history with this man is a sign of misplaced trust and foolish thought processes. A key difference between gullibility and the related construct of credulity is that gullibility typically involves some concrete action, such as handing over a check to a con artist, or tying the knot to the same person for the third time, as in the example just presented. Thus, gullibility involves some degree of being coerced, and can be understood as resulting from a special, psychological, form of coercion.

As mentioned, a related construct is *credulity*. This term refers to a tendency to believe things that on their face are ridiculous or that lack adequate supporting evidence. Credulity differs from gullibility in that, as mentioned, there is an action component to gullibility (e.g., writing a check to pay for the Brooklyn Bridge), whereas credulity mainly involves a state of belief or conviction (e.g., that someone actually can own it). The two terms are related, in that gullible outcomes typically come about through the exploitation of a victim's credulity. Thus, when the early 20th-century con artist Charles Ponzi sought money for his bogus pyramid investment scheme (involving trading of prepaid overseas postal vouchers), the success of the scam depended on the credulity of his, mostly unsophisticated, immigrant victims in believing the feasibility of the money-making scheme.

Gullibility builds on credulity (which may be considered a largely cognitive factor), but has a coercive element that also takes advantage of affective factors (in the case of a Ponzi scheme, greed) and also has situational elements (such as a salesperson making false claims or a neighbor telling you how much money he made on the scheme). Despite the action component in gullibility, however, gullibility and credulity are actually quite close in meaning, and public usage of the term *gullibility* may be closer to the term *credulity* as I have defined it.

Trust is a construct that is obviously related to gullibility. Gullibility always involves an act of trusting someone or some assertion, when skepticism or inaction might have been more appropriate. Exploiters are people who understand the reluctance of others to appear untrusting and are willing to take advantage of that reluctance. So is gullibility nothing more than trust, and is mistrust the antidote to gullibility? One hopes not, as that would make for a pretty cynical and grim world. No, as pointed out by the late psychologist Julian Rotter (1980), gullibility is not so much equivalent to trust as it is to a foolish or naïve application of trust in situations where the warning signs are fairly evident. Trust is a very positive and healthy trait to possess, and the challenge is not to always withhold trust but to be able to recognize those (hopefully infrequent) occasions when wariness is appropriate and even necessary for one's wellbeing.

WHAT ARE THE CAUSES OF GULLIBILITY?

Probably the main reason why there has been so little research on gullibility is that there are many factors that can contribute to a gullible outcome, and it is difficult to say for any individual which one was most important. In discussing

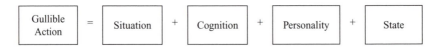

Figure 1.1 Proposed explanatory model of gullibility.

the various cases in this book, I touch on four broad explanatory factors, each of which can be subdivided further. These factors are situations, cognition, personality, and state. These factors can be put into an additive model, as depicted in Fig. 1.1. What this means is that a gullible outcome occurs out of a mix of these four factors, which make variable degrees of contribution to the outcome depending on the situation and the person.

Briefly, this model (a more complex version of which can be found in Greenspan, Loughlin, & Black, 2001) can be expressed by the formula:

$$\text{Gullible Action} = \text{Situation} + \text{Cognition} + \text{Personality} + \text{State}.$$

What this means is that a gullible outcome (such as handing over a check to a con artist) is the result of a complex interaction among four sets of factors:

1. the social situation (presumably the con man was very persuasive, or there may have been others who vouched for his honesty);
2. cognitive processes (perhaps the victim was bad at reading people or naïve about the type of investment covered by the scam);
3. personality (perhaps the victim was a highly trusting or weak person who has difficulty saying "no"); and
4. state (perhaps the victim was exhausted or inebriated or highly infatuated with the con man).

Individually, any of the four factors could, if the valences were strong enough, explain a gullible outcome. However, in most cases of gullible behavior, at least two of these factors are at work.

By portraying the equation as additive (or, if one prefers, multiplicative), it is my intention to suggest that any gullible action could be a result of one or several of these factors acting in combination. Because gullibility is a relative outcome, the model could be used to explain a nongullible act just as well as it explains a gullible act. Thus, if someone is able to resist a con man's pitch and not hand over a check, it could be a result of the con man being unskilled, or the potential victim might have possessed the smarts or personality strength

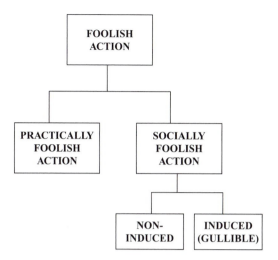

Figure 1.2 Types of foolish action.

to have seen through or resisted him, or it might have been that the victim was in a highly alert and vigilant state.

In each of the gullibility stories discussed in this book, one or more of the elements in the model are mentioned as a likely contributor to behavior described in that story. I save a more detailed treatment of the full model until the last part of this book, in which I discuss some general questions such as "How does self-deception contribute to gullibility?" and "How can naïve individuals be helped to be less gullible?"

GULLIBILITY AS A FORM OF "FOOLISH ACTION"

To fully understand the nature of gullibility, it is useful to consider it a form of "foolish action" (for a fuller discussion, see Greenspan, 2009). There are two major categories of foolish action, as depicted in Fig. 1.2: "practically foolish action" and "socially foolish action." Socially foolish action is further subdivided into "noninduced" and "induced" subtypes, and gullibility can be considered synonymous with induced socially foolish action.

Foolish action involves behavior that has a high likelihood of backfiring, sometimes with disastrous consequences because of a failure to take into account one or more serious risks, which are obvious to most people of the same age and should have given the actor pause. A practically foolish act is one in which the potentially serious consequence is physical. An example would be smoking a cigarette near a gasoline can or driving a pickup truck with children sitting in the bed. A socially foolish act is one in which the potentially serious consequence is interpersonal.

DEVELOPMENTAL FACTORS IN GULLIBILITY AND ITS DIMINUTION

Although many adults behave gullibly, children are far more likely to behave gullibly. Understanding this fact, and the process (particularly the cognitive or credulity process) by which children develop into less gullible adults, is likely to come from an examination of the ideas of the great Swiss developmental psychologist Jean Piaget.

A major finding of Piaget's is that the thinking of young children is "precausal." That is, young children tend to assume that two events that occur at the same time are causally related, without attempting to understand logically the possible mechanism that might explain such a causal relationship. An example would be wanting something to happen, and when it happens assuming that one's wanting brought it about. Precausal thinking may be considered magical, in that events are not viewed as conforming to laws of nature but to supernatural forces, especially one's own thoughts and actions. And magical thinking, as I argue throughout this book, is a contributor to many of the beliefs and behaviors that are considered gullible.

In *The Child's Conception of the World*, Piaget (1926/1969) described four types of magical thinking in young children (the typology and my choice of examples borrows heavily from Vyse, 1997):

1. "Participation between action and things" occurs when a child superstitiously believes that his or her action (such as drawing a curtain quickly) will stave off something bad (such as being attacked by robbers while one sleeps).

2. "Participation between thoughts and things" involves the belief that one's thoughts can influence outcomes. An example is a girl practicing being a teacher who gives good grades to her friends, and then believes that this is what actually caused them to later get good grades).

3. "Participation between objects" refers to the belief that the action of an object at one occasion influences its action at another time (one example reflecting the pervasive belief that inanimate objects are conscious, is a girl who would no longer play competitively with a set of marbles again,

because she was convinced that they would want to be returned to the girl she had won them from).

4. "Animism," or the idea that all inanimate objects are volitional living things (an example can be seen in a boy who believes that the moon follows him around as he walks at night).

The magical and superstitious thinking of children was explored by Piaget in a number of studies, in which he used the "semi-clinical" method, which relies on somewhat free-form verbal interviews. Piaget found that underlying the magical and precausal thinking of young children was what he termed *egocentrism*, a style of thinking that reflects a confusion between the child and others, and a form of solipsism, in which the child believes that everything revolves around him or her (e.g., if a parent became sick it was because the child had a bad thought). Egocentrism is a process that persists in different forms in middle childhood and adolescence, and may explain why vestiges of magical thinking persist in many individuals throughout their lives, despite their general abandonment of primitive thinking styles in favor of the more systematic modes of thinking characteristic of adults.

At the heart of Piaget's research on cognitive development is the finding that children's thinking develops universally through invariant stage sequences. Although he was mainly interested in exploring cognitive development as it manifests typically across the broad population of children and youth, Piaget (1926/1969) did raise the possibility that vestiges of magical thinking persist in some adults and are at the root of their gullible susceptibility to various superstitions. He believed that magical thinking in adults was most likely to manifest itself "when the boundary between the self and the external world becomes momentarily vague and uncertain" (p. 162).

Three circumstances, in particular, are most likely to pull for a magical response in adults: "involuntary imitation, anxiety, and the state of 'monoideic' desire" (p. 162). An example of the first circumstance (not used by Piaget, who doesn't appear to have been interested in sports) is when a man watching a horse race rides in his seat along with the jockey in an effort to help his favorite horse win. An example of the second circumstance, magical thinking triggered by anxiety, is the routine that Piaget attributed to a "lecturer" (who I strongly suspect was him) that required him to walk to the podium in a certain manner to ensure that the lecture would be successful.

Piaget did not define the term *monoideic*, but from his examples it appears to involve a state of appeal to some higher power to keep a bad thing from happening. An example of monoideic desire given by Piaget was when a man (again likely him) riding home in a storm on a bicycle became concerned that a tire would burst, and engaged in various mind exercises to keep that catastrophe from happening.

At the heart of the magical thinking of adults, according to Piaget, is a residue of precausal *artificialism*. This term refers to the idea that all things in the universe were manufactured by people. Although on first glance, this notion might appear to be derived from conventional religious beliefs (e.g., about God creating the world in 7 days), Piaget marshaled considerable evidence to suggest that this is not the case. Instead, he built on the ideas of his famous predecessor at the University of Geneva, Pierre Bovet, who argued that the origins of religious feelings (and the receptivity of children to externally communicated conventional religious beliefs) can be found in the magical powers attributed by a young child to his or her parents.

Piaget wrote that the "real religion" of the young child, which "he will later transfer to God" (p. 354), grows out of the child's initial view of his parents as all powerful and, essentially, as the creator of both natural and social objects and laws. Piaget cited a case, first described by Bovet, in which a young boy named "Hebbel" expressed amazement at seeing his father upset over a wind that had blown down some trees. This was Hebbel's first realization that his father was not omnipotent. Similarly, Piaget cited the case of a little girl who begged her aunt to make the rain come. The artificialism of the child does not stem, according to Piaget, from "the pressure of education," but is "an original tendency, characteristic of child mentality, and penetrating...deep into the emotional and intellectual life of the child" (pp. 354–355).

Central to the various forms of precausal and magical thinking is the notion of *participation*. This term refers to the idea that two beings or phenomena are in a relationship to each other, even though there is no logical causal connection or contact between them. The decline in magical thinking that occurs in middle childhood and adolescence is not a reflection of experience, as "no direct experience can prove to a mind inclined towards animism that the sun and the clouds are neither live nor conscious" (pp. 384–385). Nor is it attributable to adult instruction, as children and adults do not talk about such things (Piaget's great genius lay in getting children to talk about things they had never talked about before and that neither scientists nor caregivers had ever thought to ask them about before).

The abandonment of participation, and of related concepts such as animism and artificialism, results from, according to Piaget, the decrease in egocentrism that occurs throughout middle childhood and early adolescence, a decrease that reflects the development of language and thought in general and that undoubtedly reflects in large part biological processes of brain maturation.

The "child gradually comes to assume an objective standpoint in regard to things and consequently to abandon the ideas of participation on which animism and artificialism are nourished" (p. 385). Nevertheless, residues of magical thinking can be found in most adults (more in some than in others) and, this undoubtedly, explains in part why humans are such a gullible species.

IS GULLIBILITY UNIQUE TO HUMANS?

The use of, and susceptibility to, deception is not confined to human beings, so it is worth asking the question "Is gullibility a purely human phenomenon?" The answer is "probably not," although the focus of this book, except for the following brief discussion, is entirely on the human manifestations of gullibility.

The question of gullibility in machines was raised by Steven Spielberg and his late collaborator, Stanley Kubrick, in the movie *AI* and, even more so, by Carlo Collodi (1881/1968), in his classic children's book *Pinocchio*, on which *AI* was loosely based. (See a more in-depth discussion of these two works in chap. 2.) Both works deal with artificial boys—an electronic version in *AI* and a wooden one in *Pinocchio*—who become separated from their imprinted human parental figures (mother in *AI*, father in *Pinocchio*) as a result of their extreme gullibility. For Spielberg and Collodi, there is no question that machines are inherently gullible; the real challenge is to make them sufficiently less gullible to survive in a human world filled with cruelty, deception, and manipulation. In fact, the message of these works (especially *Pinocchio*, where the theme of gullibility is much more fully developed) is that the hallmark of being a competent grown-up human is the ability to move from childish gullibility to adult skepticism in the face of interpersonal deception. The challenge in creating a machine that can have any hope of replacing humans is, thus, to give it the ability to see through the double dealing of humans.

Implications of machine gullibility for human adaptation come into play when considering various computerized devices intended to assist physically and mentally handicapped individuals in performing various everyday tasks. Most of the attention by computer scientists and disability professionals has been directed at addressing physical or routine social challenges (such as getting to work, cooking a meal, or paying one's bills), but successful independent functioning also depends on the ability to cope with nonroutine social challenges, such as deceptive financial or sexual manipulation. (Interestingly, a possible partial explanation for the general failure of computers to defeat the top chess champions may be an inability to use or see through deceptive chess moves.) Thus, what is generally viewed as a wholly nonsocial problem may sometimes turn out to have a significant sociocognitive component.

The topic of gullibility in the plant world was raised by Michael Pollan (2001) in his book *The Botany of Desire* (actually, he mentioned gullibility not in the book but in a radio interview in which he talked about the book). For Pollan, the issue of gullibility arose not so much in the gullibility of plants as in the gullibility of humans, and other animals such as bees, toward plants. Pollan stated that his inspiration for writing the book came when he was working in his garden and decided to take the perspective of the plants he was tending. When he did that, Pollan had the insight that his plants would be saying to themselves something along the lines of "boy, those bees (and humans) are really gullible." What he meant by this is that humans, and bees, exist in a symbiotic relationship with plants, and they do the plants' bidding as much, or more, than the plants do their bidding. Thus, when humans clear trees to plant a grain crop, they are creating an environment in which that crop can get its need to survive and expand met, as much as the crop is getting the humans' need for food met.

The specific nature of plant deception is addressed by Rue (1994). He described deception by plants as "morphological," rather than "behavioral." By this he meant that certain deceptive structures or physical processes have been developed through evolution to attain certain plant ends, and there is no element of motivated behavior on the part of the plant to use or activate those elements. An example would be the presence of certain colors, shapes, and smells in certain plants (such as orchids) that serve to lure bees into pseudo-copulation, thus pollinating the plants. The bee in such a scenario is described by Rue (1994) as a "dupe," indicating gullibility on its part.

As one moves up the phylogenetic chain, deception is more likely to be behavioral (i.e., motivated and intentional) and gullibility is more likely to occur in response to such behavioral deception. Certainly, anyone who owns a dog or a cat knows that these pets can be duped. In the children's book *Across Five Aprils* by Irene Hunt (1965/1986), Jethro noticed that his sheepdog Shep was missing. Billy, a neighbor boy, told Jethro that "he had seen a man patting Shep, and when the man whistled Shep went running after him. . . . Jethro was annoyed at Shep's gullibility" (p. 106). My late dog Sheba, a shepherd mix, was similarly likely to go off with anyone who showed an interest in her. This came in handy sometimes, as when I wanted to put her out of the house, all I had to do was to pretend that I was leaving. It was not enough to merely open the front door (Sheba became wise to that) but as soon as I stepped part way out the door, she would exit, after which I could step back and close the door behind her. This trick always worked, no matter how many thousands of times I used it. The reason, of course, is that going out for a walk or ride was one of Sheba's great pleasures, and I actually stepped through the door with her enough times (thus giving her "intermittent reinforcement") that she was willing to bet on my coming out with her, and she was unwilling to run the risk of being left alone in the house, if she could help it. Thus, Sheba's gullibility in such a situation was a function of the very strong motivation she had to be in my presence, and to go for walks or rides with me outside. What makes dogs and other animals, such as cats, so "gullible" is the ease with which they can be tricked by using some simple physical ruse (such as luring a cat out of a hiding space using some favorite food item).

Behavioral deception is sometimes seen in nonprimate mammals. This usually is triggered by simple threat or aggression situations, and does not involve complex role-taking ability. Examples include female coyotes who sometimes use sexual wiles to lure unsuspecting male dogs into ambushes by coyote confederates (Warner, 2000); opossums and some species of fox, who feign death to avoid being attacked (Rue, 1994); and a dog, who has been observed (Rue, 1994) to lure its owner out of an easy chair by feigning a desire to go outside, only to jump on the chair when it is vacated (this may be termed "Sheba's revenge").

Systematic observations (as opposed to informal reports) of complex deceptive behavior have been done mainly for nonhuman primates. This is because primates are the only animals, other than humans, who show evidence of possessing "theory of mind," an ability that normally develops in humans in early or middle childhood, and that appears to be a prerequisite for social deception. Theory of mind involves the ability to put oneself in the shoes of other organisms, or to think about the mental processes going on inside the heads of other organisms. Obviously, successful duping in humans (as seen in con men) depends, to a large extent, on this ability. Theory of mind on a simpler (i.e., nonlinguistic) level is seen in nonhuman primates, as in the following examples of deceptive behavior: Byrne and Whiten (1987) report on a baboon who diverted other baboons from attacking him by feigning alarm at a far-off danger; there have also been several reports (Rue, 1994) of chimps looking away from food—to avoid signaling its location to other chimps—and then recovering the food at a later time.

CHAPTER 2

Gullibility in Literature and Folktales

Although gullibility has received relatively little attention by social scientists, it has been a very central theme in many works of literature, including both fiction and folklore. A few of the more prominent examples are discussed in this chapter. These include *Pinocchio*, *The Emperor's New Clothes*, *Little Red Riding Hood*, *Tom Sawyer*, *Othello*, *Gulliver's Travels*, and Melville's *The Confidence Man*. As can be seen from the titles, several of these works are aimed at a young audience, and have the purpose of warning them against the perils of being overly trusting.

PINOCCHIO WAS ONE GULLIBLE PUPPET

Disney's animated film *Pinocchio*, in its second theatrical release in 1945 when I was 4 years old, was the most memorable movie of my early childhood. Its message about the fate awaiting boys who misbehave and lack a conscience was quite chilling. A few years ago, I was inspired to read the original 19th-century children's book, by Italian author Carlo Collodi, after watching Steven Spielberg's 2001 movie *AI: Artificial Intelligence*. The Spielberg film, about a robot boy named David who yearns to be human, and who embarks on an epic adventure to find his mother, is loosely based on the Pinocchio story and has many Pinocchio references in it, such as to the "Blue Fairy."

The hero of *AI* is portrayed as quite gullible, particularly when his need to emulate humans is activated. In one such incident, the human son in David's family (miraculously recovered from a seemingly permanent coma, after David was procured as a replacement) tricks him into eating food, with almost fatal consequences for David's internal robot electronics. In another incident, which contributed to the decision of David's parents to get rid of him, David was again tricked by his jealous human brother into sneaking into their mother's bedroom to cut off a lock of her hair while she slept.

Gullibility is a relatively minor theme in *AI*, and mainly appears in the early segments, leading up to David's long search for his mother. Pinocchio, a marionette made of wood who also yearns to be a real boy, engages in a long series of adventures seeking to reunite with his "father" and creator, the lonely old man Gepetto. Gullibility is the central theme in this story, and it appears in every episode in which Pinocchio is sidetracked from his quest. In fact, one can argue that this story, written in the land of Machiavelli, is really more about the need to develop the ability to see through manipulations than it is about the need to be good or to develop a conscience (a word that is used in a recurring song in the movie, but that is never uttered in the book). Although Pinocchio berates himself after each duping episode for being bad, others continually berate him for being dumb. It is only after he starts to listen to such warnings, as from "the talking cricket" (squashed by Pinocchio early in the book), that Pinocchio becomes reunited with Gepetto and earns the right to be human.

A listing of Pinocchio's many mishaps shows his gradual movement from gullible puppet to more socially wary human being. After Pinocchio tells Gepetto he is willing to go to school, the old man sells his coat to buy Pinocchio a spelling book. On his way to school, Pinocchio is duped into selling the book for 5 cents so that he can procure a ticket to attend a puppet show. The theater owner feels sorry for Pinocchio and gives him five gold coins to buy Gepetto another coat. But a fox and a cat trick Pinocchio into going with them to the "Wonder Field" to turn his 5 coins into 2,000 by planting them over night. (In addition to being gullible, Pinocchio is also guileless, as he quickly tells others of his treasure.) A bird tells Pinocchio "do not heed the advice of bad companions," but Pinocchio ignores him. When confronted by robbers (the fox and cat in obvious disguise), Pinocchio hides the coins in his mouth but reveals the hiding place when they threaten to kill Gepetto. Pinocchio gets away and is rescued by the Fairy with Blue Hair (this is where his nose grows as punishment for telling her a lie). He promises the fairy that he will wait for Gepetto to arrive but he again is duped by the fox and the cat into following them to a city called "Fools-Cap," to plant his remaining coins in the Wonder Field. Returning 20 minutes later, Pinocchio finds the coins missing, while a parrot laughingly proclaims: "I laugh at those simpletons who believe every tomfoolery that is told them and who fall into every trap." Even then, it takes some time for Pinocchio to understand what has happened to the coins.

The first sign of nongullibility appears when Pinocchio is chained to a dog-house by a farmer who is annoyed that Pinocchio has stolen his grapes. Some weasels come by and try to trick Pinocchio into letting them steal some chickens in exchange for giving him one (an arrangement they claim to have had with the farmer's late guard dog). But Pinocchio sees through this ruse, which earns him his freedom from the grateful farmer. Another sign of social intelligence occurs when he recognizes the Fairy with the Blue Hair in disguise (previously, Pinocchio was always taken in by disguises). Pinocchio promises the fairy that he will go to school and be a responsible boy. Some boys trick Pinocchio into skipping school by telling him that the dog-fish (a giant shark, not the whale of the movie) that ate Gepetto has been sighted, but Pinocchio quickly figures out the trick and becomes quite assertive, easily parrying the verbal ploys used by the boys. Pinocchio is chased by a mastiff and jumps in the ocean. The mastiff starts to drown and begs Pinocchio for help. The marionette understands that this may be a trick. He decides to risk helping the dog, but does it in a very careful manner, thus demonstrating both goodness and social wariness. This combination, of kindness and nongullibility, continues to mark Pinocchio's future behavior, promulgating Collodi's apparent message that being nongullible does not require one to become selfish and uncaring.

Before becoming fully human, however, Pinocchio suffers one major setback. The Fairy, impressed with Pinocchio's improved school attendance, proposes to make him human at an evening ceremony at her house, to which she allowed Pinocchio to invite all his friends. Pinocchio promises to be home in time for the event, but is tempted by his best friend, Lampwick, into accompanying him to "Playtime Land," a reputed paradise where the residents are on perpetual vacation. At first, Pinocchio resists, but Lampwick makes all sorts of promises and inducements (e.g., 100 other boys have already committed, they will be traveling in a nice coach, the Fairy won't really be mad at him, they will never have to work or go to school, etc.) and Pinocchio finally caves in. After a short time of merry-making in Playtime Land, Pinocchio turns into a donkey and is sold to a circus, where he is lamed. Pinocchio is thrown into the ocean to drown so he can be skinned, but he turns back into a marionette and is swallowed by the dog-fish, in whose stomach he has a tearful reunion with Gepetto. They escape, and start to walk home. Along the way, they encounter the fox and the cat, but this time Pinocchio resists them, saying "Good bye, cheats. . . . You tricked me once but you can't catch me again." Pinocchio returns home with Gepetto, and is rewarded for several months of hard work by being made human by the Fairy, who says: "My good Pinocchio! Because of your kind heart I forgive you for all of your misdeeds. . . . Always listen to good counsel, and you will be happy." The Fairy appears to know that as an empathic person, Pinocchio will always be a little vulnerable to deceptive manipulation, but that he now has a strong enough will, and sufficient social intelligence, that there is a good chance that he will be able to survive in society.

DANGEROUS GULLIBILITY: LITTLE RED RIDING HOOD AND THE PIED PIPER

Pinocchio was hardly the only children's book to have avoidance of gullibility as its central message. Gullibility is a common theme in children's literature. As with *Pinocchio*, the main message of these stories is "resist the lures of deceptive others" and "listen to good advice" if you expect to survive and grow up. A good example of this is the German fairy tale *Little Red Riding Hood*. Red Riding Hood is given a basket of food to bring to her ailing grandmother. Red Riding Hood's mother warns her not to loiter in the woods or go off the path. On her journey, Red Riding Hood encounters a wolf. She has no prior experience with wolves, and thus is not sufficiently wary in the face of his lies and deceptions. The wolf tells her that her grandmother would appreciate some nice flowers, which are to be found a short way off the trail. When Red Riding Hood gullibly goes in search of the flowers, the wolf rushes off to eat the grandmother and dresses up in her clothes. The girl again proves gullible, in that she does not see through the wolf's disguise, even though she senses that her grandmother now has too big ears, eyes, hands, and teeth. The wolf eats Red Riding Hood, but a hunter saves her and her grandmother. Afterward, "Little Red Riding Hood thought 'I will never again wander off into the forest as long as I live, if my mother forbids it'" (Cole, 1983, p. 114). As told by the Brothers Grimm (Zipes, 1992), there is a sequel to the usual ending. In this version, after the demise of the first wolf, "Little Red Cap" revisits her grandmother and is confronted by a second wolf. This time, the girl is wise to the wolf's intentions. She pretends to be taken in by the wolf, but instead rushes over to her grandmother's, where the two of them set a trap and kill him. Thus, the heroine learns from her former experience and this time is able to dupe the duper. The message here seems to be that to survive in the world one must not only avoid being deceived but must become proficient at using deception oneself.

Another classic folktale that addresses the potentially fatal danger to children from their gullibility in the face of manipulation by predatory adults is *The Pied Piper*. Angered when the town elders of the German town of Hamelin (Newtown or Franchville in the British version) reneged on a promise to pay him for ridding the town of rats, the piper got his revenge by getting the children of the town to follow him as he played his pipe, in the same manner as he had earlier lured the town's rats into a watery death. "In and out among the oak trees you might catch glimpses of the Piper's many-colored coat. You might hear the laughter of the children break and fade and die away as deeper and deeper into the lone green wood the stranger went and the children followed. All the while the elders watched and waited. They mocked no longer now. And watch and wait as they might, never did they set their eyes again upon the . . . children" (Cole, 1983, pp. 230–231).

A fairy tale, you might say, but one that repeats itself, typically on a smaller scale, all the time. Witness the February 2004 chilling security camera video in Sarasota, Florida, of 11-year-old Carlie Brucia passively taking the hand offered by her abductor and killer, Joseph P. Smith, as he led her away. So too, newspapers in June 2001 showed the awful security photo of 3-year-old Jamie Bulger walking off holding the hands of the two 10-year-old boys who beat and stoned him to death a short time later and then left his body on railroad tracks in Liverpool, England, to make it look as if a train had killed him. Fourteen-year-old Elizabeth Smart, abducted in the middle of the night in her own bedroom in Salt Lake City, Utah in 2002 by fringe Mormon polygamist Brian David Mitchell, did not struggle or make any noise as he led her away, presumably because she believed his threats to harm her or other family members. Happily, in the Smart case, Elizabeth was eventually reunited with her family, although her initial passivity in leaving the house with Mitchell was compounded by her failure to make any attempt to escape during the 9 months when she lived (sometimes unsupervised) with Mitchell and his co-kidnapper wife Wanda Barzee.

The moral of the Pied Piper story seems aimed mainly at the town elders whose greedy mistreatment of the Piper caused him to turn on them and take their children. But this folktale, along with *Little Red Riding Hood*, conveys a chilling message about the importance of being wary in the face of the lies and manipulations of predators pretending to have benign intentions.

THE EMPEROR'S NEW CLOTHES AND THE POWER OF GROUP MODELING

The archetype for all folktales about gullibility is the *Emperor's New Clothes*, by Hans Christian Andersen. The story depicts gullibility on the part of the emperor and his immediate aides, and what might be termed *credulity* on the part of the populace in his empire. This is because, as described earlier, *gullibility* involves action resulting from a manipulation, and *credulity* involves a willingness to believe something that is untrue, without necessarily involving any action. As told in Anderson's classic fairy tale, "one day, . . . two rascally swindlers arrived in town, pretending to be weavers and claiming to make the most beautiful cloth you can imagine . . . clothes made of it had the wonderful property of remaining invisible to anyone who was either unfit for his job or remarkably stupid" (Zwerger, 1991, p. 74).

The emperor thinks this a great idea, not only because he loves to wear beautiful clothes, but also because he thinks this a useful sort of IQ test to apply to his court and empire. He gives the two swindlers a great deal of money to start their weaving, and they pocket the money and pretend to work. The king sends out a government official to check on the work. Although he cannot see anything, he doesn't want to admit that he is stupid, so he reports back to his highness that the work is going well. The swindlers ask for more money to finish the weaving, and the emperor agrees. Another official is sent, with the same result. Finally, the emperor comes to see for himself, and the two swindlers and the two ministers (who each believe that everyone else can see it) points out to the emperor the beauty of the patterns and colors in the cloth.

The emperor, not wanting to admit that he is unfit for his job, says the cloth is "very beautiful! I like it very much." The swindlers continue to pretend to make clothes for the emperor to wear in an upcoming procession. They get the emperor to strip to his underwear and put the clothes on him, saying they're "as light as a cobweb! You might think you were wearing nothing at all, but that's the beauty of these clothes!" The chamberlains pretend to pick up the king's train, as they "were afraid to admit that they couldn't see a thing" (p. 78). The emperor walks in the procession, and the people (none of whom want to admit they are stupid or unfit for their jobs) cry out, "Oh, how wonderful the emperor's new clothes look." Suddenly a child called out "But the emperor has no clothes on." The people start to tell each other what the child has said: "The child over there says the emperor has no clothes on." Pretty soon, all the people are shouting: "The emperor has no clothes on." The emperor realizes that what the people are saying is the truth, but he manages to make it through the ceremony and the chamberlains keep carrying the train that doesn't exist. The emperor now knows who the true fools in his empire are, namely those who were duped by the two swindlers.

This classic story is rich in moral messages. The main one is probably that children should trust their own instincts and not allow their beliefs or perceptions to be shaped by others. That this is the case is shown in the dedication of a Chinese version of the story, which is to "all the children of the world who dare to see things as they really are" (Demi, 2000). The story shows how clever con artists can be in using their knowledge of human psychology (in this case, that people take their cues from others) to get what they want. The *Emperor's New Clothes* is, thus, a warning to children to be on the lookout for clever manipulators who will take advantage of them if they are too trusting and gullible. The story also suggests that adults sometimes let their egos and thought processes get in the way of common sense, and that young children, using a simpler approach, can sometimes see the truth more easily than can adults.

The gullibility theme pervades the many "trickster" stories, ranging from Native American coyote folktales, to animated short films such as Bugs Bunny (in which Elmer Fudd is constantly being duped), Tom and Jerry (the cat constantly being duped by the mouse), etc. An example of a trickster story in a recent children's book is *The Tale of Tricky Fox: A New England Trickster Tale* (Aylesworth, 2001), which is dedicated to "the teachers, who are not easy to fool." In this story, Tricky Fox brags to Brother Fox that he can fool a human into putting a pig in a sack for him. He puts a log in a sack and, acting old and infirm, he asks a kind lady to let him spend the night. He puts the sack down on the floor and asks the lady not to look in it. She says she won't but then looks in and sees it is a log.

During the night, the fox throws out the log, and in the morning he looks in his bag and asks "what's happened to my loaf of bread?" The lady knows that there was never a loaf of bread in the bag. Embarrassed to admit that she broke her promise by looking in the bag. she puts a loaf of bread in the bag. The fox repeats this trick with another woman getting her to upgrade the loaf of bread to a chicken. Then he tries it a third time, hoping to upgrade the chicken to a pig. "But Tricky Fox hadn't counted on one important thing, and that was that this particular lady was a teacher. And Tricky Fox didn't know that teachers are not so easy to fool as regular humans are. And this lady had gotten suspicious, and she'd come around the side of her house, and she'd watched through the window as Tricky Fox danced and laughed and sang that sassy sing of his." So instead of getting a pig from her pigpen, the teacher puts her bulldog in the sack. When Tricky Fox returns home and opens the sack, the bulldog jumps out, bites Tricky Fox, and chases him into the woods. And because of that, foxes are now much more respectful of humans and are no longer heard singing sassy songs.

The message in this tale is similar to that in other gullibility stories, namely that one must be on one's guard against those who would exploit one's trust and kindness. The fox is shown using his knowledge of human psychology (namely, that people would be tempted to look in the bag, and at the same time too embarrassed to admit it) to manipulate others. The fact that a teacher was the one who outwitted the fox suggests both the need to respect teachers but also that education provides one with the wisdom to know how to handle people like the fox. There is also an element of moral judgment here, in that otherwise dubious methods such as breaking a promise (looking in the bag), spying (looking in the window at the fox), and using deception (substituting the dog for the pig) are justifiable when defending oneself from manipulation and exploitation.

MARK TWAIN, CHRONICLER OF A CREDULOUS AGE

One of the most famous treatments of gullibility in fiction is Mark Twain's fence-painting scene in his novel *The Adventures of Tom Sawyer*. In that episode, Tom's guardian, Aunt Polly, orders him to whitewash a stretch of unpainted wooden fence, 30 feet long and 9 feet high. Tom sees Jim the slave, and proposes to switch chores with him, fetching water from the community pump in exchange for Jim painting the fence. Jim resists, saying that Aunt Polly had foreseen this offer and ordered him to refuse it. Tom tries several more ploys, and Jim starts to waver after Tom offers to let him see his sore toe.

Aunt Polly then comes out and breaks up this conversation by beating Tom with her shoe. Tom later has an inspiration when he sees Ben Rogers walking by. Tom starts to paint very thoughtfully, appearing to be very absorbed in his painting. Ben makes a comment about how it's too bad that Tom has to work and Tom replies, "What do you call work?" When Ben asks "Why ain't that work?" Tom replies "Well, maybe it is, and maybe it ain't. All I know, is it suits Tom Sawyer." Ben asks "Oh come, now, you don't mean to let on that you like it?" to which Tom replies "Like it? Well I don't see why I oughtn't to like it. Does a boy get a chance to whitewash a fence every day?" Ben then implores Tom to let him paint, and Tom resists, finally relenting only when Ben offers him the remains of his apple.

When Ben becomes tired out, Tom then lets Billy Fisher take over in exchange for a kite, Johnny Miller in exchange for a dead rat, "and so on, hour after hour. And when the middle of the afternoon came, from being a poor poverty-stricken boy in the morning, Tom was literally rolling in wealth....He had had a nice, good, idle time all the while—plenty of company—and the fence had three coats of whitewash on it! If he hadn't run out of whitewash, he would have bankrupted every boy in the village." Tom reflects on the afternoon's experience and derives a general law of human behavior, "namely, that in order to make a man or a boy covet a thing, it is only necessary to make the thing difficult to attain," as reflected in the various unpleasant and difficult recreational activities that people engage in mainly "because the privilege costs them considerable money."

Twain dealt with the topic of gullibility at greater length in other works, including his masterpiece *The Adventures of Huckleberry Finn* (which was peopled with all kinds of swindlers and con artists). In *Puddn'head Wilson*, Twain took on the topic of mass gullibility, as reflected in a whole town that has been hoodwinked over a couple of decades by a slave woman's switching her baby in the nursery with the son of a wealthy landowner. The theme of financial gullibility, in the context of the bubble investment mania that existed in the United States after the Civil War, was the focus of Mark Twain's first novel, *The Gilded Age* (subtitled "A Tale of Today," which still holds in light of the dot.com and Enron collapses), which he co-authored with Hartford newspaperman Charles Dudley Warner.

The book was written by Twain and Dudley on a bet with their wives, to the effect that they could in a few weeks produce a novel better than the blockbuster, *Uncle Tom's Cabin* (credited by Abraham Lincoln with starting the American Civil War) written by Twain's next-door neighbor, Harriet Beecher Stowe. It is a riveting and amusing treatment of the topic of financial gullibility, both on a macro level (the pressure on individuals and institutions not to miss out on the riches that others seem to be amassing) and also on a micro level (the difficulty that some people have in saying "no" to a charismatic and enthusiastic scam artist, even one who has victimized you repeatedly in the past).

The macro insanity of the bubble mentality was satirically captured by Twain and Dudley in the following passage:

> Beautiful credit! The foundation of modern society. Who shall say that this is not the golden age of mutual trust, of unlimited reliance upon human promises? That is a peculiar condition of society which enables a whole nation to instantly recognize point and meaning in the familiar newspaper anecdote, which puts into the mouth of a distinguished speculator in lands and mines this remark:—"I wasn't worth a cent two years ago, and now I owe two millions of dollars." (p. 193)

Although the macro level of analysis helps to explain the group context in which mass financial gullibility flourishes, it is the micro level, that is the level on which one individual, pressured by another, makes a stupid decision, in which I—as a psychologist—am particularly interested. One of most sympathetically treated characters in *The Gilded Age* is Eli Bolton, a mildly prosperous small-town Pennsylvania businessman, whose motivations have more to do with kindness than with greed. The authors noted that "all his life Eli Bolton had been giving young fellows a lift, and shouldering the losses when things turned out unfortunately" (p. 190). Although Bolton is overextended in bankrolling several dubious schemes by enthusiastic young men, he is unable to turn down a request from a Mr Small, who comes to him with a sob story, in which a loan of $10,000 more would make the difference between a failed venture (and calamity for his unsuspecting wife and daughter) and a certain bonanza.

Although Bolton has placed several other debts of Small's in a file labeled "doubtful," and although he has pressing financial needs of his own, Bolton falls under the sway of Small's persuasiveness and "devoted the day to scraping together, here and there, ten thousand dollars for this brazen beggar, who had never kept a promise to him nor paid a debt" (p. 193). Near the end of the book, after teetering on the brink of ruin, and finally recouping some of his fortune, Bolton is again approached by Mr Small for an investment in a dubious scheme. Mr Bolton, having learned from his experiences, is finally able to cut Small off with the use of a firm and not-so-friendly "no."

The Gilded Age is, in many respects, Twain's most cynical piece of writing. It would be difficult to imagine a more corrupt place than the Senate depicted in that book; the same is true for the judicial system. Nevertheless, it is also a moving and persuasive morality play on the perils of gullibility. I should note that I used to live near Hartford, and learned from a visit to the Mark Twain House that he himself was once seriously damaged financially in a failed get-rich-quick investment scheme. So, like most people who write about gullibility, Twain had some personal experience from which to draw.

WAS GULLIVER GULLIBLE?

There have been a number of books, most of them collections of essays, with the word "gullible" substituted for "Gulliver," as in *Gullible's Travels: The Adventures of a Bad Taste Tourist*, by Cash Peters (2003), *Gullibles Travels: Writings*, by Jill Johnston (1974) and *Gullible's Travails*, edited by Brian Rix (1996). Given this literary use of the name "Gullible" as a stand-in for the hero of Jonathan Swift's 19th-century novel *Gulliver's Travels*, I wondered if Swift himself had such a meaning in mind when he came up with the name of his hero.

My curiosity was rewarded, when Irma Ned Bailey—an English professor at San Antonio College, whom I tracked down through a Jonathan Swift Web site started by her late husband Roger Blackwell Bailey—sent me the following message: "Gulliver is always gullible, in that he accepts at face value whatever he sees without analyzing it." Bailey (personal communication, May

12, 2004) also pointed out that Gulliver's "first name, you recall, is Lemuel, like 'lemming', the little animal that follows other lemmings over the cliffs whenever they overpopulate." Bailey's view that the *Travels* is about gullibility was confirmed in an e-mail from Michael Seidel (personal communication, May 14, 2004), a Columbia University literature professor, and the author of the introduction to my 2003 edition of the *Travels*. This view is confirmed in many works, although in only one did I find specific reference use of the word "gullible."

In writing about the last, and most comedic, of Gulliver's four voyages, A.D. Nuttall (1995), a professor of English at Oxford, commented on Gullliver's extreme gullibility (which he saw as a sign of his increasing madness) in praising the rationality and other virtues of the Houyhnhnms (horses) and missing their many flaws, including cruelty. Nuttall believes that he may have cracked the mystery of the *Travels* when he noted that

> if we try to write "Gulliver" in the "little language" of the *Journal to Stella* we get "Gullible" and this, it might be said, is the key. There is, however, a snag. *Gullible* is not known to the *Oxford English Dictionary* before the 19th century, though the puzzling word *cullible* (having the same meaning) appears to have been in use in Swift's time (see, for example, Swift's letter to Pope of 16 July 1728). Meanwhile, the word, *to gull*, was of course common currency [used by Shakespeare to describe Othello-SG]. Certainly, Gulliver is from the first entirely deceived by appearances. (Nuttall, 1995, p. 265)

This phenomenon is perhaps most evident in the third book, which dealt with Gulliver's voyage to the country of Balnibarbi with "the flying or floating island of Laputa." In that country, scientists and mathematicians were held in the highest esteem, and on a visit to the capital city of Lagado, Gulliver was treated to a presentation at its Grand Academy of some of the most absurd scientific experiments imaginable. One of these experiments was carried out by a senior scientist whose "employment from his first coming into the Academy was an operation to reduce human excrement to its original food." Another scientist, who had written "a treatise concerning the malleability of fire" was currently "at work to calcine ice," while "there was a most ingenious architect who had contrived a new method for building houses, by beginning at the roof and building downwards to the foundation."

The work that perhaps most explicitly explores the emphasis on gullibility in the *Travels* is *Swift's Anatomy of Misunderstanding*, by Frances Deutsch Louis (1981). In it, she cites a 1714 letter to the Earl of Peterborough, in which Swift wrote about the tendency of people "to reason themselves into a thousand various conjectures" (p. 24). Swift noted that he was not immune from this tendency, as he had "thought myself twenty times in the right, by drawing conclusions very regularly from premises which have proved wholly wrong." Much of the *Travels* may thus be seen as an exploration of the contribution of dogmatism to mistaken, and thus gullible, thinking. This theme was explored further by Douglas Lane Patey (1995), who argued that Swift's attack was not aimed at science per se, but on quacks using pseudo-scientific concepts to justify irrational beliefs.

Contrary to the tendency of leading thinkers in the Enlightenment to celebrate the triumphs of science, Swift ridiculed those claims by showing "men in the act of looking at smaller and smaller pieces of experience and learning less and less" (Louis, 1981, p. 27). The Grand Academy of Lagado is an obvious stand-in for England's Royal Society, which in the 17th century took great pride in its mathematical and positivistic approach to knowledge. An obsession with counting and measuring pervades the *Travels*, and is seen in all of Gulliver's descriptions as well as in the behavior of the people whom he describes. Those contemporaries, such as Locke and Bacon, who believed that precise observation and measurement provide the path to true understanding are gullible, in Swift's view. This point is made in the *Travels*, according to Louis (1981) when she noted that "the Lilliputians measure Gulliver's hat in every way, know each numerical proportion, and learn everything from their quantitative analysis except that it is a hat–a fact that is not evident, despite precise mathematical data" (p. 14). She argued that

> measurement is not always the road to meaning. Swift also illustrates the appalling poverty of a people whose faith in quantitative analysis interferes with their ability to feed, clothe and house themselves adequately and Gulliver assumes that it is the physical proportions rather than the morality of the Lilliputians and the Brobdingnagians that will interest his readers. Swift illustrates that a new way of looking at things may also be a new way of mistaking them. (p. 14)

The essential point made by Swift in the *Travels*, according to Louis, is "that much of the faith men had in their own learning was based on their mistaken identification of seeing with knowing" (p. 37). Swift "shows how seeing can become a dangerous substitute for thinking itself, and how a man might lose himself amid 'deceitful resemblances of objects and signs'" (p. 37). Gulliver's gullibility comes through repeatedly in his tendency to give approval to dubious ideas, solely on the basis of superficial impressions. That a "confirmation bias" is operating in Gulliver can be seen in his quickness to believe the nonsensical if superficially appealing theory that a way to manufacture colored silk is to have spiders eat colored flies. Gulliver's gullibility on an action (as opposed to a belief) level can also be seen in the quickness with which he is talked into leaving his wife and family, despite his belief in the "prudence and justice" of staying home, and despite his increasing disillusionment over the benefits to be obtained from such journeys (Boyle, 2000, p. 45). "Gulliver does not learn from his previous mistakes, or indeed from anything he experiences" (Hunter, 2003, p. 224). If the essence of true gullibility is a failure to learn from past episodes of duping, then Lemuel Gulliver can be considered a serial gull.

GULLIBILITY AS A THEME FOR HERMAN MELVILLE

In 1857, the last, and some would say strangest, novel by Herman Melville was published. It was devoted entirely to the topic of human gullibility. Its title, *The Confidence Man*, was derived from the widely publicized 1849 arrest of William Thompson, whose scam was to walk around the financial district of New York in a well-dressed manner, going up to a gentleman and pretending that he had met him three or four times previously. Then, after an exchange of small talk, Thompson would ask the stranger "have you confidence in me to trust me with your watch until tomorrow?" The victim, not wanting to admit that he could not remember Thompson, or that he lacked confidence in him, would hand over his expensive watch and Thompson would walk away laughing to himself. The scam always worked and Thompson was caught only when a former victim spotted him.

The novel, dedicated to "victims of *auto da fe*" (the burning and dismembering of accused devil worshippers during the Spanish Inquisition) takes place on a Mississippi river boat, the *Fidele*, cruising from Saint Louis to New Orleans. The first part of the book is a demonstration of the universality of human gullibility, in which the confidence man (the devil in various disguises) shows how easily anyone, from the most suspicious to the most trusting, can be taken advantage of by appeals to the widest array of motives. Two particularly hilarious examples are the scamming by a snake oil salesman of a man resolutely skeptical about natural remedies and the cheating of a tough-nosed barber (who has a sign over his chair saying "No Trust") out of the price of a shave.

The second part of the book consists largely of a series of commentaries by the confidence man about how it is better to be too trusting and be gulled than to be so pinched off that one is incapable of ever giving one's confidence. This is widely interpreted as a satirical portrayal of Ralph Waldo Emerson and the fatuously optimistic pronouncements of his Transcendental school. Melville portrays Emerson as the archetypal American con man, and his followers as gullible, as when they are taken in by his hypocritical platitudes about friendship.

Melville was known to have an interest in P.T. Barnum, the great showman, who uttered the famous words "there is a sucker born every minute." Although Melville worked briefly on a Mississippi paddle steamer during his youth, it is possible that some of the inspiration for *The Confidence Man* came from Barnum's 1855 autobiography. In that book, Barnum tells a long story about how he used magic tricks and a practical joke to convince a credulous barber on a Mississippi steamboat that he was in league with the devil. An earlier satirical piece by Melville, titled "Authentic anecdotes of 'Old Zach'," was published in the magazine *Yankee Doodle* (it is reprinted in a 1997 Everyman edition of Melville's Shorter Fiction, edited by John Updike). In that piece, Melville, who saw the Mexican War as a pretense for the expansion of Southern slave-holding territories, pretended to be a war correspondent covering the doings of General Zachary Taylor, and hilariously lampooned ads for Barnum's newly opened American Museum. One of these ads was titled "Prodigious Excitement: Old Zach's Pants," and poked fun at the gullibility of the American people (still going strong today) for anything having to do with celebrities and their possessions.

To me, as a developmental psychologist, one of the most interesting passages in *The Confidence Man* has to do with the possible role of experience and development in inoculating an individual against his or her gullible tendencies. This passage involves a debate about whether or not Adam and Eve would have been able to hold their own with the serpent in the apple-eating incident had they come into the Garden of Eden as fully formed adults with more worldly experience. Both sides of this debate are argued effectively, and it is not clear what Melville's own position was. Melville sometimes agonized over the immature and competing aspects in his own personality, as when he wrote a critical review of a work by his staunch supporter Nathaniel Hawthorne and later apologized for it. Indeed, one of Hawthorne's sisters had written a letter in which she characterized Melville as still being a work in progress, in terms of his difficulty in taking consistent positions on various matters, such as slavery. This tendency is manifested in the sharp differences between the first half of *The Confidence Man* (written when Melville was depressed) in which all trust is portrayed as foolish, and the second half of the book (written when he was manic) in which distrust is portrayed as a fault.

It has been suggested that the book would have been a comic masterpiece, on par with the tragic *Moby Dick*, had Melville managed to weave these two notions more tightly together throughout the book (a problem partly reflecting that it was written as magazine installments, at a time when he was financially distressed). We know that Melville, a skeptic on religious matters, and a general cynic about the state of humanity, had strong impulses toward belief and optimism, and that these tendencies sometimes were ascendant. Like many people, Melville struggled to balance his competing tendencies toward gullibility and excessive distrust.

OTHELLO AND OTHER SHAKESPEAREAN DUPES

Deception and ruses are found in many Shakespeare plays, typically as a plot device rather than as a central focus. For example, in virtually all of the comedies a character pretends to be someone else, and is usually able to manipulate one or more other characters as a result. A good example of this is in *Measure for Measure*, where numerous examples of successful disguise can be found. Although gullibility is thus used as a plot device in many of Shakespeare's plays, it is a more central topic in some of his other plays. An example of gullibility in falling for tall tales can be found in Shakespeare's last sole-authored play, *The Tempest*. The prankster Stefano persuades Caliban, the monster-like original inhabitant of the island, that he is the man in the moon. Caliban replies that indeed he had seen him on the moon along with his dog. This causes the jester Trinculo to comment: "By this good light, this is a very shallow monster. . . . A very weak monster. The man in the moon! A most poor credulous monster."

Gullibility takes on a more serious tone in Shakespeare's tragedies, where it sometimes has fatal consequences. It has been suggested by the Australian film scholar Lisa Dethridge (2003) that the continuing popularity of *Romeo and Juliet* stems from the fact that "it's about youth and gullibility" (p. 37), a topic that Dethridge sees as of universal and never-ending interest. Although gullibility is not the central theme in *Macbeth*, the hero's undoing undoubtedly is traceable mainly to his inability to resist and see the dangers in the ceaseless regicidal urgings of his ruthless and overambitious spouse.

The play in which Shakespeare most fully explored the topic of gullibility is, undoubtedly, *Othello*. In that tragedy, set in Venice, the title character is a dark-skinned general of Moorish descent, who becomes convinced by his scheming servant, Iago, that Desdemona, Othello's devoted wife, is carrying on an affair with Othello's lieutenant Cassio, whom Iago jealously seeks to do in. The convincing bit of evidence, in Othello's mind, is that a handkerchief that he gave to Desdemona winds up in Cassio's possession. The handkerchief was in fact planted by Iago, who celebrates Othello's falling for the trick by uttering the lines "Work on, my medicine, work! Thus credulous fools are caught; and many worthy and chaste dames even thus, all guiltless, meet reproach."

Showing no awareness that he may have been manipulated by Iago, Othello strangles Desdemona. Emelia, the maid servant to Desdemona (and also Iago's wife) discovers her mistress' dying body. She confronts Othello, who justifies the deed by saying that "Cassio did top her. Ask thy husband." Emelia is incredulous that anyone would be foolish enough to have believed her husband, and says to Othello: "O gull! O dolt! As ignorant as dirt!" Othello sticks to his guns for awhile, mentioning the handkerchief, but then Emelia says: "O thou dull Moor! That handkerchief thou speak'st of I found by fortune and did give my husband; For often, with a solemn earnestness, more than indeed belong'd to such a trifle, he begged of me to steal it." Then, looking piteously at Othello, she asks, "what should such a fool do with so good a woman?" A light bulb finally goes off in Othello's head and he rushes at Iago. Now racked with guilt, Othello asks the assembled nobles to inquire of the "demi-devil" Iago "why he thus ensnared my soul and body?" Othello wishes to be remembered as "one who loved not wisely but too well" and also as "one not easily jealous, but being wrought perplex'd in the extreme." Then he stabs himself and dies.

The Othello story is rightly seen as showing how extreme jealousy can cause a normally rational person to become irrational. Thus, when Desdemona complains to Emelia toward the end of the play that she "never gave him cause" to suspect her of infidelity, Emelia responds that "jealous souls will not be answer'd so; they are not ever jealous for the cause, but jealous for they are jealous; 'tis a monster begot upon itself, born on itself." In the words of Daniel Goleman (1995) in his book *Emotional Intelligence*, Othello becomes so "emotionally hijacked" by jealousy that he becomes essentially a "dolt" and "ignorant as dirt." Of course, it is possible, as suggested in several racially tinged remarks, that Othello was no mental giant to begin with, and that his lack of intelligence, combined with his being "perplex'd in the extreme," caused him to kill the wife he loved.

Othello is also a commentary on the evils of lying and of spreading false rumors, and about the natural tendency to believe liars, especially ones as skilled and malevolent as Iago. Shakespeare's views about the universality of human lying, and gullibility, are stated in Sonnet CXXXVIII: "when my love swears she is made of truth, I do believe her though I know she lies. That she might think me some untutor'd youth, unlearned in the world's false subtleties.... O love's best habit is in seeming trust.... Therefore, I lie with her and she with me." To Shakespeare, successful deception requires some degree of self-deception, whether conscious (as in his case) or unconscious (as in Othello's case). This view has some truth to it, as countless stories in this book illustrate.

CHAPTER 3

Gullibility in Religion

Religion has proved to be a fertile field for the expression of gullible behavior, both in the portrayal of gullibility in religious characters, and in the unquestioning acceptance by followers of supernatural notions. In this chapter, a number of topics related to religious gullibility are explored. These include both conventional forms of religious expression (the story of Samson, Satan, belief in miracles) and less conventional forms (Spiritualism, apocalyptic sects, Christian Science). Although anti-Semitism could be treated as a form of political gullibility, it is included in this chapter because it is so often justified on religious grounds.

SAMSON AND OTHER BIBLE STORIES

The Bible, as a moral teaching tool, contains many stories in which the trust of unsuspecting individuals is violated by those who use deception and dishonest manipulation.[1] With a few exceptions, such as Samson, the emphasis is on the motives and actions of the deceiver, many of whom are major Biblical figures, and not much is written about those who are deceived. The bulk of the Bible's deception stories are found in the Old Testament, particularly in the *Book of Genesis*, which predates the Ten Commandments and the other behavior prohibitions that are laid down in the Pentateuch. In fact, Alan M. Dershowitz (2000) argued, in *The Genesis of Justice*, that the Ten

---

[1] All Biblical quotes are taken from the *Oxford Family Edition*, New Revised Standard Version, 1989.

Commandments, and indeed much of Western law, can be seen as attempts to erect barriers against the kinds of acts that are routine in *Genesis*.

Following is a partial list of incidents that involve exploitation of unsuspecting gulls in *Genesis*:

1. Lot escapes from doomed Sodom with his wife and two daughters, but his wife looks back and is turned into a pillar of salt. The two (unnamed) daughters, desiring to keep their father's lineage alive, get Lot drunk and seduce him. Lot wakes up with no memory of his having been raped, and the daughters become pregnant.

2. God, speaking through an angel, tricked Abraham into agreeing to sacrifice his only son, Isaac. At the last second, Abraham is told "never mind."

3. Jacob tricks his older twin brother Esau into giving up his rights as firstborn son in return for a bowl of lentils; later, Jacob deceives his blind and ailing father Isaac into giving his blessing to him rather than Esau.

4. Laban tells Jacob that he will have to work 7 years before he can marry his younger daughter Rachel, but he tricks Jacob into marrying the older daughter Leah. Jacob then has to work another 7 years before he can take Rachel as his second wife.

5. Shekhem, the Hamorite, who later asks for Dina's hand in marriage, rapes Dina, the daughter of Jacob and Leah. Jacob's sons (Dina's brothers) respond that they are agreeable, but only if Shekhem and all of his male relatives become circumcised, so that they can enter into an alliance together. While the Hamorites are in a weakened state following the surgery, they are slaughtered in an act of mass revenge.

6. Judah has three sons, Er, Onan and Shelah. Er, the first-born, is married to Tamar. Er dies and Judah orders Onan to have sex with Tamar (in line with the "Leverite duty") so that Er's inheritance rights may be preserved. Onan, whose own interests are better served if the order is defied, "spilled his semen on the ground whenever he went in to his brother's wife" (resulting in use of the term "onanism" to refer to masturbation, when it actually should be used to refer to *coitus interruptus*). Tamar, despairing of the situation, disguises herself as a prostitute and seduces her father-in-law, and becomes pregnant. She protects herself against punishment by producing Judah's ring (given as an IOU for later payment) at what Dershowitz describes as the first judicial proceeding in the Bible

7. Joseph is sold into bondage by his jealous brothers, who tell their father, Jacob, that a lion ate him. Joseph is then falsely accused by the wife of his

master of attempting to rape her, in retaliation for spurning her advances. Joseph becomes a prisoner, where his talents as a dream interpreter cause him to become a high advisor to the Pharaoh. During a famine, Joseph's brothers come to beg for food and (without revealing his identity) Joseph sends them on their way with food and a supply of silver and gold, including a silver cup. He later sends the soldiers after them and has them arrested for stealing the valuable objects. Joseph's brothers are terrified and fear for their lives. Joseph then reveals his identity and tells them it was just a joke. Jacob is sent for and has a happy reunion with the son he thought was dead.

A prominent gullibility tale, and one of the few in the Old Testament that pays much attention to the victim, is the story of Samson and Delilah (*Judges*, 16). Samson was a fearsome Israelite warrior who had killed many Philistines. When Samson falls in love with Delilah, "the Lords of the Philistines came to her and said to her, 'Coax him and find out what makes his strength so great, and how we may bind him in order to subdue him; and we will each give you eleven hundred pieces of silver.'" Delilah asks Samson, "Please tell me what makes your strength so great, and how you could be bound, so that one could subdue you?" Samson falsely tells Delilah, "if they bind me with seven fresh bowstrings that are not dried out, then I shall become weak, and be like anyone else." The lords of the Philistines bring Delilah seven fresh bowstrings that had not dried out, "and she bound him with them. While men were lying in wait in an inner chamber, she said to him 'The Philistines are upon you, Samson!'"

Samson, of course, snapped the bowstrings and prevailed. This scenario was repeated twice more, with Samson telling two more lies ("bind me with new ropes that have not been used," and "weave the seven locks of my hair with the web and make it tight with the pin"), with the same results. Delilah comes to Samson a fourth time and asks "how can you say 'I love you,' when your heart is not with me?" Finally, "after she had nagged him with her words day after day, and pestered him [so that] he was tired to death," Samson told her the true secret of his strength, namely that he has never had a haircut. This time, the Philistines were successful in capturing Samson and gouging out his eyes, after which he gets his revenge (with the help of some grown-back hair and divine intervention) by pulling down the pillars of the Philistine temple, killing himself and 3,000 Philistines in the process.

My first reaction after reading the Samson and Delilah story was one of amazement at Samson's stupidity. Samson may indeed have been the Biblical prototype for the "dumb jock." I could understand Samson spilling the beans if Delilah had used some guile, but she was pretty direct, saying, in effect, "Tell me what it would take to overpower and capture you." True, he showed some coyness in giving her phony information, not just once but three times (with an obvious betrayal by Delilah following each disclosure). One wonders why Samson continued to keep Delilah around after the first betrayal, let alone after three. Then on the fourth occasion, Samson gives Delilah the key to his own destruction, after she uses an obvious "if you really loved me..."ploy and because he was getting tired of her nagging. In chapter 9, I discuss how exhaustion contributes to gullibility (as in the giving of confessions to military or police interrogators who make deliberate use of sleep deprivation). Samson is thus not the only notable person who sacrificed his long-term wellbeing to get a good night's sleep.

Undoubtedly, the main moral of the Samson story, like much else in the Bible, is "keep it in your pants if you know what is good for you." It may also, however, be read as a cautionary tale about the risks of extreme gullibility. The most famous example of gullibility in the Bible, and perhaps in world literature, was triggered not by a human but by the serpent, who tricked Adam and Eve into eating from the forbidden tree, an act that got them expelled from the Garden of Eden and that allegedly doomed the rest of us to being mortal. The serpent "was more crafty than any other wild animal that the Lord God had made" and Eve—gullible and unworldly—was no match for him. The serpent assured her that God had not meant it when he threatened death as the punishment for eating from the forbidden tree. Furthermore, the serpent promised Eve that eating from the tree would make her and her husband a co-equal of God's. Eve fell for this trick and talked Adam into going along with her. The serpent turned out to be correct in assuring Eve that God's death threat was a bluff, but she undoubtedly came to regret her moment of weakness, as many bad things were inflicted on her and her husband, and succeeding generations, as a result.

This story is in many ways a prototype of the "gullible moment," as emphasized repeatedly throughout this book. That is, gullibility often occurs in a complex and demanding micro-context, where various cognitive, emotional, and other challenges come together. Eve is not the only one who would make a poor choice when placed in such a situation, given the pressures and inducements used and her own experiential and cognitive limitations.

BELIEF IN GOD AND SUPERNATURAL PHENOMENA

In his book *A Devil's Chaplain*, evolutionary biologist Richard Dawkins (2003), explores the role of gullibility in mainstream religious belief. In a chapter titled "Viruses of the Mind," Dawkins alluded to "the programmed-in gullibility of a child, so useful for learning language and traditional wisdom, and so easily subverted by nuns, Moonies and their ilk" (p. 135). For Dawkins, gullibility is a quality that has important survival value for the species, as unquestioning acceptance of "memes" (cultural units for transmitting information) keeps children from being exposed to danger, such as from hot stoves or passing cars. The basic gullibility of humans continues into adulthood, albeit somewhat abated (Dawkins did not explain the abatement mechanism), and accounts for the susceptibility of many adults to supernatural beliefs and dubious religious doctrines.

Dawkins considered supernatural beliefs to be "mind viruses," that is unworthy and untrue memes masquerading as legitimate ones. Just as biological and computer viruses worm their way into organisms and computers by masquerading as normal and safe microorganisms and computer programs, so too mind viruses worm their way into the mind by their similarity to legitimate memes and by the built-in gullibility of humans who have been programmed to accept memes passed on by authority figures such as parents and religious leaders. Richard Brodie (1996) further explores these ideas in *Virus of the Mind*.

A personality quality that Dawkins (2003) sees as important for the ability to resist toxic memes (and, thus, to be skeptical about religion) is "any impulse to solve mysteries" (p. 138). He used as example the Catholic notion of transubstantiation, which comes into play when one takes communion. Dawkins said that "it is easy and nonmysterious to believe that in some symbolic or metaphorical sense the Eucharistic wine turns into the blood of Christ" (p. 138), but the Catholic doctrine of transubstantiation demands more, namely a belief that the wine literally turns into Christ's blood, despite the "accident" of it still looking like wine, through the "Mystery of the Transubstantiation." For Dawkins, calling this a mystery makes it easier for Catholics— conditioned by a "belief in infallible authority"—to accept it as a miracle that does not have to be questioned further. This is because he sees Catholics having "mind[s] well prepared by background infection" (p. 139) to react to mysteries not with questioning but with awe.

A personality quality that Dawkins sees as critical to escaping the clutches of religious ideas is a willingness to stand up to authority. Dawkins noted that it is very rare for a person to adopt a religion other than the one followed by his parents, and said that when that happens it is typically because "[one] has been exposed to a particularly potent infective agent" (p. 143) rather than through one's independent seeking and questioning. Dawkins illustrated the authoritarian nature of traditional religions by referring to a conversation he had with a London rabbi who was given the job of figuring out whether it was acceptable for observant Jews to use cough lozenges made with menthol imported from China. The rabbi figured that the menthol was probably kosher, but needed to put someone on a plane to China just to make certain. When Dawkins asked him what was the point of such nonsense, the rabbi responded by saying that there was no point other than to have something to be obedient to. "It is very easy not to murder people," said the rabbi. "But if He [meaning God] tells me not to have a cup of coffee with milk in it with my mincemeat and peas at lunchtime, that is a test. The only reason I am doing it is because I have been told to so do. It is doing something difficult" (p. 140).

For Dawkins, religious gullibility is not only an illustration of, but may be a precursor to, a more global form of gullibility. As he said, if you can believe "something as daft as the transubstantiation [then] you can believe anything, and (witness the story of Doubting Thomas) these people are trained to see that as a virtue" (p. 141). In other words, training children to accept nonsensical religious notions may predispose them to accept all kinds of other nonsense with a similar blind trust.

A considerably less hostile treatment of the role of gullibility in conventional religious belief is contained in a book by Michael Shermer (2001) titled *How We Believe*. Although a prominent skeptic, as well as an atheist, Shermer's position is that one can be a skeptic toward irrational beliefs, including official religious doctrines, and still believe in God (in fact, as many as one-third of the members of Shermer's Skeptics Society, and an even larger percentage of scientists, claim to hold religious beliefs). This is because for most people belief in God is a matter of faith, that is, an emotionally-driven stance, and for Shermer that is acceptable. Where he draws the line, however, is when one begins to use rational arguments to justify such a stance, by pointing to various supernatural and miraculous phenomena as evidence. Then, Shermer's skeptical juices begin to flow.

For Shermer, the explanation for why people believe in God is that "humans are pattern-seeking animals. Our brains are hard-wired to seek and find patterns, whether the pattern is real or not" (p. 61). He cited Bart Kosko's (1993) book *Fuzzy Thinking*, to suggest that belief in God is analogous to what we do when we look at an optical illusion, such as the Kanizsa-square illusion, in which the mind fills in a square where all that is really on the page are four Pac-men turned at right angles. For Kosko, "God glimpses, or the feeling of God recognition, may be just a 'filling in' or deja-vu type anomaly of our neural nets" (cited in Shermer, 2001, p. 62). Shermer noted that in the Kanizsa illusion, "there is no square.... The square is in our mind. There appears to be Something There, when in actual fact there is nothing there. As pattern-seeking animals it is virtually impossible for us *not* to see the pattern. The same may be true for God. For most of us, it is very difficult not to see a pattern of God when looking at the false boundaries and bright interiors of the universe" (p. 63). An alternative explanation of religion, based on transferring to "God" the young child's initial quasi-religious worship of his parents, was provided in a developmental study of magical thinking by Jean Piaget (1926/1969) discussed in chapter 1.

Shermer posited a "Belief Engine" to explain why most people (90% of Americans, the highest of any Western population) profess a belief in God, but also a belief in magic and various supernatural phenomena, such as an ability to talk to the dead. The best modern treatment of the connection between religion and belief in magic is contained in a book titled *Believing in Magic: The Psychology of Superstition*, by Stuart A. Vyse (1997). Magic is integral to religion, because the very concept of a personal God responding to prayer is magical, because many religious practices (e.g., sprinkling of holy water, the transubstantiation of the communion wine, the healing miracles attributed to saints) do not conform to natural laws and processes, and because in some religions priests are believed to have magical (e.g., shamanistic) powers.

Vyse sees belief in magic as a variant of superstitious thinking, which is the notion that performing or not performing certain acts can affect certain outcomes that are not logically connected to the act in question. Superstitions are fairly universal and are mechanisms for anxiety management rather than signs of mental illness. Engaging in a superstitious ritual does not in itself imply belief in magic. There are people, however, who engage in superstitious ritual and who do see a causative connection to some outcome. Then we are in the realm of magical (and gullible) thinking. An illustration can be found in the famous Swiss psychiatrist Carl Jung, who believed there was no such thing as a coincidence. One day he was psychoanalyzing a woman who told him of a dream in which she was given a golden scarab. Just then Jung looked up and saw a scarabaeid beetle, the closest thing to a golden scarab that one could find in Switzerland. It was banging against the window pane, trying to get into the darkened room, contrary to its usual practice of going toward the light. Jung was convinced that the woman's telling of her dream is what brought this unusual event about. This tendency to see the working of magic, rather than coincidence, in unusual events is fairly universal and explains not only Jung's belief in UFOs, alchemy, and other supernatural phenomena, but explains why so many people believe in God, prayer, and miracles.

SATAN AS A MANIPULATOR OF THE GULLIBLE

The various Bible stories involving the devil, which many commentators consider a later manifestation of the serpent, all involve a variation on the theme of an evil trickster who tries to prey on the gullibility of others. A Massachusetts Bay Colony law of 1647, termed the "Old Deluder Satan Act" (Cremin, 1970), mandated establishment of grammar schools and universal instruction in reading and writing, to foil attempts by the devil to take advantage of gullible individuals who are unable to read scripture. It is interesting to discover that public education in North America began not (as generally believed) to prepare young people for work or other aspects of adult life, but rather to make them less gullible and vulnerable to exploitation.

Nongullibility in dealing with the devil is a quality attributed to Christ, as reflected in the following exchange in Matthew, 4: "Then Jesus was led up by the spirit into the wilderness to be tempted by the devil. He fasted forty days and forty nights, and afterwards he was famished. The tempter came and said to him 'If you are the Son of God, command these stones to become loaves of bread.'" Jesus answered "One does not live by bread alone." Then the devil dares Jesus to jump off the roof of the temple, to see if he will be saved by angels, and Jesus answered: "it is written, 'do not put the Lord your God to the test.'" Finally, the devil tries to bribe Jesus by offering vast tracts of land if he "will fall down and worship me." Jesus tells the devil, in no uncertain terms, to get lost.

The notion of Satan as a manipulative trickster who preys upon the gullible and weak is still alive and well in some religious circles, especially among Fundamentalist preachers such as the late Reverend Jerry Falwell, who warned constantly of the lures of "Satan the Great Deceiver." As detailed in a book by Joan O'Grady (1989) titled *The Prince of Darkness: The Devil in History, Religion and the Human Psyche*, the idea of an evil super demon is a logical outgrowth of the notion of an omnipotent deity, in that one needs to take God off the hook as an explanation for evil deeds. In the earliest Jewish writings, Yahweh was responsible for all that happened in the world, good and bad, but contact with the Persian religion during the period of Jewish exile in Babylon brought about the introduction of the idea of Satan (a Hebrew word) as the adversary of God and man.

In the Book of *Job*, Satan is introduced as tempter, but is still seen as a subject of God and under his commands. This shift to a splitting off of Satan as an independent entity is seen by comparing an early book, *Samuel*, in which Samuel was tempted by God, to a later book, *Chronicles*, in which David was tempted by Satan. The story of how Satan was cast out of heaven by God appears in an Apocryphal book, *Enoch* (a book that had all but disappeared before it was rediscovered), written in 200 BCE, shortly before the Christian era. *Enoch*, which tells the story of the exile of the fallen Prince of Darkness, never became an official part of Jewish scripture, but apparently had important influence over the much fuller development of the devil concept in Christianity.

A host of names, such as Beelzebub (literally "Lord of the Flies") in late Judaism and Lucifer, in Christianity and Islam, have been used to refer to this personification of evil in the world. The core motive underlying the fall of Satan (who is usually portrayed as having at one time been God's favorite angel) is pride and self-love. The central mechanism used by Satan to tempt men into evil deeds is deception, specifically involving a false presentation by the devil of himself as good and as interested in the victim's wellbeing (an early prototype for this use of deceptive flattery is the serpent in the Garden of Eden). According to O'Grady, it was Saint John of the Cross, in the 16th century CE, who most fully developed the notion of the Devil as one who tricks the worthy, by preying on their pride and self-complacency. For Saint John, and later Christian writers about the Devil, the focus is really on the process by which one is deceived and tempted by others or oneself into behaving badly, a process that capitalizes on one's own worst needs and self-deceptions. The idea of a personified devil as the tempter, while a useful metaphor, is secondary, and almost irrelevant, to the advice these writers give as to how to live a worthy and gullibility-free life.

As described in Elaine Pagels' (1995) *The Origin of Satan*, and Peter Stanford's (1996) *The Devil: A Biography*, the devil concept proved to have important political uses, and played an expanded role in Christian theology as a means to the end of social control and consolidation of power by religious and other leaders. Thus, there is a double edge to the role of gullibility and the Devil, first in the gullibility of those who are led astray by evil thoughts or devil-like tempters, and second in the gullibility of those who are manipulated by leaders who use the devil concept to do in their enemies and achieve political or other ends. Thus, Pagels noted that in 90 CE, Clement (a successor to Peter as Bishop of Rome), believing that church opponents were in the process of caving in to his authority, "avoids associating them with Satan, as later leaders would do with more entrenched dissidents" (Pagels, 1995, p. 153).

The end to which the devil concept proved most useful in early Christianity was as a rationale for the suppression of various heresies, including many teachings that today would be considered quite tame. The most influential tome in this effort was *Against Heresies*, written around 180 CE by Irenaeus, Bishop of Lyons. Heretics, according to Irenaeus, are those " 'who claim to be Christians . . . [but] use the name of Christ Jesus only as a kind of lure', in order to teach doctrines inspired by Satan" (p. 155). According to Pagels, this document was used for succeeding centuries as a basis for Christian persecution of other Christians. In one of the suppressed heretical documents, *The Testimony of Truth*, the anonymous disaffected author takes this notion even further: describing the majority of Christians as heretics and "gullible disciples, subject to seduction" (p. 158) by church authorities.

The two high (actually, low) points in the political use by the Roman church of the Devil concept came in the medieval period, as reflected in the Crusades and the suppression of the Cathar heresy and, later, in the Inquisition and the witch hysteria. In the 16th century, Martin Luther—the founder of Protestant Christianity but conventional in his thoughts about the Devil—took the concept to its logical extreme, labeling as agents of Satan the following: Jews, Roman Catholics, all who fought against landowners (Luther needed their support), and all Protestants who were not Lutherans (Pagels, 1995). Luther, plagued by constipation, even blamed his gastric problems on the Devil.

BELIEVERS IN END-OF-THE WORLD PREDICTIONS

Shortly after we moved to Colorado, in mid-1998, I struck up a conversation with our postman, "Tom." I knew he was a member of a fundamentalist Christian church (he had tried to recruit me) and I was curious to learn about his beliefs. I asked Tom what he thought about the coming of the year 2000. He told me emphatically that the world was about to end. I asked him why he thought that and he told me that some very significant things were happening in the world that all pointed to that conclusion. Tom was particularly impressed by a story told by a member of his church who had emigrated to Colorado from Mexico. According to this person, a Mexican woman had recently given birth to a baby who came out of the womb with horns like the Devil's. Although a newborn, this baby spoke in perfect Spanish and said "the world is about to end." Then the baby and its mother both abruptly died. What amazed me was Tom's unquestioning belief in the story's veracity, and his apparent lack of interest in asking questions such as "how did the parishioner come to learn of this story?" and "what evidence did she have that it actually happened?" To Tom, the truth of the story lay in its congruence with the tenets of his religious belief system and the fact that others in his church believed it.

An interesting aspect of the gullibility of believers in an imminent apocalypse is that it does not seem shaken by the failure of earlier predictions by the same cult leader. Social psychologist Leon Festinger and his colleagues explored this question in their book *When Prophecy Fails* (Festinger, Riecken, & Schacter, 1956). Their explanation made use of the notion of cognitive dissonance, a theory initially developed by Festinger. Cognitive dissonance is a state of tension caused by the fact that an aspect of reality is in conflict with a strongly held idea or value. When this happens, according to the theory, one either abandons the belief or finds a way of reframing reality to fit with the belief. Although most of the research on the theory took place in the laboratory, the prophecy study was done in the field, using observational methods. The study was inspired by a publicized prophecy by a "Mrs Keech," that on a certain date there would be a great flood. Mrs Keech was very interested in space ships and other occult phenomena, and she claimed that the message about the flood had come to her through automatic writing, done while in a trance state, from superior beings on a planet called Clarion.

The researchers managed to infiltrate Mrs Keech's group (using deceptive methods that would today likely be considered unethical) and described what happened when the appointed day came and went without the predicted apocalyptic flood. Although a small number of members, whom the researchers considered among the least committed, did drop out of the group, the majority of the members had their beliefs actually strengthened by the failed prophecy. This was done by reframing the episode as a test, by interpreting various other events (such as a mysterious visit from five young men who the group decided were aliens in disguise) as a sign that something was still going on, by Mrs Keech continuing to get clarifying messages (such as that when the ship came for them, they would not be returning to Earth), and (the spin always put on failed apocalyptic prophecies) that the predicted catastrophe was averted by their own actions and beliefs.

The history of the Jehovah's Witnesses shows how a fringe religious sect can survive, and flourish (today it has millions of members), even in the face of multiple failed apocalyptic prophecies. Barbara Grizzuth Harrison (1978) who, as a child was raised in a family of Jehovah's Witnesses, gives a fascinating account of this phenomenon in her book *Visions of Glory: A History and a Memory of Jehovah's Witnesses*. The founder and first president of *The Watchtower Bible* and Tract Society (the official name of the Jehovah's Witnesses, later changed to Zion's Watch Tower Tract Society) was Charles Taze Russell, born in Pittsburgh in 1852. A successful haberdasher, Russell became interested in his late teens in the teachings of the Second Adventists, who taught that Jesus would physically return and the world would end in 1873 or 1874. Russell felt that the methods used to make these predictions were unsound, and in 1873, at age 22, he published his own ideas, in a book titled *The Object and Manner of the Lord's Return*. His basic idea was that Christ would come silently, not in visible form, and that his purpose was to bless, not destroy, the people on the earth. In 1877, Russell merged his Pittsburgh group with one in

Rochester, New York that held similar ideas, started calling himself "Pastor Russell," and traveled around the United States giving sermons.

At age 26, in 1877, Russell published a book with N.H. Barbour (the leader of the Rochester group) titled *Three Worlds, and the Harvest of This World*, in which they laid out a highly intricate theory regarding the coming apocalypse. They wrote that 6,000 years of human existence had ended in 1872, and that the invisible Christ returned to earth in 1873. Beginning in 1874, a 40-year period began in which righteous ones would be "harvested." At the end of this period, in October 1914, the world would end, but not before Russell and his followers would disappear, called away to be with their Lord in 1878. Of course, 1914 was the year that World War One began, but Russell was still around.

Although Russell had earlier written that the 1878 date could not be altered, he proceeded to periodically present new mathematical calculations, on the grounds that Biblical dates were hidden by God and the exact formula could not be known until God saw fit to reveal it. This formulation, which could explain away all "miscalculations," was later buttressed by a change in the nature of the predicted event itself. In the new version, the prediction was changed from one in which believers were to be called away to one in which they were to enjoy everlasting life on earth, with the added wrinkle that they could die but later be called back to life. There were obvious advantages to this new prediction, as nothing happening could be taken as confirming evidence for the truth of the prediction, and the death of a follower could always be blamed on his or her lack of piety.

As with many cult founders, Russell was highly autocratic, and was accused of numerous sexual and financial improprieties. He was the target of many lawsuits, with his opponents always depicted by him as agents of Satan and his own persecution always used as evidence of his identification with Christ. Russell was associated with various financial scams, the most successful of which was to sell "miracle wheat" seeds, advertised in *The Watchtower*, for $60 a bushel (at a time when regular wheat seeds sold for $1 a bushel and produced twice as much yield) and then funnel the proceeds into a dummy corporation that he controlled.

Russell died in 1916, 2 years after his failed prediction that the earth would end in 1914. Although one might have expected the sect to fold, it owed its survival in large part to World War One. One reason was because many of its members were imprisoned because of their refusal to serve in the military, thus shifting the focus of sect members away from internal disputes and towards external persecution. More importantly, the conflict (which began in 1914) was interpreted as a sign that Jesus had begun his war with the Devil, but in heaven rather than on earth. The fact that the earth survived was also interpreted (in line with the Cognitive Dissonance theory of Festinger and his colleagues) as a sign of God's benevolence. As quoted by Harrison (1978):

> Had Jehovah's great warrior, the Lord Jesus, continued his assault against Satan and his angels after that first skirmish which dusted those rebels from heaven, ... no flesh would have been saved. So, for the sake of God's own people, and to fulfill his purpose, Jehovah "cut short" those days of tribulation against the invisible rebel spirits by stopping his war for a period before ... Armageddon. (p. 165)

Thus, what could have been seen as complete failure was used as the basis for an altered theology, one that emphasized a dual road to salvation: a few living saints would be called to heaven immediately after their deaths, whereas other (not yet worthy) followers would have the opportunity to live forever once the earth was cleansed and perfect.

This continual reframing of its belief system to explain away disconfirming reality explains, in part, the survival and growth of the Jehovah's Witnesses. It is also likely that the makeup of church members (many of them unsophisticated, some with marginal mental health) is a contributing factor. The rigid nature of the church's hierarchy, the convoluted dogma, and the movement's tarnished history would likely cause more sophisticated people to respond with great skepticism.

THE GULLIBILITY OF THOSE WHO BELIEVE IN MEDIUMS

Spiritualism is an alternative religious movement that sprang into being in spring 1848, in the Hydesville, New York, home occupied by farmer John Fox, along with his wife and two teenage daughters, Katie and Margaret. For several nights, there were mysterious rappings and other strange sounds. One of the girls was able to induce the raps by snapping her fingers, thus suggesting that some conscious agent was responding. The girls developed a system for communicating with the presumed spirit, asking questions and then having it answer with one rap for "yes" and two raps for "no." Similar phenomena began to appear throughout upstate New York, and later throughout the region. A movement, termed Spiritualism, began to make converts throughout the world, and within 15 years after its humble beginnings, it was estimated that there were more than 11 million adherents in the United States alone. An excellent account of the origins of this movement, including the likely faking by its originators, can be found in *Talking to the Dead: Kate and Maggie Fox and the Rise of Spiritualism* (Weisberg, 2004).

The appeal of Spiritualism lay in two factors:

1. It offered an alternative to establishment religion, and a means for individuals to communicate directly with God, at a time when reform of many institutions was in the air.

2. More importantly, it provided an opportunity for people to communicate with loved ones at a time (predating antibiotics and modern medicine) when life expectancy was short and child mortality was rampant.

For this reason, Spiritualism probably reached its zenith in the immediate aftermath of World War One in England, when a huge percentage of the young adult male population had died in the trenches of Europe. Another part of the appeal of Spiritualism is that it lent itself to entertaining theatrical acts, at a time before the invention of radio, motion pictures, and television. Many professional magicians found second careers as Spiritualists, whereas other magicians reproduced Spiritualist effects in their magic shows, and scientists and other magicians (most prominently Houdini) set out to expose the fraudulent nature of mediums and various Spiritualist phenomena.

One of the most ardent believers in Spiritualism was the English physician and author Arthur Conan Doyle, the creator of Sherlock Holmes, who wrote several popular books in support of Spiritualism and was a star on the lecture circuit, where one of his main attractions was the showing of slides purporting to show faint images of ghosts and fairies in the background. Doyle, whose conversion to Spiritualism reportedly stemmed from a desire to communicate with his son who had been killed in World War One, was so committed a believer that even when mediums were exposed (or self-confessed) as frauds, his explanation was that they sometimes became tired and only resorted to fakery on those occasions. Even after the most famous of his fairy photos were shown to be fake (through evidence of double exposures and switched photographic plates), he continued to use them in his lectures, and in a book he wrote in defense of fairies.

There is a fascinating account of the friendship between Doyle and the great magician and escape artist Harry Houdini (the Wisconsin-reared son a Reform Jewish rabbi who had emigrated from Germany) in a book by Kenneth Silverman (1996) titled *Houdini!!!: The Career of Ehrich Weiss*. Although Houdini became interested in Spiritualism initially after the death of his mother, his intellectual honesty and deep understanding of conjuring tricks made him one of Spiritualism's leading opponents. Doyle was fascinated by Houdini because he believed him to be a secret medium, whose amazing escapes from locked and submerged trunks and the like resulted not from his physical and intellectual skills but from a supernatural ability to dematerialize and rematerialize himself. Doyle, who believed that Houdini was concerned that his popularity would wane if he admitted he was a medium, dismissed the fact that Houdini consistently and vehemently denied this explanation. Doyle used Houdini's denials as further evidence that he actually was a medium, for why else, reasoned Doyle, would Houdini be so adamant unless he wanted to divert people from knowing the truth.

For his part, Houdini thought that Doyle was one of the most gullible men he had ever met. For example, Houdini recounted the time that he accompanied Doyle and his wife in a taxi back to their hotel after a dinner at Houdini's home in upper Manhattan. Houdini entertained them with simple magic tricks, such as making a coin disappear. Doyle was dumb-struck and expressed great amazement.

To me, the most interesting thing about Spiritualism is the fact that many of its adherents—such as Doyle—were people of great education and accomplishment. One would like to think that intelligence provides some protection against nonsense of this sort, but obviously in many cases it does not. Cognitive psychologist, Ray Hyman (2002), provided an interesting example of this at a lecture I attended of the Rocky Mountain Skeptics (and that I understand will be included in a forthcoming book by Hyman on Nobel-caliber scholars who fall for crazy ideas). The example involves a late 19th-century professor, Johann Carl Friedrich Zoellner, a leading German scientist who is considered the father of astrophysics. One evening, Zoellner attended a demonstration put on by a visiting American spiritualist, Harry Slade. The demonstration consisted of a number of tricks—a rope untying itself, writing appearing on a slate, and so on—all of which Hyman, a magician in his younger years, was able to replicate in his lecture. Zoellner was so blown away that he converted to Spiritualism and wrote a book claiming the existence of a fourth dimension accessible only to people with supernatural talents.

Hyman (2002) devoted much thought to the question "Why are great scientists sometimes so stupid?" Part of his answer is that the stereotype of scientists as coldly rational and always analytical is a myth, and that the truly great scientists, such as Zoellner, are risk-takers and contrarian thinkers whose greatest insights often occur through intuitive flashes of insight. Unfortunately, such reliance on intuition and emotion can sometimes lead even the greatest of thinkers astray.

A puzzle about Doyle concerns how someone so dismissive of evidence (his response to any finding critical of Spiritualism was to ignore it because

"everyone knows it exists") could have created so rational and scientifically
oriented a fictional character as Sherlock Holmes. Some have suggested that
Doyle hated Holmes for this reason, as reflected in an often expressed desire
to kill him off. But Holmes lacked the one quality of a true scientist, which
is a willingness to consider the possibility that he might be mistaken. His
deductions were typically based on the flimsiest of evidence (appropriately
seen as a kind of wizardry) and his intuitions were, magically, almost never
proved wrong. If he were a real-life character, Sherlock Holmes would almost
certainly have been as gullible as Doyle.

GULLIBILITY IN ANTI-SEMITISM

Anti-Semitism is a religiously inspired quasi-political movement that ex-
ploits the gullibility of people who are quick to believe all sorts of negative
things about Jews, particularly that their machinations are at the root of everything bad in the world. One modern twist on this theme is that the Nazi
extermination of Jews didn't happen, was greatly exaggerated, and, in any
event, was not ordered by Hitler. In this view, the story of the Holocaust was
a lie orchestrated by the Jewish establishment.

According to cognitive psychologist Keith Stanovich (1999), people who
are gullible enough to believe such nonsense are not necessarily lacking in
intelligence (which Stanovich viewed as the possession of cognitive schemas)
as they are guilty of being "irrational" (i.e., unable to apply those schemas
adequately to accord with reality). He gave the example of two Illinois
teachers who were fired after they sent out letters to parents protesting the
requirement that the curriculum include a unit on the Holocaust, an event
that the teachers were convinced was a historical fiction. To Stanovich, such
irrationality/gullibility is fueled by what he terms an *intuition pump*. In other
words, when people hold on to a powerful affective notion, such as that Jews
are at the root of all evil, the only truth that matters to such individuals is the
truth that resides inside their heads.

Anti-Jewish sentiment is an old phenomenon, going back to Biblical times,
and in its early forms it was based primarily on the fact that Jews had different
religious beliefs. It has played a central role in Christianity, primarily because
of the importance given to the story of how the Jews, and Judas Iscariot (the
only one of Jesus' disciples who bore the name of the Jews), betrayed Christ.
This story, of how Christian leaders increasingly came to scapegoat Jews for
the death of Christ, is explored in *Judas Iscariot and the Myth of Jewish Evil*
(Maccoby, 1992).

The early view of Judas was that he was a fool, a gullible schmuck tricked by the Romans. A later shift to viewing him (and by extension, Jews) as evil was, according to Maccoby, an accommodation to the anti-Semitism that was already widespread in the Greco-Roman world. Maccoby wrote that "the incipient anti-Semitism found in Paul's epistles developed into a full-blown indictment of the Jewish people as the rejecters, betrayers, and finally murderers of Jesus" (p. 27). After the disastrous Jewish war against Rome (which resulted in the destruction of the Temple), the Pauline Church was careful to deny any Jewish connection, or any notion that Jesus was a rebel against Rome, and developed the idea that Christ was an opponent of the Jewish religion as opposed to someone whose main goal was to reform the Jewish religion from within.

To blacken the reputation of the Jews, and thus cement their position with the Romans, the post-Pauline leaders developed the notion that Judas, and by extension the Jews, were evil arch-sinners who brought divine retribution down on their heads for their skepticism in rejecting and betraying God's son. In particular, Jews were portrayed as schemers who manipulated the Romans into killing Jesus and were responsible for all of the bad things that happened in the world.

The use of Jews as a Christian scapegoat was cemented in the Middle Ages (which began around 1100 CE), and was best exemplified in the Passion Plays that depicted the life and death of Christ. Those plays began around 1300 CE, and were enormously popular. In them, Biblical Jews were portrayed as evil moneylenders, when in reality most of them had been farmers. Again, contrary to historical reality, Jews were depicted carrying out all of the evil deeds against Jesus, including piercing his side with a lance. The negative portrayal of Jews in Passion Plays is still alive, as seen in the film *The Passion of the Christ*, produced by actor Mel Gibson.

The Pauline and medieval myth of Jews as evil conspirators has continued into the modern era and lies at the core of 19th- and 20th-century anti-Semitism, as described in a book by Robert S. Wistrich (1991), titled *Antisemitism: The Longest Hatred*. The book contains an especially good account of the 1890s "Dreyfus Affair," in which the defeat of France by the Prussian army was blamed on espionage by Captain Alfred Dreyfus, the highest-ranking Jewish officer in the French Army. Although the evidence against Dreyfus was later determined to be a forgery, it took years for his name to be cleared, and the affair showed how deep-seated anti-Semitism was in France, a country in many ways tolerant of Jews.

The emotional hatred of many Christians against Jews made them likely to gullibly accept two notorious anti-Semitic rumors: the "blood libel," which began in the Middle Ages, but continued (in various guises) to the modern era, and the *Protocols of the Learned Elders of Zion*, which was a 20th-century phenomenon. These two rumors were widely believed, especially by the unsophisticated masses, and were used as the basis for untold numbers of anti-Jewish riots and pogroms.

An account of the origins and influence of the blood libel can be found in *The Blood Libel Legend: A Casebook in Anti-Semitic Folklore* (Dundes, 1991). The basic form of the legend is the belief that Jews capture non-Jewish children, and then torture and kill them and use their blood in satanic rituals. The first known example of the blood libel took place in 1144, in Norwich, England, when the body of a Christian child named William was discovered. The rumor that developed around this death was that the Jews of Norwich had bought this boy for the purpose of crucifying him on Good Friday, and that his grave was discovered because of divine intervention intended to punish the Jews for their crime. In this story, the monks at a monastery were directed by the Lord to bury William as a holy martyr. A book was written by Thomas of Monmouth, purporting to detail both the crime against William (who became sainted) and the many miracles attributed to him.

The earliest accusation that Jews engaged in ritual murder was made in the second century BCE, in a story told by the historian Posidonius about a rumor that every 7 years the Jews captured a Greek, cut him up and ate parts of him, and swore an oath of hatred against Greeks. Such accusations were rare, however, until the Middle Ages. Following the story of William of Norwich, blood libel rumors began to crop up regularly in countries throughout Europe, and were used as a pretext for killing rampages against Jews, or anti-Jewish policies such as the mass expulsion of Jews from Spain in 1492.

A modern equivalent of the blood libel, which has been used throughout the world as a justification for anti-Semitism is a pamphlet known as the *Protocols of the Learned Elders of Zion*. A historical account of this notorious anti-Semitic tract is provided in *A Rumor About the Jews: Reflections on Antisemitism and the Protocols of the Learned Elders of Zion* (Bronner, 2000). The tract, which first appeared in 1903, consists of "the supposed minutes from twenty-four sessions of a congress held by representatives from the 'twelve tribes of Israel' and led by a Grand Rabbi, whose purpose was to plan the conquest of the world" (p. 1). It actually was a crude forgery, created by the Imperial Russian secret police, and used as a justification for blaming the Jews and the Freemasons (who supposedly were in cahoots with them) for the revolutionary political turmoil in Russia and the military weakness of the country after its defeat in the Russo-Japanese War.

Although the pamphlet was a ludicrous and obvious fake, it was exported around the world, was treated as serious by any number of political and intellectual leaders, and was, according to Bronner, made required reading by the Nazis. As described by Bronner, the document (along with the blood libel) was used to justify many notorious pogroms in Russia and other countries in eastern Europe. Reportedly, the Protocols can still be found in book stalls in Russia and various Muslim countries, among other places. It has even been serialized as a TV mini-series in Saudi Arabia, a country where Jewish travelers are refused entry.

Industrialist Henry Ford was a big fan of the Protocols. In 1920, he launched an anti-Semitic campaign in a newspaper he controlled, the Dearborn *Independent*, by authorizing a serialization, and later mass distribution, of the Protocols and a series of editorials on "the Jewish question" (a euphemism for "should Jews be allowed to be citizens?"). As detailed by Neil Baldwin (2001) in a book titled *Henry Ford and the Jews: The Mass Production of Hate*, Ford always believed that "history is more or less the bunk." Believing that history was a series of unpublicized conspiracies, and because of his pre-existing anti-Semitism, Ford promoted the Protocols as a way of setting the historic record straight. Thus, in a bizarre twist, a conspiracy theory fueled by prejudice became the "real history."

CHRISTIAN SCIENCE AS A MAGNET FOR GULLIBLES

In addition to the many failed prophecies, one reason why the Jehovah's Witnesses call on more than the normal amount of religious gullibility is because its members follow a highly dangerous prohibition against blood transfusions. This prohibition has caused many deaths to followers and to their minor children. Christian Science is another religious sect, also founded in the United States, where prohibition against modern medical practices plays an even more central role than is the case with the Jehovah's Witnesses, where such a prohibition is limited mainly to blood transfusions (although some Witnesses have naïvely applied the prohibition to vaccinations because of a mistaken belief it involves a transfer of blood).

Mary Baker Eddy, who was born in New Hampshire in 1821, founded Christian Science, which last reported its membership numbers in the 1930s when the estimate was 500,000. The religion, and its charismatic founder, has been the subject of a number of books exploring the possibility that Mrs Eddy was a fraud and her followers highly gullible dupes. Among these were *The*

Life of Mary Baker G. Eddy and the History of Christian Science, co-authored by Willa Cather (Cather & Milmine, 1909/1993). Cather was fascinated by Eddy's neuroticism, and supposedly used her as the model for Mrs Cutler in her novel *My Antonia*.

A more in-depth treatment of Eddy is *The Healing Revelations of Mary Baker Eddy: The Rise and Fall of Christian Science*, by the mathematician and skeptic Martin Gardner (1993). Gardner provided evidence that predating her founding of Christian Science, Eddy engaged in a variety of spiritualist practices (which Eddy later denied) in which she communicated with the dead through such means as automatic writing and séances. The turning point in Eddy's life was her discovery of a quack doctor named Phineas Parkhurst Quimby. A clock repairman, Quimby developed an interest in mesmerism (a healing method based on a hypothesized electromagnetic field in the body termed *animal magnetism*) and a belief that he possessed the ability to detect illness with his mind. His key idea was that all illness was a result of wrong thinking, and that he could cure illness by teaching a patient to think correctly. In Quimby's view, all illness is in the mind and the cure for illness is to give up a belief that sickness and pain actually exist.

Quimby was a highly charismatic figure, with deeply hypnotic eyes, and it is likely that some of his "cures" were brought about in hysterical patients through the force of hypnotic suggestion. Eddy, a woman with little formal education, became a follower of Quimby and his ideas, after she went to his Portland, Maine, office in 1862 (when she was 41) for treatment of what she called her "spinal inflammations," which had kept her for years in a state of bedridden invalidism. Achieving some relief, Eddy went to study with Quimby for several months in 1864 and later became a devoted disciple of his methods and theories.

Quimby died in 1866 at the age of 64, attended by a homeopathic doctor, and later that year Eddy was injured in a fall, which restored her to her former state of invalidism. Without Quimby to help her, Eddy said that she lay in bed leafing through the Bible and ran across Matthew 9:2, which told the story of Jesus healing a man with palsy. Eddy was inspired by this passage, which convinced her that Quimby's method was congruent with Christian beliefs, and she termed her synthesis "the Science of Divine Metaphysical Healing," later changed to Christian Science. Eddy later wrote that she cured herself using this new belief system, although Cather suggested that her recovery resulted more from the effects of repeated doses of morphine. In fact, Eddy had periods of recurring illness for the rest of her life, and she became quite dependent on morphine to deal with the pain. However, because pain did not exist for Eddy, she justified her use of morphine by claiming that it helped to combat her false belief in the pain.

Eddy claimed that there was no religious emphasis in Quimby's ideas, and that the Christian rationale for her movement came from her alone. In fact, Quimby was very religious and made many references to Christianity in his writings. Eddy came to downplay Quimby's contribution, and even claimed that he had been her disciple rather than the other way around. In fact, Quimby's ideas had influenced a movement called New Thought, and were filtered into a number of its books, such as Walter Evans' 1869 *Science and Health: The Mental Cure*, that antedate Eddy's books, likely influenced her, and anticipated all of the ideas published in 1875 in the first edition of her book, also titled *Science and Health*.

By all accounts, Eddy was a highly unstable woman, who for her entire life had anxiety attacks (as a child caused by fears of Satan) and needed to be rocked every night to sleep. Although she gave up mesmerism as a healing force, she continued to believe in it as a force for evil, and was convinced that her illnesses were brought on by her enemies who directed "malicious animal magnetism" (MAM) her way. She was attended by students and followers in her evolving church, and from time to time she directed her disciples to work in round-the-clock shifts in her home, using their own thoughts to create a barrier that would ward off the MAM that was aimed at her (modern day Christian Science has largely expunged mention of MAM from its writings, in an effort to erase evidence of its founder's paranoia and to avoid the destructive practice whereby church members used to accuse each other of MAM whenever they had a disagreement). Eddy constantly railed against her servants, accusing them of stealing and of acting under the influence of MAM. Eddy attributed the death of her last husband, clearly of a heart attack, as revealed in an autopsy, to MAM and to poisoning.

The tremendous growth of Christian Science in the 1890s provoked concern that what appeared to be a wacko cult was in danger of surpassing traditional Christianity in numbers of adherents. Among those who criticized Eddy in print was America's greatest satirist and commentator on gullibility, Mark Twain (1907). Aside from being concerned about Eddy's empire building and cult following, Twain was offended by the third-rate quality of her writing. He was convinced that Eddy's major work, *Science and Health*, had been ghost-written, because it was somewhat less incoherent and ungrammatical than her letters and some of her articles. But Twain was unable to get his hands on the original 1875 edition of *Science and Health*, which to this day has been kept from examination by scholars.

To my mind, the great scandal of Christian Science is the willingness to endanger the lives of followers by discouraging them from seeking traditional medical treatment. A prominent example involved the great puppeteer Jim Henson, who sought medical attention for pneumonia only when he was literally on his death bed. Even in Eddy's lifetime, there were some high-profile deaths of church members. A notorious case involved Mrs Abby Corner, of West Medford, Massachusetts, who handled, without medical assistance, the birth of her daughter's child, using "metaphysical obstetrics," a technique taught by Eddy in her lectures. Both her daughter and grandchild died during the delivery, and Mrs Corner was arrested for manslaughter.

The lack of empirical validity for the effectiveness of Christian Science healing can be found in a number of studies. For example, it has been found that the death rate from cancer of church members is twice that for the general population, that the life expectancy of church members is significantly lower than for non-church members, and that nearly 20% of deaths of church members are preventable. So why do Christian Scientists, many of them well educated and affluent, continue to participate in a religion that endangers their lives and the lives of their loved ones?

One assumes that most practitioners believe that the practice does work, as reflected in the fact that they are still alive, and may have a somewhat lower incidence of minor illnesses. There is, in fact, some evidence that the immune system is influenced by the mind, although none that illness is an illusion. The ideas behind Christian Science have some superficial validity and it is, therefore, understandable that they would appeal to many people. Furthermore, one can always attribute a major failure, such as the death of a member, to the fact that she didn't pray hard enough and thus wasn't close enough to God. Such a "blame the victim" stance explains why people stay in snake-handling Christian sects, despite the many families that have been decimated by deaths from snake bites (Brown & McDonald, 2000).

CHAPTER 4

Gullibility in War and Politics

The stories in this chapter address the role of gullibility in politics and war (which was described by von Clausewitz as the use of force to attain political aims). In the military domain, gullibility is explored in the fable of the Trojan Horse, and in two notable military fiascos: Vietnam and Iraq. Conventional political gullibility is explored on the Right, on the Left, and in the rise of spin doctoring. Paranoid political gullibility is explored in a common form (belief in conspiracies) and a more extreme form (suicide bombers).

THE TROJAN HORSE AND MILITARY DECEPTION

Deception has always been a big part of warfare, as seen 2,000 years ago in Sun Tzu's classic book, *The Art of War*. In another book with the same title, Renaissance political theorist Niccolo Machiavelli, best known for writing in *The Prince* about the uses of deception by political rulers, made a similar case for the uses of deception by military leaders. Most of the writing on this topic has focused on the skill of those doing the deceiving but, given the focus of this book, I am more interested in the factors contributing to the gullibility of those who were deceived. As with other cases of gullibility throughout this book, two sets of factors explain most of the gullibility in war: stupidity and emotion.

Deception has contributed to many notable military victories, and gullibility is often one of the reasons, sometimes the major reason, why the losing side loses. Given that opposing forces are often evenly matched (and sometimes the eventual loser's forces are superior), deception can make the critical difference in winning a battle or war. There is an extensive literature on military deception, with one of the best recent treatments being Jon Latimer's (2001), *Deception in War: The Art of the Bluff, the Value of Deceit, and the Most Thrilling Episodes of Cunning in Military History, from the Trojan Horse to the Gulf War*.

One clue to the gullibility of military dupes can be found in Norman Dixon's (1976) *On the Psychology of Military Incompetence*. Dixon noted that armies tend to operate on the basis of collective wisdom, by leaders who for the most part have attained senior status by playing it safe, that is by going along with group consensus. Given the ambiguity and unreality of much battlefield information (something that may be less of a factor, at least for advanced militaries, in the age of satellites and remote-controlled video drones), this creates room for wishes and preconceived ideas, not to mention collective delusions, to operate.

The key to being a successful military deceiver is to provide misinformation that plays into the enemy's wishes or ideas. The classic example of this is the story of the Trojan Horse, told sparingly in Homer's *The Odyssey*, and in more embellished form in Virgil's *The Aeneid*. In spite of its subtitle, there is no discussion of the episode in Latimer (2001), but Tuchman (1984) begins her marvelous study of what she terms "pursuit of policy contrary to self-interest" with an analysis of the story as a prototype for all later political and military stupidity.

The basic story goes as follows: After a bloody and inconclusive 9-year siege of Troy by a Greek coalition sent to recapture Helen, the kidnapped wife of the king of Sparta, the Greeks gave up, got in their ships, and took off. Outside the walled city, they left a large wooden statue of a horse. Hidden inside the horse was a band of soldiers, led by Odysseus (Ulysses). Inscribed on the horse was a dedication to the Goddess Athena, asking her aid in ensuring a safe return. The Greeks knew the horse would appeal to the Trojans, who considered it a sacred animal, and they hoped they would move it inside the city walls, to a temple of Athena located there.

There was considerable debate among the Trojans as to whether the horse was a trick and should be destroyed (in Virgil's version, Laocoon gave his famous warning: "I fear Greeks bearing gifts"). The balance was tipped in favor of gullibility by a captured Greek soldier, Sinon (actually, a plant), who told them the horse was a true offering to Athena. According to Sinon, the horse had been made deliberately too large to enter into the city, because the Greeks did not want to admit that the Trojans had defeated them. This story made sense to the Trojans, as they did, in fact, have to dismantle a gate to bring the horse inside. The story also obviously appealed to their vanity. Relieved that the long war was finally at an end, the Trojans brought the horse inside the city, and proceeded to have a drunken celebration. While the city slept, Sinon opened the horse's trap door and Ulysses and his men opened the gates to the city. In the ensuing battle, the Trojans were slaughtered, the victims of their own emotion-driven trust.

Often the seeds of gullibility lie in past victories, in that a victor sometimes comes to underestimate an opponent and to overestimate one's own ability to predict, and counteract, the opponent's actions. Certainly, this is the best explanation of the almost fatal lack of preparedness of the Israeli military to the surprise crossing of the Suez Canal by the Egyptians in 1973. As detailed by Latimer (2001), Israel's military and political leaders were unable to see through a very sophisticated and carefully carried-out program of deception by the Egyptians (involving large-scale clandestine moving of men and equipment, and use of various political and communication ruses), partly because they never imagined that the Egyptians were capable of such a coordinated and difficult feat, and partly because they assumed that they would, as in the past, be able to deal easily with whatever the Egyptians came up with. These factors made them inclined to ignore signs that otherwise might have been taken more seriously. Again, affective factors on the gullible side tipped the balance in favor of the deceptive side.

Perhaps even more than in other forms of gullibility, self-deception plays a major role in the gullibility of military leaders. Self-deception contributed to the gullibility of the Germans in North Africa, and on both the eastern and western European fronts in World War Two. In the face of exceptionally skilled deception campaigns by the British, Americans, and Russians, the resulting gullibility contributed significantly to the collapse of the Third Reich, according to Latimer (2001). In the Normandy invasion, British and American deception consisted of two parts: the use of double agents and the creation of a false order of battle. Although this two-headed deception campaign was used throughout the war, it reached its zenith in the D-day invasion, a story that is told in *Fortitude: The D-Day Deception Campaign* by Roger Hesketh (2002).

The Germans knew that an invasion was coming, and they had a rough idea of when, but they were not certain where the landing would be. Tremendous efforts went toward convincing the Germans that the main landing would be from southeast England, across the Channel at Pas de Calais, and that the first landing from southwest England, in Normandy, was actually a feint. The ruse was so successful that many German divisions were held in reserve near the Pas de Calais region, and were never brought to bear in Normandy, where they might have repelled the Allied forces. The ruse worked because the Germans considered the Pas de Calais to be the most likely invasion location, as it had a natural harbor, lacked Normandy's deadly cliffs, and was closer to

Germany. Thus, the deception campaign worked because it took advantage of the preconceived ideas of the German military leaders. This tendency to let one's ideas and preferences color one's judgment is at the heart of many gullibility episodes.

GROUPTHINK IN THE PLANNING OF THE VIETNAM WAR

Gullibility played an important role in the many mistakes committed by U.S. military and political leaders in their conduct of the Vietnam War. As detailed in Robert Mann's (2001) *A Grand Delusion: America's Descent Into Vietnam*, U.S. gullibility was fueled by the anti-communist hysteria that existed during the Cold War against the Soviet Union and the Chinese communists, and by the fear of Democratic presidents (John F. Kennedy and Lyndon Johnson) that they would be blamed for the "loss" of Vietnam as an earlier Democratic administration, that of Harry Truman, had been blamed by Joe McCarthy and other Republicans for the communist takeover of China. Kennedy's vulnerability was also affected by his need to counter the perception of him as a weak leader after the botched landing at Cuba's Bay of Pigs. Many attribute that earlier fiasco to Kennedy's gullible acceptance of flawed advice from military and CIA advisers. If so, Vietnam is an example of a "neurotic paradox," in which one compensates for a past mistake by repeating it again, but on an even grander scale.

As with the Germans in regard to the Normandy invasion, U.S. gullibility was an outgrowth of assumptions and beliefs that affected judgments about reality. But unlike the earlier situation, where German gullibility was helped by an Allied deception campaign, the U.S. gullibility toward Vietnam was almost entirely the product of an abiding obsession with communism. An example can be found in then Vice President Hubert Humphrey, an early skeptic about the war but whom Johnson bullied into becoming an ardent supporter of American escalation. After returning from a 1966 trip to Saigon, Humphrey exclaimed to his staff " 'I want to show that there is a master plan, . . . a designed strategy' by the communists to subjugate South Vietnam" (Mann, 2001, p. 501). Mann further wrote that "Humphrey saw not a nationalist struggle for control of a single country, but an international communist plot to seize all of Asia. . . . 'The danger of China is a plague—an epidemic, and we most stop that epidemic'" (p. 501).

Barbara Tuchman (1984), in *The March of Folly: From Troy to Vietnam*, described several cases in which institutions (mostly governments, but occasionally other entities, such as the Catholic Church just before the Protestant secession) have persisted in disastrous policies even after it should have become evident that the policies were not working and that the beliefs and assumptions underlying the policies were incorrect. U.S. policy in Vietnam was one of the cases detailed by Tuchman. Among the mistaken assumptions underlying U.S. policy were that (a) America would lose Asia if South Vietnam fell (it did not happen when the United States pulled out and the North Vietnamese prevailed); (b) the war was a reflection of a unified communist world initiative rather than a continuation of Vietnam's colonial fight to free its country from France (the preponderance of evidence now supports the latter view); (c) pouring massive amounts of U.S. aid and manpower into Vietnam would prop up a corrupt and unpopular regime and make it a viable nation (that argument was what the British call a "nonstarter" from the beginning); and (d) massive bombing would cause the will of the Vietcong and North Vietnam to crumble (instead, as is usually the case, it had the opposite effect).

Although affective factors (a deep-seated fear of world communism) played the dominant role in explaining the gullibility of U.S. policymakers and the public, there was undoubtedly a cognitive factor as well. This reflected the relative absence of sophisticated knowledge about Vietnamese history, politics, and culture among the so-called "best and the brightest" (Robert McNamara, McGeorge Bundy, and other mostly Ivy League technocrats who devised the initial U.S. intervention) and also among congressional leaders and the public. In the absence of knowledge, mythology and mutual group reinforcement have more of a chance to become a basis for policy.

The likelihood that a smart individual will behave foolishly (and gullibly) is, paradoxically, often increased when that person is participating in a group decision process that is made up of other smart individuals. This "groupthink" process is part of a more general phenomenon in which people suspend their doubts about a course of action advocated by one's peers. We are all influenced, to a greater or lesser extent, by the opinions of others as to whether or not a particular course of action is correct. Yale social psychology professor Irving Janis (1980) coined the term *groupthink*. Groupthink refers to a process in which individually intelligent people, when in a certain group context, convince each other of the rightness of an incredibly stupid course of action. Janis first presented this concept more than 30 years ago in a book with the revised title, *Groupthink: Psychological Studies of Policy Decisions and Fiascos*.

Janis studied several fiascos from recent U.S. history, as examples of groupthink at work. The starting point for Janis' analysis is the fact that major policy decisions by governments, as well as nongovernmental entities, almost always emerge from a group process rather than, contrary to myth, mainly from the initiative of a president or other leader. It is appropriate to characterize such a group as "gullible" when it adopts a recommended policy that is based on totally wrong assumptions, often promoted by one or more especially persuasive advocates within the group.

What are the characteristics of groupthink that make possible a decision such as the escalated U.S. involvement in the Vietnam War, or before that, the failed U.S.-backed invasion of Cuba's Bay of Pigs (which Janis described as "the perfect fiasco")? The main predisposing factor is that "members of any small cohesive group tend to maintain *esprit de corps* by unconsciously developing a number of shared illusions and related norms that interfere with critical thinking and reality testing."

There are two shared illusions underlying most groupthink-influenced decisions:

1. an illusion of invulnerability (how could such a smart collection of people fail to be successful?); and

2. an illusion of unanimity (there is usually never any critical questioning of the group's decision or any willingness to open the discussions up to consider alternatives).

These illusions are maintained through the operation of "mind guards" (silencers of dissent, as when President Kennedy's brother Robert took adviser Arthur Schlesinger, Jr. aside and told him to keep his objections about the Bay of Pigs invasion to himself) and the establishment of a group norm of docility, encouraged by the leader (in these two cases, John F. Kennedy and, later, Lyndon Johnson). The maintenance of group cohesiveness is reinforced by the exclusion of outsiders who might have access to critical information. Ignorance plus the emotional attractiveness of a desired goal is a formula, as in other cases, for gullible action.

GULLIBILITY IN THE BUILDUP TO THE SECOND IRAQ WAR

As discussed in *Fiasco: The American Military Adventure in Iraq*, by Thomas E. Ricks (2006), gullibility played into the Iraq War[1] in two ways:

1. In the gullibility of a naïve President George W. Bush, and his coterie of advisers, in persuading themselves that pacifying and unifying Iraq would be an easily-obtainable goal.

---

[1]The United States fought two against Iraq. The first is commonly referred to as the Gulf War. The Second War in Iraq is referred to here as the Iraq War.

2. In the gullibility of Congress, the media, and the public, in believing the false argument that Iraq possessed weapons of mass destruction (WMDs) and bore heavy responsibility for the attack on New York's World Trade Center.

The gullibility of President Bush and his advisers is a two-part issue, the first having to do with Bush as an individual and the second having to do with the deliberation processes in the Bush Administration out of which the decision to invade Iraq emerged. With respect to Bush, the question—resulting from his verbal dysfluency and malapropisms—has sometimes been framed as "is Bush retarded?," as in a December 2007 MS NBC telecast on which news anchor Keith Olbermann characterized Bush as "transcendently stupid" and wondered if he should be viewed as America's "idiot-in-chief."

I happen to believe that Bush has average or above-average IQ, but has a cognitive style that is remarkably passive and incurious. As a consequence, Bush is profoundly ignorant of the world and relies on others to come up with (often disastrously) simple solutions to complex problems. Such a "supported presidency" (analogous to supported living and supported employment in the disability field) can work if two conditions are met:

1. Wise and competent people need to be put in place to tell the president what to do.
2. The president still needs to be able to recognize and put the brakes on a proposed course of action that is unwise and potentially catastrophic.

Unfortunately, Bush met neither of these conditions, unlike another intellectually lazy president, Ronald Reagan, who chose good advisers but was also strong enough to stand up to them on occasion. In contrast, Bush chose advisers who led him down the path to the fiasco of Iraq, and his lack of intellectual curiosity made him unable to recognize the pitfalls in their advice.

The decision process used in coming up with the flawed decision to overthrow Iraqi dictator Saddam Hussein through an unprovoked U.S. invasion has been described, even by many of the participants themselves, as an example of groupthink in action. In a March 17, 2004, article in the *San Francisco Chronicle*, science writer Keay Davidson quoted Jonathan B. Tucker of the Center for Nonproliferation Studies, and a former UN weapons inspector in Iraq. Tucker said: "I was very surprised that no WMDs were found. I was taken in by this groupthink, this set of preconceived notions, as well as anyone else'" (Davidson, 2004, P. A-1).

Jim Lobe wrote an article titled *"Chickenhawk Groupthink?"* that was published by the Inter Press Service on May 12, 2004. Chickenhawk is the somewhat pejorative term widely applied to "an 'in-group' of tough-talking advocates of military intervention, whose captain is Vice President Dick Cheney and that has had a decisive influence on Bush himself" (Lobe, 2004). Lobe contrasted this in-group to "an 'out-group' of 'realists' . . . which ironically boasts men . . . with real war experience." In contrast, "the in-group is dominated by individuals, particularly Cheney and virtually the entire civilian leadership of the Pentagon, who have none at all. Hence the moniker 'chickenhawks', defined as individuals who favor military solutions to political problems but who themselves avoided military service during wartime."

As in the examples of groupthink discussed previously in regard to Vietnam, various factors contributed to the Iraq disaster: a small and cohesive group with a long history together (Cheney, Rumsfeld, Wolfowitz, etc.) who thought they had all the answers, who believed in their group's inherent morality, and who shared stereotypes, particularly of the enemy; a disinclination to examine alternative or contingency plans for any action; being highly selective in gathering information; avoiding expert opinion; protecting the group from negative views or information; and having an illusion of invulnerability. Lobe further noted:

> Middle East experts at the State Department and the Central Intelligence Agency (CIA) were likewise scorned and excluded from both planning and the immediate aftermath of the invasion, while the creation . . . of ad hoc intelligence analysis groups that 'stovepiped' evidence of Iraqi WMD and ties to Al Qaeda was a classic illustration of selective intelligence gathering that would confirm pre-existing stereotypes. (Lobe, 2004)

As noted by Lobe and Ricks, Army Chief of Staff Shinseki's stated opinion that many more occupying troops were needed to provide security in Iraq had to be publicly denounced to protect the group's sense of its own omniscience.

The role of gullibility in the Iraq War pertains not only to the deluded arguments used by decision makers to convince themselves of the need to invade, but the failure of outsiders who should have known better than to accept official explanations noncritically. The editors of *The New York Times* later chided themselves (2004) in an editorial apology, for believing what they termed *official gullibility* in accepting the WMD rationale for the war.

Outside the United States, there was a widespread belief that U.S. voters were gullible in voting to re-elect Bush in the 2004 presidential election. This was expressed most famously the day after the election, when Britain's *Daily Mirror* ran a picture of Bush on its cover, over the caption "How can 59,054,087 people be so DUMB?" By this, the editors of the paper were indicating that a majority of U.S. voters had been tricked into voting for a deceitful candidate whom they believed had demonstrated considerable incompetence in his first term, particularly in his handling of the Iraq crisis. The topic of political gullibility, especially the success of conservative candidates in using emotionally charged symbols, is covered later in the next section. Here I discuss the Bush victory briefly in relation to the four factors portrayed in Fig. 1.1 in chapter 1.

The first factor, "situation," came into play in two ways. First, evidence of the nonexistence of WMDs had not, at the time of the election, become as overwhelming as it was later; neither had evidence of the terrible cost and protracted nature of the conflict become as clear as it was to become a few months later. Second, negative advertising, such as the breathtakingly devious campaign to discredit John Kerry's Vietnam War hero status, has rarely been used so effectively, or responded to so ineffectively. The second factor, "cognition," came into play in that the majority of voters have almost no historical background information sufficient to know when a candidate is feeding them a line of baloney. The third factor, "personality" comes into play in that most voters are unwilling to challenge authority. The fourth factor, "affect/state," is probably most relevant to understanding this, as it is of other, examples of mass gullibility. The portrayal of Bush as a courageous wartime president standing up against the forces of evil called forth strong emotional reactions in many voters. The diminished stature of Kerry gave the hero role squarely to Bush, despite his having evaded military service and in spite of evidence of a failed policy.

Clearly, the adjective "gullible" can be applied to U.S. voters as well as institutions such as the media and Congress, who allowed themselves to be hoodwinked (the title of a 2004 book about Iraq by John Prados) into supporting the Iraq adventure. This gullibility was helped not only by the lack of adequate background knowledge in those who were hoodwinked but also by the ambiguity of the facts themselves. The wise course of action when one has conflicting and ambiguous facts is to stand pat and do nothing. Gullible people have a hard time, in most cases, of being able to admit uncertainty. In the case of Iraq, as in a majority of the stories told in this book, the deciding factor was probably affect. The 9/11 tragedy was a profoundly upsetting national event, and the success (and later failure) of Bush lay in his ability to use that tragedy as an "affect engine" to manipulate others into doing his bidding.

GULLIBILITY ON THE POLITICAL RIGHT

Ronald Reagan, who died in 2004 at the age of 93, was a second-tier movie actor, and before that a radio sports announcer, who became a phenomenally popular president of the United States. His popularity was unaffected by the fact that his actions (e.g., producing runaway budget deficits) rarely lived up to his rhetoric (e.g., the need to reduce the size of government). Nor did the public seem bothered by his shaky grasp of the details of policy and history. He was typically quite detached, telling movie stories at serious meetings, and relying heavily on direction from his aides and his wife Nancy. The oldest person ever elected president, it is likely that the Alzheimer's disease with which he was later diagnosed had already begun to manifest itself during his second term. Although his last year in office was severely tarnished by the Iran-Contra scandal, he was still revered enough to have Washington's National Airport renamed for him and for it to be seriously suggested that his likeness be added to Mount Rushmore.

To me, this seemed like mass gullibility, so I was intrigued to run across a book by Stephen Ducat (1988) titled *Taken In: American Gullibility and the Reagan Mythos*. Although overly reliant on half-baked Freudianism, Ducat still came close to capturing the essence of Reagan's appeal. He described Reagan's talent as a leader as providing "tender music that warms our hearts" or "a kind of lexical Muzak—bland, soporific, but subliminally evocative" (p. 90). Using Milan Kundera's definition of *kitsch* (an object, usually art, of poor quality that appeals to low-brow taste) as "the absolute denial of shit," Ducat described Reagan as the political embodiment of kitsch. By this, he meant that Reagan provided a "Hallmark card rendering of social reality" (p. 90), which, despite its banality and seeming emptiness, "touches Americans in deep and unexpected ways" (p. 91).

The appeal of Reagan's brand of kitsch, according to Ducat, is that he came across not as an all-powerful father figure but as an all-comforting mother figure, singing us a lullaby that tells us that all will be safe, perfect, magical, and happy. In this lullaby (or bedtime story), shit happens, "but always as the excreta of the Outside Agitator, as a contamination introduced by a demonic enemy" (p. 90), namely the "evil empire" of the Soviet Union and its allies. But just as the big bad wolf is always slain in children's fairy tales, Reagan reassured us that the wolf of communism would be slain. No ambiguity here, no hugs for Brezhnev (as Jimmy Carter, Reagan's predecessor, was photographed doing), no talk about our national malaise (another Carter no-no). And the evil empire did die, arguably through internal economic and political forces that had little or nothing to do with Reagan. Fairy tale come true, *ipso* Reagan a great president.

Garry Wills (1987), who has written several books about U.S. presidents, provided a similar analysis of Reagan's appeal in his book *Reagan's America*. But for Wills, the more appropriate metaphor is not the fairy tale or lullaby, but rather the sports fable or pep talk. One needs to keep in mind that Reagan in many ways remained the sportscaster that he started out becoming. Most of his often repeated stories involved sports or war heroes, which are sort of the same thing. Many of these stories were embellished or, quite typically, completely made up. One example is a story Reagan told about a football game between his high school from Dixon, Illinois, and a rival team from Mendota. In this story, the Mendota players yelled for a penalty at a crucial point in the game. The official had missed the play and asked Reagan what had happened. Reagan's sense of sports ethics required him to tell the truth, Dixon was penalized, and went on to lose the game by one touchdown. Wonderful story, except that it never happened.

One quality of Reagan's that has been much noted is that he never bothered himself too much with the detailed facts, or complexities, of a situation. He believed in his stories so completely, that they became the only reality that mattered. In terms used by Swiss developmental psychologist Jean Piaget, Reagan was all "assimilation" (reliant on existing schemas) and no "accommodation" (modification of existing schemas to fit the facts of a situation). To me, this is a sign of intellectual laziness, and of a rather one-sided adaptation. But it was a good fit with a public equally uninterested in, or unknowledgeable about, complex reality.

Undoubtedly, Reagan's acting skills contributed to his success. Although by no means a great film actor, he had considerable success playing the kind of middle-American icon, such as doomed Notre Dame sports hero George Gipp, who the public loved. As others have noted, Reagan's greatest acting job came in playing the role of a strong, benevolent, and reassuring president. The gullibility of the public came in mistaking this for the real thing.

Undoubtedly, one reason why Ronald Reagan is so venerated by Republicans is that he probably had more to do than anyone else with the triumph of conservatism as the dominant political philosophy in the United States. To understand the gullibility of so many toward the idea that Reagan was a great president, it is necessary, therefore, to understand the gullibility of so many to the conservative message. The best explanation of the dominance of the conservative message is probably to be found in a book by George Lakoff (2002), titled *Moral Politics: How Liberals and Conservatives Think*. Lakoff is a cognitive linguist with an interest in everyday categorization, and this was his first effort to apply his methods to politics. His core message in *Moral Politics* was that the appeal of the conservatives lies less in their policy proposals than in their consistent use of an underlying "strong father" metaphor. Lakoff sees this metaphor as more appealing to the public than the underlying liberal metaphor of a "nurturing parent." An additional reason for the success of the conservatives is that they are more conscious of the metaphor they are using, and thus are better able to hone their message.

The strong father metaphor is based on an ideal view of the family, particularly popular among fundamentalist Christians as being hierarchically ordered, headed by a strict father who (a) sets firm limits, (b) expects instant obedience, (c) sends his children out into the world to succeed on their own and will not rescue them if they fail, (d) brooks no meddling with his authority within the family, and (e) defends the family from external threats. Translated into government policy, this strong father model has the following components: (a) the government seeks to build character in the people, and expects them to stand on their own feet; (b) success or failure is a function of character (one's inner strength) and it is immoral to interfere by helping people who have failed (i.e., who lack character); (c) people who succeed (the rich) have higher character and are morally superior to those who do not succeed (the nonrich) and thus are more deserving of government attention than are those of weaker character; (d) good and evil are clearly demarcated, and there cannot be any compromise with evil (e.g., bad people should be locked up or cast out without sympathy); (e) there should be no meddling (such as through economic or environmental regulations) with the natural moral order or with the process by which those of superior character get ahead; (f) there should be no redistribution of income (such as through progressive taxation) that interferes with that natural order; (g) moral authority and obedience are absolute, and moral deviance (such as homosexuality) or questioning of hierarchy (such as by feminists) are not to be tolerated; and (h) just as the father must protect his family, the government should be firm and unyielding in protecting the nation from its enemies (such as Saddam Hussein and, formerly, the "evil empire" of communism).

The strong father model explains two aspects of conservatism's appeal that are puzzling to liberals:

1. Policy positions that appear inconsistent on the surface (e.g., reducing the size of government combined with massive increases in military spending) are not experienced as inconsistent by people who hold to this model because they are both consistent with the strong father metaphor (strong fathers let their adult children sink or swim on their own;

however, strong fathers also carry a big stick in protecting their families from enemies).

2. Blue-collar workers and union members who used to vote for liberals have been increasingly voting for conservatives because they are very enamored of the strong father metaphor.

GULLIBILITY ON THE POLITICAL LEFT

If gullibility involves a tendency to be taken in by appearances or one's own fantasies, even in the face of strong disconfirming reality, then no aspect of political gullibility is more dramatic than the infatuation that untold numbers of Western intellectuals had with Communism and the Soviet Union. This idealization of Soviet society was widespread in the late 1920s and throughout the 1930s, and persisted in many individuals even at a time when the horrible realities of Soviet life under Stalin and his successors was becoming quite evident. In a review of a book by G. Edward White (White 2004) about Alger Hiss—the U.S. diplomat accused of spying for the Soviets—journalist Max Frankel (Frankel 2004) wrote that "we will need novelists to recreate the angry idealism of the Depression years that led so many Americans to feel a kinship with Communists" (p. 23).

The cynical use of the Hiss case as an anti-communist rallying cry by ambitious politicians such as Joseph McCarthy and Richard Nixon caused many left-leaning people to assert Hiss' innocence. Although the consensus today (aided by the release of Soviet intelligence files) is fairly strong on the side that he had indeed been a spy, "Hiss sold himself to gullible college audiences, [and] survived the scrutiny of skeptical journalists" (p. 23). Frankel noted that Hiss became a symbol of a highly emotionally charged cultural schism in American life, and the gullibility of his supporters was driven less by the truth of his assertions (which most were not in a position to evaluate) as by the fact that he was a convincing liar and he told a story of innocence and persecution that his supporters wanted to hear.

Paul Hollander, a University of Massachusetts sociologist who experienced life in Hungary under both the Nazis and the communists, has devoted several decades to an attempt to understand the gullibility that led Hiss and so many other well-educated Westerners toward Communism and the former Soviet Union. In a book titled *Political Pilgrims: Travels of Western Intellectuals to the Soviet Union, China, and Cuba 1928–1978*, Hollander (1981) examined the curious phenomenon of Westerners who traveled to communist societies and then returned home to write laudatory travel books, articles, or speeches that contained the most incredibly naïve and mistaken of utterances. This was by no means confined only to left-leaning figures. For example, the Reverend Billy Graham once returned from a trip to the Soviet Union with praise for the substantial degree of religious freedom that he observed there. For the most part, however, such flagrant misstatements were made by people of the left, such as Susan Sontag, who returned from a trip to Cuba in the 1960s and affirmed her belief that no Cuban writer "has been in jail or is failing to get his works published" (cited in Hollander, 1981, p. 266), shortly before evidence surfaced of numerous lengthy prison terms handed out to writers and widespread suppression of their writings.

Three of the factors in the four-factor model of gullibility described at the beginning of this volume can be called on to explain these mistaken perceptions. The first explanation is situational. The host countries went to great effort to select what the visitors could see and to give them a positive experience. The social reciprocity rule described in Robert Cialdini's (1984) book *Influence*, also explains why people who were the recipient of tremendous hospitality, often at the expense of the host countries, would feel some reluctance to write anything bad about their hosts. The second explanation is cognitive. Many of these visitors had little in-depth knowledge of the societies they were visiting and, thus, lacked an independent ability to judge the truth of what they were seeing or being told. This, combined with the tendency of these very bright people to overestimate their own ability to figure things (and people) out, made them easily fooled. The third, and probably most important explanation for this (and most other varieties of) political gullibility is affective. Many of these visitors went on these pilgrimages with tremendously positive expectations, and they were unable or unwilling to seek out or notice any disillusioning evidence.

Hollander (1981) quoted Jonathan Mirsky writing in 1979 about his attitudes during a trip he took to North Vietnam in 1972, during the Vietnam War: "Throughout our trip ... we sheathed the critical faculties which had been directed against our own Government and ... humbly helped to insert the ring in our own noses" (p. ix). Mirsky quoted one of his former guides, whom he met again in 1979, as saying "*We* wanted to deceive you. But *you* wanted to be deceived" (p. ix).

The affective/state force that drove the tendency of Western intellectuals to see the good and ignore the bad in communist societies was made up of a combination of idealism (a hope for the establishment of a utopian future) and alienation (disgust over the perceived failure of their own society to become sufficiently utopian). The irony and naïveté in such a perception, of course, is that most of the people living in the communist countries would have traded places with the visitors in a heartbeat.

The idealism that Western communists and fellow travelers (the largest category, made up of sympathizers who never formally joined the party) was based mainly on a belief that Marxism provided a formula for a more just and egalitarian society. Marxism became a kind of religion or, as Mexican writer Octavio Paz described it, "Marxism . . . is the superstition of the 20th century" (cited in Hollander, 1981, p. 419). Hollander noted that the appeal of Marxism lay in the notion that a socialist society would "bring about better material living conditions in combination with the maintenance (or renewal) of community and thus provide the blessings of technology, industry, and urban life without the ruptures, conflicts, and disturbances associated with them under capitalism" (pp. 417–418).

The pioneering French sociologist Emile Durkheim put this in more eloquent terms when he noted, more than 100 years ago, that those attracted to Marxism have "a thirst for a more perfect justice . . . [and utter] a cry of grief, sometimes of anger, . . . by men who feel most deeply our collective *malaise*" (cited in Hollander, 1981, p. 417). It is not surprising that those who feel such grief over the injustices in their own society might be slow to give up their hope that another, more perfect, society was being created. Belief in the Marxist ideal (which, like belief in psychoanalysis, survived among literary types long after it ceased to be taken seriously elsewhere) made it difficult to recognize the perversion and unworkability of those ideals in practice.

Gullibility toward communism can be found in more general form, in the excessive trust that was sometimes shown by governments when dealing with the former Soviet Union around issues such as arms control. This form of gullibility is addressed in a pamphlet that Hollander co-authored with the late philosopher Sidney Hook and the former Soviet dissident Vladimir Bukovsky, titled *Soviet Hypocrisy and Western Gullibility* (Hook, Bukovsky, & Hollander, 1987). Hook, a former Marxist theorist who become an avowed anti-communist after learning about the true nature of Soviet society under Stalin, hammered away at the theme that the wish to maintain the peace at all costs made public opinion in the West too willing to excuse away Soviet actions (such as their December 1979 invasion of Afghanistan) or believe their "big" lies, based on the earlier Nazi theory, variously attributed to Goebbels or Hitler, that "a lie must be monstrous to be convincing."

Hook, who sometimes came across as a bit crazed on the topic of communism, saw Western behavior toward the Soviet Union as analogous to the gullible belief by British Prime Minister Neville Chamberlain that his appeasement of Hitler had obtained "peace in our time." Vladimir Bukovsky took this theme a bit further, alluding to the Soviet mastery of brainwashing techniques, and their skillful use of the notion of "absolute value" (an extreme concept such as "everlasting happiness for mankind"; Hook et al., 1987, p. 19), combined with the threat of global destruction, to manipulate a Western public into over-looking Soviet atrocities and too quickly believing in their good intentions. Again, wishful thinking sometimes led to gullible action.

MANY PEOPLE WHO ACCEPT CONSPIRACY THEORIES ARE GULLIBLE

One of the shocking things about the 9/11 tragedy is how many people, both in America and in the rest of the world, remain convinced that the event was allowed to happen by the U.S. government, or was actually carried out by the Israelis. Shortly after the attack, New Jersey's poet laureate Amiri Baraka (a Newark-born African American formerly known as LeRoi Jones) gave a public reading of his poem "Somebody Blew Up America." It contained the lines (question marks added by me): "Who knew the World Trade Center was gonna get bombed? Who told 4,000 Israeli workers at the Twin Towers to stay at home that day? Why did Sharon stay away?" (The full poem is at counterpunch.org/poem1003.html.) Although the tone is paranoid, it is quite funny. My favorite stanza (again, question marks added) is: "Who do Tom Ass Clarence Work for? Why doo doo come out of the Colon's mouth? Who know what kind of Skeeza is a Condoleeza? . . . "

Although there are other passages in which Baraka made statements that seemed sympathetic to Jews (e.g., "Who put the Jews in ovens, and who helped them do it"), Baraka's poem was met with accusations of anti-Semitism, and calls were made for his resignation. He remained defiant, stating in an interview that "The Israelis knew about it just like Bush knew about it, just like the Germans knew about it, just like the French knew about it." As proof of his assertion, Baraka stated that no Israeli citizens died in the attack; in fact, five Israelis were killed in the collapse of the Towers and two were on one of the doomed planes. Unable to get Baraka to resign, the New Jersey legislature eliminated the position of poet laureate.

The view that Osama Bin Laden, and his terrorist organization al-Qaeda, had nothing to do with the 9/11 attacks is endemic within the Muslim world. A Gallup poll conducted in nine Muslim countries in January 2002 found that an amazing 61% of the respondents did not believe that Arab groups were behind the attacks. As that poll included non-Arab Muslim countries such as Turkey, where the United States still is relatively well thought of, it is likely that in some parts of the Muslim world this paranoid view of 9/11 is nearly unanimous. This was confirmed in a 2003 segment of the CBS news magazine *60 Minutes II*, titled "The Big Lie." CBS reporter George Crile attended a wedding party in a small town in Pakistan. The thing that surprised Crile was that everyone at the party, including members of the elite such as a pediatrician, the mayor, and a successful businessman, all made comments such as "Osama is totally innocent" and "the Jews did it." These comments were not offered as opinions or suspicions, but rather as absolute certainties.

The widespread view of 9/11 described above has obvious roots in underlying anti-Jewish and anti-Israeli prejudices found among many American Blacks and among many Muslims around the world. But the origins of this specific rumor can be traced to a news story that appeared in Jordan 2 days after the tragedy and that mentioned rumors of Israeli involvement. The next day, an Israeli diplomat mentioned to reporters that 4,000 telephone calls had come into his government from people in Israel worried about their inability to contact relatives in New York. Then on September 17, a television station in Beirut controlled by the radical Islamic group Hezbollah issued what it termed an official investigative report, in which it mentioned that 4,000 Israelis employed at the Twin Towers had failed to show up for work on 9/11. The next morning, this story began appearing on one Islamic Web site after another, and began surfacing on news broadcasts and TV talk shows in Egypt, Iran, and many other Muslim countries. The story became embellished with other false details, and now this fantasized "Big Lie" is believed throughout the Muslim world and by gullibles in the United States such as Amiri Baraka.

To me, the scary thing about this story is not just the implications for American foreign policy (the United States, as well as Israel, certainly earned some of the animosity they received), but rather to the lesson it teaches about gullibility in the age of the World Wide Web. Baraka, presumably, is not a stupid person, and neither are the notables who were interviewed at the wedding party in Pakistan. Yet none of them seemed to ask questions such as "How do we know that this rumor is true?" "Why are we so distrusting of the Americans but so trusting of the things we read on the Web or hear on our own broadcasts?" and "If Arabs had nothing to do with the attacks, what were Muslim fundamentalists from Arab countries, all of whom had taken flight training, doing on the planes?" This unwillingness of even educated people to question dubious sources of information, combined with their all-too-willingness to believe things that fit with their prejudices, has very disturbing implications for a world in which rumors can make it around the world in a matter of hours.

SUICIDE BOMBERS ARE SUPER-GULLIBLE

Mentally ill people are likely to have personality traits, such as submissiveness, which place them at increased risk for gullibility and exploitation. For the most impaired, such as those with schizophrenia, cognitive and judgment impairments contributing to increased gullibility can be found as well. Thus, it is undoubtedly the case that mentally ill people are, as a class, highly gullible, as reflected in the fact that they are disproportionately represented in exploitative cults that are run by individuals who themselves are mentally ill and, in some cases (e.g., Marshall Applewhite, David Koresh, and Jimmy Jones) suicidal and homicidal as well. Mentally ill people are vulnerable to such cults both because of impaired reasoning, but also because of a pervasive unhappiness they hope will be relieved.

The Heaven's Gate tragedy that took place in California in 1997 was a dramatic example of exploitation of the gullibility of many cult members. Their leader, Marshall Applewhite, ordered 38 people, some of whom had previously been persuaded to castrate themselves, to commit suicide so that they could be picked up by an alien spaceship parked behind the Hale-Bopp comet. Timothy Ferris (1997) put it well when he wrote:

> Stripped to its essentials, the question of what happened at Rancho Santa Fe looks less like a psychopathological riddle and more like an object lesson in the hazards of living a life innocent of empirical rigor. It's hard to avoid the reflection that the mass suicide might have been averted had just one of the observers declared "Gee, the evidence [of the space ship] fails to support our belief. Maybe the belief is wrong." (p. 31)

Among the class of mentally ill people, those who have paranoia are most likely to be gullible, especially in their susceptibility to calls for terrorist or hate-filled acts. In using the term *paranoia*, I am referring both to the larger universe of people who have a paranoid personality style, as well as to the smaller subgroup that qualifies for a formal diagnosis of "paranoid schizophrenia." The key feature of paranoia is a fixed idea of reference, in which one believes that a certain individual, group, or entity is persecuting oneself or is otherwise responsible for various outcomes that are damaging to oneself. Because suspiciousness is a central trait of paranoid people, one might assume that they are less likely to be gullible but, paradoxically, paranoids are probably among the most gullible people one will meet. That is because paranoid individuals are sitting ducks for any information, no matter how unlikely, that supports their fixation, and they are completely uninterested in questioning the possibility that the information is bogus.

In a book titled *Wings of Illusion: The Origins, Nature and Future of Paranormal Belief*, Schumaker (1990) suggested that highly gullible people suffer from a form of psychopathology that he termed *monodeistic*. That term was used earlier by Kallman (1981) in an article titled "Monodeism in Psychiatry:

Theoretical and Clinical Implications" that appeared in the *American Journal of Psychiatry*. Monodeism, according to Schumaker, is a form of "private religion," an idea that was first advanced by Ernest Becker (1973) in his book *The Denial of Death*, which conceptualized mental illness mainly as a lack of courage to face the complexities and difficulties of the world. This private religion serves to make the world more manageable by making reality narrower. Such a constriction of reality is part of the normal self-deception process that, according to Becker, allows us to function in various anxiety-producing situations. However, in certain people this monodeistic process is overly dominant, and becomes controlling and restricting, rather than self-regulating and expanding. Schumaker also considered paranoia to be a form of *suggestive* disorder, a term that implies susceptibility to influence by those who reinforce their "clumsy lie." Such a lie (e.g., that a conspiracy by Israel and/or Jews is responsible for all of the problems in the world) becomes all-consuming, and interferes with, rather than enhances, a paranoid person's everyday social and nonsocial adaptation.

The role of paranoia in susceptibility to recruitment of terrorists is explored at some length by the psychiatrist and ethicist Willard Gaylin (2003) in his book *Hatred: The Psychological Descent into Violence*. Gaylin noted that "paranoid mechanisms are at the heart of the phenomenon of hatred" (p. 108), and focused on the distortion of reality that is caused by a "quasi-delusional view of the world and one's place in it" (p. 108). Gaylin distinguished between hatred—an all-consuming feeling that draws one to engage (often violently) with members of a despised class without accepting the possibility that any members of that class may have value—and prejudice. Gaylin sees prejudice as a less intense dislike, that generally makes one indifferent toward members of a class, and that accepts the possibility of some variability within the class. He made a distinction between terrorists such as Ted Kaczynski, the Unabomber who sent bombs in the mail to academics and industrialists, and terrorists such as the 9/11 airplane hijackers, according to their degree of mental illness. To Gaylin, Kacyznski is undoubtedly a psychotic paranoid schizophrenic, whereas the 9/11 terrorists were probably not psychotic. Rather, they were "the paranoid extremes in a generally paranoid culture" (p. 112).

A paranoid culture, such as is found in some of the Arab countries today, "is not a population of paranoids. Rather, it is a group led by psychotic individuals who encourage paranoid elements endemic in the culture." These paranoid elements, are shared by paranoid psychotics as well as by people with paranoid personalities, with the exception that those in the second category are still able to function in the real world (i.e., they are "still holding onto a modicum of reality"; p. 113). This explains how suicide bombers are able to carry out, and sometimes plan, complex operations in foreign countries. Among the elements found in paranoids are a pervasive negativism; constant suspiciousness and wariness; chronic anger (which can be empowering, especially when contrasted with fear); egocentrism (negative events are always referenced as directed against oneself); narcissism (the idea that one has been chosen by some unseen force and that there is a purpose in every action or event); and finally, what Gaylin termed the "paranoid shift" or projection, in which one's own feelings are projected onto others.

With respect to this last attribute, Gaylin noted that "it is not just our unconscious desire that we shift or project. It is the total responsibility for our failed existence that is transferred. In the process, rage supplants guilt" (p. 115). The paranoid shift always is expressed in the form of a conspiratorial view of life and often leads one to become what Gaylin termed a "grievance collector." Gaylin explained the gullibility of those who are at risk of becoming suicide bombers partly in situational terms, as a function of paranoia-inducing processes operating in cultures as well as in families. Gaylin sees paranoid communities, such as are found in Arab refugee camps, as "ideal environments for nurturing a paranoid view of life and a culture of hatred" (p. 118). Such a climate, fueled by real grievances and hardships, pervades not only the overall culture but is also expressed within families, in the messages that parents share with their children.

In line with Richard Dawkins' view of children as meme-absorbing machines, Gaylin noted that "children are more than ready to accept their parents' views of the world. A paranoid parental atmosphere ... [thus] is highly contagious" (p. 118). Given the sense of anger that is slowly nursed by many of those who live in paranoid communities, young people are "ripe for manipulation" (p. 119) by those who would exploit their youthful idealism, naïveté, and gullibility. Also contributing to the decision of paranoid youths to become suicide bombers are (a) a lack of ability to empathize with those (usually innocent) people who are the targets of their attacks (a symptom of the egocentrism and scapegoating referred to earlier), and (b) a form of religious gullibility (not that terrorism is sanctioned by any legitimate religion, including mainstream Islam), in that the suicide bombers believe the absurd argument used by recruiters that in exchange for committing unspeakably barbarous acts, God will honor them with a special place in paradise.

SPIN DOCTORING AND BELIEVING SEMI-LIES

As with the earlier profiled Ronald Reagan, John F. Kennedy is another president who is lionized as a great leader, more for his charisma and television-friendliness than for his actual accomplishments. In Kennedy's case, the myth of greatness was also helped by the tragedy of his assassination and the collective need for the fable of the Kennedy Administration as America's "Camelot."

I was a college student when Kennedy was elected president, and like most people my age, I was much taken by his personality, especially when contrasted to his socially awkward and devious-seeming opponent, Richard Nixon. I remember early in Kennedy's administration sitting in a dentist's waiting room reading a very positive article in a woman's magazine about the popular new president. The article made much of Kennedy's vigor and healthy habits (a later parallel was Boris Yeltsin, an alcoholic with a debilitating heart condition, being depicted in the Russian media as a "vigorous sportsman"). In particular, the author commented favorably on Kennedy's habit of taking a nap every day at noon, when he would retire to his bedroom, put on his pajamas, get under the covers, and go to sleep.

I remember thinking at the time that noon was a little early for a man in his 40s to be taking a nap and that it seemed like a pretty unusual thing to be doing, more a sign of invalidism than of vigor. Nevertheless I believed the story, believed that President Kennedy was in good health, and believed that he actually took a nap every day at noon. Now of course, we know that President Kennedy was a man with serious debilitating illnesses, specifically, Addison's disease, chronic gastritis, and a severe degenerative back condition (Dallek, 2003). It has also been alleged (Hersh, 1998) that Kennedy may have been taking his clothes off at noon for reasons other than taking a nap.

Part of my gullibility in stifling my skepticism about the pajamas story was because of my relative youth and inexperience; I was still under the Candide-like impression that only people of high moral character occupied high office. But that was also a more innocent age, not very far removed from the heroic events and leaders of the 1940s and 1950s. In the ensuing 40-plus years, I have become less naïve but then so has the country. We are now much more used to the possibility that presidents will lie (Johnson on Vietnam, George W. Bush on Iraq), cheat (Nixon in Watergate), steal (Reagan to finance the contras), and fool around (Clinton with Monica Lewinsky) and that the natural tendency of our leaders when in trouble is to cover up. Could Kennedy's handlers get away with the pajama story today? Maybe for a few days, even given that the art of spin doctoring has advanced considerably in the last 20 or 30 years.

The Kennedy pajama story was an early example of the use of "spin," which is a propaganda technique by which a politician's handlers take a story that is potentially embarrassing (in this case, the fact that Kennedy had a gap in his published calendar many days around noon) and try to put a positive interpretation on it. Bill Press (2001), in a book titled *Spin This: All the Ways*

We Don't Tell the Truth, presents an amusing, and knowledgeable, treatment of the topic. Press described spin as "something between the truth and a lie" and borrows the definition of a "spin doctor" from the *Bloomsbury Good Word Guide* as "a person employed by a political [entity] . . . to present or interpret facts or events in a favourable light" (Press, 2001, p. 2). Press discussed various possible origins of the term, including the spin that a baseball player puts on a pitch, and the spin that a storyteller (such as Homer in *The Iliad*) uses when he or she weaves a yarn.

The growth of spin doctoring in the years since Kennedy are a reflection of the fact that the press, made cynical by the Vietnam War and competitive by the tabloids, is no longer willing to play by the old rules of keeping a potentially newsworthy item, such as a politician's philandering, secret as a matter of courtesy or fairness. In fact, the pendulum seems to have swung too far in the other direction, such that any sign of a skeleton in a public person's closet is fair game for exposure and gloating.

Sometimes spin backfires, as when a politician uses spin in an inappropriate context or tries too hard. This happened when former Congressman Gary Condit tried to spin his way out of admitting his affair with missing intern Chandra Levy (when dealing with such a tragedy, spin will always be seen as tacky), and the latter happened when Bill Clinton gave his ridiculous answer to a question about marijuana use by saying "I didn't inhale" (that reflected a lawyerly tendency on Clinton's part to lie by parsing words). The rule of spin is to avoid using it so egregiously as to give fodder to the late-night comedians. Short of that, there is a good chance that many people will be gullible enough to believe anything fed to them by the spin doctors.

CHAPTER 5

Gullibility in Criminal Justice

In this chapter, I explore the role of gullibility in the criminal justice system. A number of topics are covered, ranging from gullible lawyers and juries to the gullibility of a public that is taken in by crime stories and unjustified claims of redemption. I also address the gullibility of those talked into committing crimes, those talked into confessing to crimes they may not have committed, and those (particularly children) talked into describing crimes they may not have witnessed.

GULLIBILITY AMONG MURDER ACCOMPLICES

Although most of the recent spate of tragic school shootings involved only one shooter, in at least two of the incidents—in Jonesboro, Arkansas, and in Littleton, Colorado—there were two shooters acting as a team: Mitchell Johnson and Andrew Golden in Arkansas, Eric Harris and Dylan Klebold in Colorado. In both of these cases, I think it is accurate to consider one of the shooters (in Arkansas, the 13-year-old Johnson) the leader, and the other (Johnson's 11-year-old cousin Golden) the follower. The leader, who in the Colorado shooting, I would consider to be Harris, may be considered the "initiator," in that he or she is more seriously disturbed than the other shooter, is more consumed with revenge fantasies, and is the person who talks the follower, whom one might consider a "foolish participant," into helping him or into carrying out the scheme. The foolish participant (sometimes more than one) does not seem to have the same angry history, does not have the same sense of victimization, and most likely is participating because he or she lacks the common sense or strength of character to say "no" to the initiative started by the more disturbed friend. Most of the literature on school shootings has addressed the problem of violence and alienation, and the situational factors (such as bullying) that contribute to these problems. However, little or no attention has been paid to the occasional group aspect, in which an impressionable young person is talked into participating.

This phenomenon is interesting from a gullibility standpoint, for it is hardly in the interest of the more passive member of the school shooting team (ignoring for a moment that it is hardly in the real interest of the initiator either) to throw away his or her life on behalf of a cause that is important mainly to a friend. A probable explanation for the gullibility of the confederate is that he or she is so involved emotionally with the initiator that a kind of contagion effect sets in, and the initiator's anger and sense of injustice becomes his or her own. In addition to this contagion effect, it is likely that the larger ramifications of what the conspirators are doing—the taking of a human life, the likelihood of winding up in jail or dead (in cases of a suicide pact, as in Columbine), the devastating effect on their families—become subsumed to the mutual excitement that comes from the group process of planning the deed. The naïveté of these young people also stems from their lack of imagination, or knowledge, as reflected in the failure to explore the many available alternatives—such as going to the authorities to report the bullying—short of committing murder.

One of the most incredible of all the group high school revenge stories, involving multiple foolish participants, occurred in the Fort Lauderdale area in 1993. Jim Schutze (1997), in his book titled, *Bully: Does Anyone Deserve to Die? A True Story of High School Revenge* tells the story (which was made into a film by the same title) of the brutal slaying of 20-year-old Bobby Kent by his closest friend, Marty Puccio, with help from Puccio's girlfriend, Lisa Connelly (who hated Kent and egged Marty on) and four of her friends, three of whom had not even met Kent before agreeing to participate in his murder.

Kent was a big guy with a very forceful personality and a very insulting, threatening, and abusive way of interacting with others, including his buddy Marty. Kent humiliated and publicly mistreated Puccio, over whom he seemed to have a Svengali-like hold, physically, verbally, and possibly sexually, and seemed to have no awareness of how resentful Puccio had become at this mistreatment. This lack of awareness resulted in part from the fact that Puccio (himself a pumped-up guy who probably could have held his own in a fight with Kent) never made a serious attempt to share his feelings with Kent, let alone to break off or alter the relationship.

Puccio's unhappiness was reflected in his repeated appeals to his parents to move, although he never told them why (according to Schutze, Puccio was afraid that his father would think him a sissy for needing help in dealing with a bully). Schutze gives a moving account of how Kent, while being repeatedly stabbed by Puccio and others, pleaded with his friend by saying "... help me Marty! ... Marty, I'm sorry! Please, whatever it is, I'm sorry, Marty, I'm sorry." Thus, this murder might have been avoided if Puccio, or the others who took part in the act, had possessed better social problem-solving skills (including the skill of knowing how to back out of the plot after second thoughts had set in). The same can probably be said about most of the school revenge killings.

The crime perpetrated against Bobby Kent was highly unusual, in that most of the participants had only a casual relationship with Puccio and, as mentioned, even less of a relationship with Kent. A more typical example of gullibility-influenced foolish participation occurred in the 1990 killing of Gregg Smart, in Derry, New Hampshire, by William Flynn, a 15-year-old high school student who was persuaded by his reported lover, Gregg's wife Pamela, a 22-year-old media coordinator in the local high school, to kill her husband. This well-known case, along with the Bobby Kent case, shows how young people can be so gullible that they can be persuaded to take on someone else's hatred and make it their own.

A TRIAL AS A TEST OF A JURY'S GULLIBILITY

On a talk show immediately following the acquittal in the criminal murder trial of O.J. Simpson, true crime writer Dominick Dunne was asked what he thought of the verdict. His reply was that "this verdict is a testament to the power of stupidity." By that, Dunne was, undoubtedly, referring both to the fact that the jurors made a grievously wrong decision, and in a ridiculously short amount of time for a case with so much evidence and testimony, but also that it was a largely working-class jury, with a heavy representation of jurors with limited education. In fact, many knowledgeable commentators, such as Vincent Bugliosi, have noted that this was an unusually weak jury, with few members having even college courses, let alone degrees. That, more than its heavy minority representation (seen by many commentators as significant mainly because one of Simpson's lawyers, Robert Shapiro, admitted "playing the race card"), may explain why the jury voted the way it did despite a mountain of physical and motivational evidence against Simpson.

Based on what I saw of the O.J. Simpson trial, and many subsequent trials on Court TV, a jury trial may be viewed as a kind of "conservation experiment" like those performed by the late Swiss child psychologist Jean Piaget. In the kind of conservation experiment carried out in a trial, the challenge to a prosecutor is to help the jury hold onto the evidence of guilt in the face of efforts by defense lawyers (and sympathetic jurors in the jury room) to obfuscate and cast doubt on that evidence. Thus, a jury coming up with an acquittal (or, more typically, a deadlock) in a case where evidence of guilt is substantial, may be considered gullible in that some or all of its members fell for specious, irrelevant, or misleading arguments by the defense attorney and fellow jurors.

Intelligence comes into play in that smarter jurors would be less likely to be diverted from the truth by such arguments as "if the glove doesn't fit you must acquit," by understanding other likely explanations (e.g., shrinkage from blood contact and storage, Simpson flexing his hand, his wearing a latex glove under it, etc.) for the observed phenomenon. Of course, the conservation/gullibility argument can be applied as well to trials in which obvious or likely innocence is obscured by one or more salient arguments or facts that create an illusion of guilt. This is most likely to occur when an innocent defendant confesses, as a confession, even when obtained under very suspect circumstances, is so affectively compelling as to obscure the importance of even the strongest evidence of actual innocence.

Neil J. Kressel and Dorit F. Kressel (2002) extensively address the issue of juror intelligence in their book titled, *Stack and Sway: The New Science of Jury Consulting*. A husband and wife team (he, a social psychologist, she an attorney), Kressel and Kressel provide an exhaustive survey of the research literature on jury functioning, with particular emphasis on the role of applied social scientists in helping attorneys to select jurors and influence jury verdicts. As a general rule, attorneys prefer a smart jury when they think an understanding of complicated technical evidence will help their side and prefer a dumb jury when they believe that such an understanding will hurt them. The reason for this is obvious: A dumb jury is more likely to be diverted by (i.e., be gullible toward) nonrational arguments if they are unable to appreciate sufficiently the power of rational (i.e., fact- or probability-based) arguments.

Sometimes attorneys can miscalculate the strength or weakness of the evidence, and this can cause them to select, through use of their challenge decisions in *voir dire*, a smart jury, when a dumb jury might have been more sympathetic to their side. An example of this, discussed by Kressel and Kressel, occurred in the case of Louise Woodard, a 19-year-old *au pair* who was convicted in 1997 in a Boston courtroom of killing (through shaking and striking) an infant, Matthew Eappen, who suffered a massive skull fracture while in her care. This case, known widely as "the British Nanny trial," received tremendous press coverage in the United States and even more in the United Kingdom.

Conflicting comments about the jury's intelligence were made by two of Woodard's attorneys after the jury returned a guilty verdict (later made moot by the judge, who released Woodard with time served awaiting trial). Lead defense attorney Andrew Good said "We [originally] thought a smarter jury would be better for [the defense]. Research showed they could follow scientific evidence better. In hindsight, that was a mistake. The people who came up to me all the time in the street [in support of Woodard]—a lot of them were working class people" (cited in Kressel & Kressel, 2002, p. 30). In other words, a dumber jury would have been less likely to have seen through the scientific weaknesses in the defense's case, and would have been more likely to have identified with the working-class defendant and to have resented the upper-class parents (especially the mother, who surveys showed was widely resented for not staying home, even though she worked a reduced schedule). The other defense attorney, Barry Scheck, on the other hand castigated the jury for not being smart enough. In other words, only a dumb jury could have failed to be swayed by the brilliance of his arguments.

An even more powerful contributor to jury gullibility than its collective intelligence is, likely, an affective orientation that often reflects jurors' backgrounds or ethnicity. Kressel and Kressel (2002) reported that a mock trial/focus group conducted before the civil trial of O.J. Simpson revealed the depth of emotion that many potential Black jurors felt about the case. They quoted Peter Gelblum, attorney for the family of murder victim Ron Goldman as saying: "By far the most important thing we learned . . . was that among Simpson supporters, the depth and strength of support for him overcame all rationality; it was mind-boggling" (cited in Kressel & Kressel, 2002, p. 145).

Gelblum noted that one group was asked: "What would you say if we had presented the following evidence to you. The murderer wore size 12 Bruno Magli shoes and this was established beyond dispute. Simpson denied ever wearing size 12 Bruno Magli shoes. A photo, which you can assume is accurate, shows him wearing size 12 Bruno Magli shoes within months of the murder. Do you think that's pretty decent evidence?" (pp. 145–146). Gelblum noted that one Black woman (a trial consultant for the earlier criminal trial determined that Black women were four times more likely to be supporters of Simpson than Black men and infinitely more than White jurors) replied "No. Somebody could have stolen them from him." When affect this strong is activated, gullibility toward specious legal arguments, and failure to "conserve" critical countervailing evidence, is quite likely to be the result.

GULLIBILITY OF LAWYERS

In watching trials on TV, I have been struck by how many criminal defense attorneys seem so caught up in the process of defending their clients as to lose any objectivity as to their guilt or innocence. One can argue, of course, that a certain degree of "lawyer gullibility" is necessary if one is to be an effective trial advocate. This is because for some defense attorneys, a trial becomes a matter of fighting the forces of injustice, and it would be difficult to muster sufficient moral outrage, or energy, if the suspicion arose that one's client might, after all, be guilty. Thus, a certain degree of self-deception about the merits of one's case might be necessary for some lawyers to be able to lie effectively about their client. This becomes a problem, however, when it blinds a lawyer to how a jury might view his or her arguments.

An extreme form of lawyer gullibility occurs when an attorney becomes so caught up in a client's cause that he or she becomes enmeshed in the client's crimes. An example of this involved Sheila McGough, whose case is chronicled in Janet Malcolm's (1999) book *The Crime of Sheila McGough*. At the time covered in the book, McGough, a woman in her 50s with no close friends and who lived with her aging parents, had gone to prison for the crime of being too gullible in trusting her client, a con artist named Bob Bailes.

Bailes was a skilled sociopath, who was very persuasive in telling his many lies. McGough seemed to have had a romantic attachment to Bailes (although there is no evidence that they were lovers), and Malcolm made a strong case that this affective dimension overwhelmed McGough's judgment and caused her to cross over the boundary between lawyer and client and to become ensnared unwittingly in one of Bailes' fraudulent schemes. There is another aspect of the McGough case that Malcolm seems to have missed, however, and that is the possibility that McGough may have a form of cognitive impairment known as nonverbal learning disabilities (NLD). This type of learning disability (related to Asperger's disorder, or high-functioning autism) was first written about by University of Windsor neuropsychologist Byron Rourke and colleagues (Rourke, Young & Leemars, 1989), and is characterized by good verbal skills but poor social and "performance" skills. For example, people with NLD are often klutzy and poor in doing arithmetic calculations or everyday tasks (Malcom wrote that McGough seemed lost in the kitchen). Some researchers view NLD as a broad spectrum disorder, with highly intelligent people such as McGough, a Georgetown graduate, at the upper end of the continuum.

Among the classic signs of NLD that McGough showed were not having a single close friend or lover, not picking up on ending cues when talking on the telephone, not being able to take the informational needs of listeners into effect (McGough was extremely verbose but could not seem to get to the point), and not being able to see through motives of others (such as Bailes' repeated using of her) or anticipate how her actions (allowing Bailes to use her client escrow account to receive a wire transfer) might put her at risk because of the way those actions would be viewed by others. An inability to let go of an obsession (in McGough's case, that Bailes was a good guy and that the criminal prosecution of her was a giant conspiracy) is also often a symptom of NLD.

Whether or not McGough has NLD, it is still appropriate to view her, as Malcolm did, as someone who was done in by her own innocence and lack of worldly experience. Her isolation probably contributed to her downfall, and that isolation was partly a function of her sheltered Catholic school upbringing (in reading about McGough, I wondered why she hadn't become a nun). It is likely that McGough's isolation was also a secondary outcome of her NLD, as there has been some discussion in the literature (Rourke, Young, & Leemars, 1989) of the fact that adults with NLD are at increased risk of depression and suicide as a result of lives characterized by isolation and under-achievement (NLD adults often have marginal jobs because of their inability to pick up on the unwritten rules of professions and work settings). We are all products of both our biology and our experiences, and there is no denying that McGough's inexperience and isolation, both as a person and as a lawyer, made her extremely gullible and vulnerable, both in her dealings with Bailes and in the self-destructive way she approached her own criminal trial.

Malcolm wrote that one of the things that put McGough at risk was that she was a sole legal practitioner, and thus did not have any colleagues or mentors around to caution her or give her advice. She became a sole practitioner because she was naïve about her choice of a law school (at age 40, after an earlier career working for a nonprofit agency). Rather than wait a few months to attend a more prestigious law school, she enrolled in a brand new law school, which essentially ruled out the possibility of landing a job with a major Washington law firm. At a time when a public defender's office had not yet been established, she was reduced, as a highly inexperienced attorney, to accepting court-appointed indigent criminal clients without the safety net of having more experienced colleagues around to warn her about clients' tricks or teach her about the importance of maintaining certain professional boundaries.

A more experienced attorney, who had represented Bailes prior to McGough, told Malcolm that Bailes had pulled similar tricks on him (including the wire transfer stunt that was at the heart of McGough's fraud conviction), but that he had been wise enough to see through and deflect these tricks and to drop Bailes as a client. He now expresses regret that he hadn't made an effort to take McGough under his wing and counsel her as to the dangers that she faced in representing Bailes. Based on what I have come to learn about McGough, however, it is possible that such advice would not have been heeded.

The one thing that might have saved McGough at her trial would have been her testimony, in which she could have portrayed herself, honestly, as the victim of a skilled con man rather than as a conscious participant in his crimes. McGough refused to testify, however, as she believed that would have been a violation of lawyer–client confidentiality and trust (McGough was willing to talk about Bailes with Malcolm only because he had since died). Bailes was a skilled liar and several people, including lawyers, were taken in by his charm and self-confidence.

What makes Sheila McGough stand out is that she refuses, even to this day, to acknowledge how profound a liar Bailes was, or to admit that he may have manipulated her. Part of the key to understanding McGough, according to Malcolm, is her deep idealism as a Catholic. Bailes became a religious cause for McGough, and that caused her to become blind to many of the things that he did. Such profound gullibility, which partly reflects McGough's lack of experience with the sharks of the world, or with people generally, made her an easy and attractive target for someone like Bailes.

GULLIBILITY TOWARD CRIME SCARE STORIES

For a number of years I lived in eastern Connecticut, in a semirural area where many people did not lock their doors and where serious crime was almost nonexistent. I was somewhat surprised, therefore, when "Marilyn," a woman who had lived in the town for a couple of years, told me one day that she was planning to move out of Connecticut because of the high crime rate. I asked Marilyn what she was referring to and she told me that she couldn't pick up the local newspaper or turn on the evening news without learning about some new murder, rape, or other horrible crime. This drumbeat of news stories had caused Marilyn to install an alarm system, and to live in constant fear of being attacked. Marilyn is an educated person, but her belief that she lives in a high-crime area is highly gullible, attributable to the increasing emphasis placed on crime stories as a way to sell media ads.

The manyfold increase in written or televised stories that emphasize crime, disasters, problems, and other kinds of risks has been profiled in two books with similar titles: *The Culture of Fear*, by University of Southern California sociology professor Barry Glassner (1999) and *Culture of Fear*, by University of Kent sociology professor Frank Furedi (2002a). Glassner asked the questions:

> How did it come about that by mid-decade [of the 1990s] 62 percent of us described ourselves as "truly desperate" about crime—almost twice as many as the late 1980s, when crime rates were higher? Why on a survey in 1997, when the crime rate had already fallen for a half dozen consecutive years, did more than half of us disagree with the statement "This country is finally beginning to make some progress in solving the crime problem." (p. ix)

Glassner attributed the paradox to the fact that news stories about serious crime did not drop during that period, but actually went up.

Scary news obviously sells. An example are the many stories in newspapers and on TV every year warning readers to check their children's Halloween candy for razor blades and poisoning. It turns out that there have been only two documented cases of child deaths in the United States associated with Halloween candy, and in both cases the candy was doctored by the child's parents. In one case the child was murdered with rat poison for insurance money, whereas in the second case the child died from heroin ingested accidentally and the parents then put heroin in the candy to divert suspicion from themselves (Glassner, 1999). There have been a few cases where children received minor cuts from objects in their Halloween bags, but in almost all cases the children placed the objects there themselves as a joke. Yet, surveys have shown that as many as 60% of parents fear that their children are at risk of being harmed from doctored Halloween candy.

Furedi (2002a, 2002b) has a particular interest in the role of the media in creating an exaggerated fear of the incidence of child abuse, and is concerned that a climate akin to a medieval witch hunt has been created. An example can be found in a case in Britain, in which a well-known news broadcaster, Julia Somerville, was arrested along with her boyfriend, on suspicion of sexually abusing her daughter. The basis for this arrest was a tip from someone working in a photo processing lab, who reported that one of Somerville's rolls of film consisted entirely of pictures of her little girl in the tub. There was nothing lewd or pornographic about these photos; in fact, they were identical to millions of such photographs that are taken every year. The basis for the tip, and for the police action, was that there were 28 such photos and that Somerville had asked for a set of duplicates. Apparently, that was considered "too many" and aroused suspicions in an age where the drumbeat of news stories about child sexual abuse has created a climate of hyper-vigilance.

The phenomenon of crime scares, aided by news stories, has existed for more than a century (centuries, if one includes the anti-Semitic "blood libels" discussed earlier). However, the Internet has added a new dimension to this problem, as discussed in *No Way of Knowing: Crime, Urban Legends, and the Internet* by "sociology of rumor" scholar Pamela Donovan (2004). A good example of this is "shopping mall and theme park abduction legends." These legends owe their origins to the hysteria in the 1880s in Britain and in the 1910s in the United States, over so-called "white slavery," in which large numbers of young women were supposedly abducted and forced into a life of prostitution. Although periodically debunked, the legend has continued unabated to the present time, with the 1970s version mainly involving teenage girls abducted in shopping mall restrooms, and the 1980s and 1990s version mainly involving children abducted from Disney theme parks.

Donovan quoted a 1996 posting on the news group alt.disney.disneyland about a restroom abduction of a young boy by two Iranians who shaved his head and changed his clothes, and were arrested just as they were leading the boy out of Disneyland. The only problem is that the incident never happened. Donovan noted that there were 580 references to shopping mall abductions in news groups in 1998, and 690 such references to abductions at Disney theme parks. A legend involving adult women (an almost exact resurrection of the white slavery myth) involves a man coming up to a woman in a shopping mall and offering to pay her $100 for appearing in a pizza commercial. The unsuspecting woman is told that the commercial needs to be shot outdoors, and when the victim walks out of the mall, she is thrown into a van and driven away. The TV tabloid news program *Inside Edition* promoted this rumor, by airing a segment in August 1998, which featured an experiment that demonstrated that the pizza ploy could be successful. The reporter then stated authoritatively that 200 to 300 people are abducted in this way every year.

James W. Moore (2002), in his book *The Internet Weather*, addressed the role of the Internet in spreading false facts, such as the myth that on 9/11 there were 4,000 Israelis who did not show up for work at the Twin Towers on the morning of the attacks. In a chapter titled "Fast Facts and Factoid Fiction Crowd Out the Truth," Moore argued that the Internet specializes in the dissemination of "factoids" (nuggets of untruth or half-truth presented authoritatively as fact). He noted that this has undermined and crowded out two sources that once were relied on to provide verified information: journalism and the scientific process. First-class journalism uses editors and fact-checkers, just as first-class science uses replication and peer review, to ensure that assertions are based on fact. Today, those processes are circumvented, as we have direct access to information on the Internet that we assume is true, but often contains serious errors.

An extreme case of gullibility toward exaggerated media stories can be found among people who read and believe the tabloids found at supermarket check-out counters. Is there any other word besides gullible to describe the people who believe the stories (sometimes accompanied by obviously doctored photographs) of Elvis still being alive, or the president shaking hands with an alien? I have always assumed that the people who read these tabloids are on the fringes of society, but that may be an oversimplification. In *I Watched a Wild Hog Eat my Baby: A Colorful History of Tabloids and their Cultural Impact*, former tabloid editor Bill Sloan (2001) revealed that the top tabloids have enormous circulations, something confirmed in a survey by S. Elizabeth Bird (1992), who found that tabloid readers are generally competent and normally functioning adults similar to readers of mainstream newspapers.

An interesting finding of Bird's is that most of the tabloid readers understand that some of the stories are false, but read them for their entertainment value. Some of the respondents see it as an enjoyable challenge to figure out which stories are true and which are false. Bird, an anthropologist, made an interesting analogy between tabloid stories and oral tales found in primitive societies. In virtually every society, one can find stories about dead people who turned out to still be alive, or about children snatched away from their mothers. That these events have a very low frequency of actually happening is less important to the tabloids (and by extension the legitimate media, which is becoming increasingly tabloid-like) than is the fact that they are highly fascinating and, in most cases, frightening. Thus, the tabloids, and to some extent the mainstream media, produce stories less because of their truth or actual importance, than because of their resemblance to already existing folk legends and beliefs. In this way, the media not only encourages mass gullibility, but also reinforces the gullibility that already exists.

GULLIBLE APPLICATION OF REDEMPTIVE AND MENTAL HEALTH NOTIONS

A form of gullibility that is common in politically liberal societies such as many Western European countries today, and the United States a couple of decades ago (before an overly harsh backlash set in), is to see criminals—even those who commit heinous acts—as victims deserving sympathy and, therefore, to be responded to with light punishment or even acquittal, rather than condemnation and harsh punishment. A related phenomenon is the tendency to be overly quick to assume that criminals who can put their experiences into words are no longer to be feared or punished. The two most famous examples of this phenomenon in the United States were Edgar Smith (with the gull being William F. Buckley, Jr.) and Jack Abbott (with the gull being Norman Mailer).

Smith, who at one time was considered America's most famous prisoner, was sentenced to die in New Jersey in 1957 for the brutal slaying of a pretty cheerleader, Vickie Zielinski. Smith claimed he was innocent and began a correspondence with Buckley, a leading conservative writer and magazine editor. In 1968, Knopf published their correspondence under the title *Brief Against Death* (Smith, 1968). Buckley became convinced of Smith's innocence and was instrumental in getting Smith's conviction overturned (largely on the basis that improper interrogation methods had been used) and in helping him to negotiate a plea deal in lieu of a retrial. Buckley considered this a formality and continued to believe in Smith's innocence.

The plea deal allowed Smith to be paroled in 1971. In 1976, unemployed, drinking, and living in California, Smith forced a woman named Lefteriya Ozbun into his car. She managed a heroic escape with a knife lodged in her back. Smith was apprehended, and at the ensuing trial he admitted that he had been guilty all along of killing Vickie Zielinski in the New Jersey murder (this was part of a failed effort to convince the judge that he was a rapist rather than a kidnapper, and thus to receive something less than a life sentence for the Ozbun abduction). In his book of essays, *Right Reason*, Buckley (1985) noted that he was severely criticized for being fooled by Smith, and even noted that one critic referred to him as a "country bumpkin."

Ten years later, a similar scenario played itself out when the left-leaning novelist Norman Mailer became an outspoken advocate for the freedom of Jack Abbott, serving a sentence in Utah for armed robbery and for killing another prisoner. Abbott began a correspondence with Mailer, who was instrumental in getting these letters published in 1981 under the title *In the Belly of the Beast*. The book, in which Abbott freely admitted his history of violence and killing, was widely acclaimed, and many New York intellectuals took up Abbott's release as a cause. Mailer wrote the Utah parole board that Abbott was a gifted writer and that, under his tutelage, he would be able to make a living.

Despite reports from prison psychiatrists that Abbott was a dangerous psychotic with a long history of violence and no evidence of repentance, he was paroled in 1981. Unlike Edgar Smith, who had the decency to wait 5 years before (almost) killing again, it only took Abbott 6 weeks. When 22-year-old aspiring actor and playwright Richard Adan, a waiter, refused Abbott's request to use the employee restroom at a restaurant, Abbott flew into a rage and stabbed the young man to death. Abbott was returned to prison, where he hanged himself in his cell in 2002. Mailer took public responsibility for Adan's death, and American intellectuals finally seem to have gotten over the naïve notion that publishing a book makes one fit to live in society.

The most eloquent and persuasive critic of the gullible misapplication of therapeutic concepts to excuse criminal conduct has been the psychiatrist and ethicist Willard Gaylin. In his book *The Killing of Bonnie Garland*, Gaylin (1982) told the story of a homicide committed by a poor Hispanic 21-year-old Yale University senior, Richard Herrin, when Bonnie, a 17-year-old affluent Yale freshman, tried to break off their relationship. Unwilling to tolerate this rejection, Herrin snuck into Bonnie's room when she was home on a visit, and bashed in her skull with a hammer numerous times while she was sleeping.

Gaylin expressed considerable dismay at the large numbers of people who rallied to Herrin's cause and attempted to portray him as a victim deserving of sympathy and lenient treatment. In particular, Herrin was supported by various Catholic clergy and lay people in Connecticut and New York, who actively raised funds for his defense, sheltered him, and put out propaganda supporting his side. Lost in all of this, according to Gaylin, was any real sympathy for Bonnie or her family, or any condemnation of Herrin and his actions.

Gaylin interviewed one supporter, Brother Richard of the Christian Brothers community in Albany, New York (where Herrin lived and attended college while awaiting trial). Brother Richard minimized the evil of Herrin's actions by insisting that anyone, even himself, would be capable of murder if they had come from Herrin's background. (Gaylin found this insulting to all of the people coming from similar backgrounds who do not kill anyone.) Although tried for murder, Herrin was convicted of manslaughter, and received what Gaylin and many others considered a too-lenient sentence of 8.3 years. Herrin showed his self-centeredness and lack of remorse by writing a letter to his supporters in which he complained bitterly about the outrageousness of his sentence. These supporters, most of them Catholic, were portrayed as doubly gullible, both by falling for the notion that all behavior should be viewed in psychiatric rather than moral terms, but also by failing to see Herrin as the manipulative and amoral sociopath that Gaylin considered him to be.

The naïveté of Catholic clergy in showing so much empathy for Herrin, and so little for the victim or her family, was replicated in the egregious response of America's bishops to the many cases of priests sexually abusing children that have rocked the church in recent years. Although the action of bishops is usually attributed to the tendency of organizations to cover up malfeasance, Gaylin (2003), in his book *Hatred*, argued that the handling of the priest scandal reflected the same emphasis on therapeutic rather than moral values that underlay clerical support for Herrin in the Bonnie Garland case.

Just as the Catholic community in New Haven felt that the right thing to do was to show compassion for a young man thought to have psychiatric rather than moral defects, so too the Catholic bishops around the United States chose to show empathy and forgiveness for priests accused of molesting children on the assumption that they were suffering from psychiatric illnesses. Without using the word, Gaylin sees this response as gullible, both because so few of the offending priests (also true of Herrin) showed any real contrition, but also because it involved an acceptance of what he sees as the unsupportable argument that the offending behavior represented an illness rather than a conscious and reprehensible choice.

GULLIBILITY IN THE INTERROGATION SITUATION

Susan Smith is a rural South Carolina woman who created a sensation in 1994 when she reported that her automobile, with her two young sons inside, was carjacked by a stranger one evening at a remote intersection. Her story attracted much attention, partly because she reported that the carjacker was Black, thus bringing an element of racial hysteria into the case in a part of the United States with a history of severe racial conflict.

Frustrated by a lack of leads, and doubting Smith's story, the local sheriff was able to get Smith to admit that she killed her children (in the hopes of holding onto an adulterous relationship) by driving her car into a lake with her two children strapped into their car seats. The sheriff used two ploys to get Smith to confess:

1. He told Smith that the state highway department had been videotaping the remote intersection as part of a traffic survey and there was no evidence of the alleged carjacking.

2. He asked her—a member of his own church congregation—to get down on her knees to pray with him, telling her that it would be good for her soul to tell him what actually happened.

Gullibility enters in here in that the story of the videotaped traffic survey of a single rural intersection is patently incredible. Smith, an unworldly and poorly educated person, was awfully credulous to have believed such a claim, especially when uttered a week after the disappearance by a sheriff who had an obvious motive to trick her. The police theory for telling such lies is that the suspect has a guilty conscience and that lies serve to loosen the person's resistance, such that her need to tell the truth, and thus assuage her conscience, causes her to confess.

The heavy emphasis on lying as a central technique in interrogations is found in the widely used text *Criminal Interrogations and Confessions* by Inbau, Reid, and Buckley (1986) and in numerous other books, such as *We Get Confessions* (Joseph, 1995) and *Make 'Em Talk: Principles of Military Interrogation* (McDonald, 1993). The book *Interrogation: Techniques and Tricks to Secure Evidence* (Paladin Press, 1991) lists 50 tricks, with all of these involving some form of deception. A relatively mild example, Trick 12, called "the file gimmick," involves writing the suspect's name on the outside of a file folder in large block letters, and referring to it in a casual manner, occasionally glancing at the suspect "as though confirming what was found in the file" (p. 30). The authors stated that the purpose of this gimmick "is to cause the subject to think you have built up a conclusive file on him and have all the evidence you need" (p. 30).

One problem with using lies to induce people to confess, noted by Gudjonsson (1992) in *The Psychology of Interrogations, Confessions and Testimony*, is that such tactics can cause highly gullible and suggestible innocent people to confess as well. Linguist Roger W. Shuy (1998), in *The Language of Confession, Interrogation, and Deception*, added that interrogators, using amateurish pseudo-psychology notions (such as that body language indicates guilt), often conclude prematurely that someone is guilty, and view the interrogation session mainly to confirm the hypothesis of guilt, while ignoring information in the session that might confirm the hypothesis of innocence.

Both of these problems are evident in a notorious case of wrongful conviction, which took place in the 1970s. It involved Peter Reilly, a Connecticut high school student residing in Litchfield County, a semirural but highly affluent area that is famous for being home to many of America's best-known artists and writers. The case was heavily covered in the media and was chronicled in two books—*Guilty Until Proven Innocent*, by Donald S. Connery (1977) and *A Death in Canaan*, by Joan Barthel (1976)—and in a film based on Barthel's book.

A reserved 18-year-old with no history of violence, Reilly drove home one night from a church youth group meeting to the house he shared with his mother, Barbara Gibbons. He discovered her near death (she later died) from a brutal beating: She was almost decapitated from a neck slashing and she had multiple broken bones; she had also been sexually assaulted. Although there were other possible suspects, including some neighboring juveniles with whom Reilly's mother had been feuding, the police focused prematurely on

Reilly, overgeneralizing from the statistical finding that such crimes often are committed by family members, but also because Reilly—socially awkward even when compared with other adolescents—was not conforming to conventional norms for expressing grief.

Although in shock from having just suffered the violent loss of his only parent, Reilly was taken down to the police station for a 25-hour interrogation. He quickly waived his Miranda rights (the right to remain silent and seek an attorney) on the mistaken assumption, often held by naïve individuals, that innocent people have nothing to fear from talking with the police. In one phase of the interrogation, Reilly was hooked up to some wires and told, falsely, as it turned out, that he was being given a lie detector test. Although polygraphs have been consistently found by scientists to have near-zero reliability in detecting lying (Ekman, 2001; Lykken, 1981) and, consequently, are almost never allowed as evidence in criminal cases, they are still widely used in police interrogations (when agreed to by suspects) because they are often part of a deception trap such as the one used against Reilly.

The dangers of relying on polygraph tests is illustrated in the case of the Pacific Northwest's "Green River Killer," Gary Leon Ridgway. Over a 21-year period, Ridgeway, considered perhaps America's most prolific serial murderer, strangled at least 48 young women and girls, the number he confessed to in 2003 in return for a life sentence. In fact, he may have killed as many as 60. Early in his career, in 1983, police interrogated Ridgway after two of the early victims were spotted getting into a truck similar to one belonging to his then girlfriend. Later, in 1984, Ridgway was suspected of choking a woman (who turns out to possibly be the only one of his intended victims to have escaped alive). Yet the police dropped Ridgway as a suspect in the Green River murders, thus allowing him to continue on his killing spree for two more decades. Why? He had "passed" a lie detector test. It seems suspects are not the only ones who demonstrate staggering gullibility.

In the Reilly case, the (phony) polygraph was used to break down his initial denials that he had anything to do with the murder of his mother. The interrogating officer told him that the polygraph showed him to be lying. When Reilly asked how this could be the case when he had no recollection of such behavior, he was told that it is common for people committing murder to black out and have no memory of their actions. In such circumstances, according to the officer, the polygraph gives a better indication of what actually happened than does one's conscious memory. Reilly then asked the officer, a resident state trooper who was well known to the youths in that town, if he had ever known a polygraph to give invalid findings. The officer replied with another lie, telling Reilly that in over 20 years of experience, he had never known that to happen. Reilly admitted that it was possible that he might have killed his mother, even though he knew of no reason why he would do so.

Although Reilly later retracted his statement, it was enough to have him prosecuted and convicted for his mother's murder. (It is well known that judges and juries in America give the greatest weight to confessions, even when obtained under questionable circumstances and even when not corroborated by physical or motivational evidence). A public outcry in Litchfield County, led by many of its famous writers and intellectuals, was successful in getting the case reopened.

The conviction was thrown out when it was revealed that the prosecuting attorney, who died while the case was being appealed, had failed to disclose a statement by an elderly couple that put Reilly in his car several miles from home at a time when the crime had already been committed. The judge was also persuaded by evidence from Herbert Spiegel, a psychiatrist specializing in hypnosis, that Reilly likely was in a trance state, triggered by grief, hunger, isolation, and exhaustion, when he succumbed to police pressure and gave his self-incriminating statement. The judge's decision was also helped by the fact that the interrogation had been audiotaped (something unusual in America at that time, and being done in that police station only on a trial basis), and his listening to it convinced him, as it would any objective person, that Reilly had been subjected to unfair pressures and interrogative tactics.

GULLIBILITY OF CHILD WITNESSES

There has been considerable interest in the gullibility of witnesses in crime proceedings, with much of that interest focusing on children. The gullibility of child witnesses reflects the ease with which they can be manipulated by an inept or overly determined interrogator into admitting things that are untrue. This has attracted so much attention because it is one facet of the "recovered memory" phenomenon that has rocked the worlds of law and human services.

The historic prototype for this phenomenon occurred in 1692, when 20 residents of Salem, Massachusetts, were condemned to death on the basis of testimony by a group of children, aged 5 to 12 years, known as "the circle girls." The Massachusetts Bay Colony was a place where fear of witches was rampant and the vicar's wife, a woman who was obsessed with sorcery and witchcraft, had influenced these girls. The girls began to accuse some of the townspeople of being witches and told fantastic stories about various feats of magic. Children of accused parents were brought in and interrogated for hours, by interrogators who believed their parents were guilty and who asked many leading questions. Eventually, some of these children began to confirm that the accused parent was, indeed, a witch.

There are those who feel that hysteria about child sexual abuse is the modern-day equivalent of hysteria about witches, and who consider the McMartin preschool trial in southern California, along with a number of other such cases, to be the modern equivalent of the Salem Witch Trials. Certainly, the McMartin case was probably the watershed event that caused the legal and human services fields to become aware that suggestibility of child witnesses is a huge problem and that great care must be taken in interrogating children if their testimony is to be believed.

A detailed, and chilling, account of the McMartin case can be found in *The Abuse of Innocence: The McMartin Preschool Trial*, by Paul and Shirley Eberle (1993). The case started in September 1983, when the chief of police of Manhattan Beach, California, pursuing a complaint by a woman with a history of mental instability, sent a letter to all of the parents attending the McMartin preschool stating that an investigation was being undertaken of possible child sexual molestation by Raymond Buckey, a 28-year-old teacher in the school. Naturally, the reaction to this letter was one of mass panic, and parents pulled their children from the school, which was forced to close (it was later burned to the ground by vigilantes).

All of the parents and children in the school were sent for evaluation to a private clinic, Children's Institute International (CII), which was owned by Dee McFarlane, a friend of the district attorney. McFarlane and her staff told the parents that every child at the school had been sexually molested. Tales of satanic ritual practices such as the drinking of blood began to circulate, and all of the preschools in Manhattan Beach were forced to close when it was asserted that children had been swapped between the various schools for the purpose of molesting them. Buckey, his mother (the school's director), his grandmother (the school's founder), and several teachers, including Buckey's sister, were arrested. Two trials ensued, and all of the defendants were eventually cleared of all charges, in Buckey's case, after he had spent 4 years in jail. One of the assistant district attorneys, bothered by the complete absence of a credible case, protested the decision to prosecute the Buckeys by resigning his position.

The interrogation of the children by the therapists at CII is now held up as a case study of how *not* to interrogate child witnesses or possible victims of crimes. Considerable research has been conducted into the induction of false memories in children, and various policy initiatives have been conducted to spell out the implications of this research for the legal system and for the conducting of interviews by mental health professionals. The two leading figures in this initiative have been psychologists Elizabeth Loftus and Stephen

Ceci. Three books that summarize the results of findings by Loftus, Ceci, and others are *Jeopardy in the Courtroom: A Scientific Analysis of Children's Testimony* by Ceci and Bruck (1995), *Children's Eyewitness Memory* edited by Ceci, Toglia, and Ross (1987) and *False-Memory Creation in Children and Adults*, edited by Bjorklund (2002).

One major mistake made by the CII therapists is that they went into the sessions already believing the allegations to be true and knowing quite a bit about the (as it turned out, completely false) allegations. Believing sexual molestation at the school to have been rampant, they saw it as their job not to find out what happened but to flesh out the state's case. They did this by refusing to accept the children's denials and they kept pushing, asking repeated leading questions, and not resting until the children told them what they wanted to hear.

An example of such persistent "closed" questioning occurred in another notorious case, also from the mid-1980s. The accused person was Kelly Michaels, a young woman who worked as a teacher at the Wee Care Early Childhood Center in Maplewood, New Jersey. According to the prosecutors, Ms. Michaels raped 10 of the 3- to 5-year-old children in her care on a daily basis with various objects over a period of 8 months with none of the other teachers, administrators, or parents noticing and without any of the children mentioning it to anyone. She was convicted of 115 counts of child sexual abuse, but was eventually exonerated when the interrogation of the children was found to be completely contaminated, as can be seen in the following transcript reported in Ceci and Bruck (1995, p.122): (adult): "When Kelly kissed you, did she ever put her tongue in your mouth?" (child) "No." (adult): "Did you ever have to kiss her vagina?" (child): "No." (adult): "Which of the kids had to kiss her vagina?" (child): "What's this?" (adult): "No that's my toy, my radio box . . . Which kids had to kiss her vagina?" (child) "Me." Another example reported in Ceci and Bruck (p. 121) went as follows: (adult): "Did she touch you with a spoon?" (child): "No." (adult): "No? Okay, did you like it when she touched you with a spoon?" (child): "No." (adult): "No? Why not?" (child): "I don't know." (adult): "You don't know?" (child): "No." (adult): "What did you say to Kelly when she touched you?" (child): "I don't like that."

Ceci and Bruck estimated that 12 different professionals interrogated the average child who testified in one of the preschool trials. One conclusion drawn by Ceci is that the first interview with a child is the one that is most likely to be accurate, and that the likelihood of false testimony increases greatly the longer the elapsed time interval between the interview and the alleged criminal event.

There are other factors besides repetitive interviewing that can influence children to change their accounts. One is to make reference to what other children have said. Again, referring to the Kelly Michaels case, Ceci and Bruck (1995) noted that an interrogator engaged in the ploy of saying that "other kids are telling me," in combination with the already discussed tactic of pushing until she got the answer she wanted: (adult): "Did you ever see bleeding in her vagina?" (child): "Umm, hmm." (adult): "Did she ever take anything out of her vagina with blood on it? Did you ever see anything like that? You did?" (child): "Noo." (adult): "Well, he said yes." (child): "No really! No," (adult): "Come on, seriously." (child): "Really! No . . . you're gross." (adult): "Well that's gross, but other kids are telling me that they saw her pull something out, and I'm wondering if you saw her bleeding from her vagina like that." (child): "Ooooh, yes." Another common interrogative mistake is to engage in stereotyping of the suspect. For example, in the Michaels case, Ceci and Bruck noted that "the investigators told 15 of the 34 interviewed children that Michaels was in jail because she had done bad things" (p. 135).

A problem with repetitive interrogations is that we now know that after some time young children will have difficulty keeping straight what actually happened from what adults suggest might have happened. Although some of the children gave multiple and widely varying accounts of what happened, the mental health and legal professionals naïvely selected as the most valid only those (typically, later) accounts that supported their opinion that crimes had been committed. They seemed oblivious to the terrible injustice that had been done, not only to the defendants, but also to the children themselves. Gullibility was, therefore, manifested not only in the children—who allowed themselves to be duped into thinking that an induced memory was truer than their real one—but also in the mental health and law enforcement professionals who deluded themselves into believing a story that fit with their justifiable revulsion against the crime of child sexual abuse.

CHAPTER 6

Gullibility in Science and Academia

Behaving gullibly can be considered a failure of one's intellectual faculties, but it is by no means limited to those of low intelligence. In this chapter, I explore common examples of gullibility engaged in by people of the very highest intelligence. These include artistic gullibility, gullibility in psychotherapy and acceptance of dubious treatment fads, academic hoaxes, pathological science, acceptance of dangerous health practices, and gullibility in the academic hiring process.

THE SOKAL HOAX EXPOSED THE GULLIBILITY OF SCHOLARS

Practical jokes prey on the gullibility of one or two individuals, whereas hoaxes prey on the gullibility of a larger group, often to make some general point. An example of a hoax that received widespread notoriety is the so-called "Sokal Hoax." It had a serious purpose, and like most hoaxes or practical jokes had a nasty aspect, but the perpetrator, his helpers, and those who shared his views, had a good laugh at the expense of those who were taken in by it. It has something to tell us about gullibility, as seen in those who were fooled by the hoax as well as those who were impressed by the type of scholarship that the hoax was parodying.

Alan Sokal, a professor of physics at New York University, carried out the hoax. Sokal's motivation for undertaking the hoax was to expose what he saw as shoddy scholarship, under the theoretical and methodological rubric of postmodernism, in the field of cultural studies. He was particularly aghast at the application of such methods to scientific topics (termed *science studies*), and those that took the extreme leftist position that all scientific findings are affected by societal, economic, and ideological (such as sexist) conditions. Sokal, a self-described leftist, who made much of having taught for a time in Sandinista Nicaragua, considered the postmodernists to be "faux leftists," who spouted nonsense to each other, and who knew nothing of many of the things they were writing about, especially the sciences. Not surprisingly, right-wing commentators and academics particularly appreciated the hoax. Sokal was also making a point about the need for the application of higher standards within the university community, as it bothered him that humanities professors were getting promoted, funded, and otherwise rewarded for publishing postmodernist drivel in poorly refereed journals.

The hoax consisted of a long article by Sokal that appeared in the May 1996 issue of *Social Text*, a respected cultural studies journal published by Duke University Press. The title of the article was "Transgressing the Boundaries: Toward a Transformative Hermeneutics of Quantum Gravity." The article contained a great deal of incomprehensible gobbledygook, interspersed with quotes from various postmodernist writers, many of them regular contributors to *Social Text*. The article was filled with several obvious scientific misstatements, many of them expressing the position that various well-established physical laws are simply social inventions. Within a few days, a second article by Sokal appeared in *Lingua Franca*, a (now defunct) gadfly journal about academia; it was titled "Revelation: A Physicist Experiments with Cultural Studies." In the second article, Sokal revealed that the *Social Text* paper was a prank, intended to expose the shoddy scholarship, ideological bias, and scientific ignorance of postmodernist scholars writing about scientific matters.

Sokal's revelation received tremendous media attention, and triggered a massive amount of commentary, both pro- and anti-Sokal, in various publications. A great deal of this commentary, including the original two papers by Sokal, is contained in a book edited by the editors of *Lingua Franca* (2000) and published by the University of Nebraska Press, titled *The Sokal Hoax: The Sham that Shook the Academy*. All of the commentary mentioned here can be found in that book.

The editors and publisher of *Social Text* undertook a spirited defense of their journal and their actions in accepting Sokal's article for publication. They basically made two points. The first point was that they believed that Sokal behaved unethically, in that he violated an implicit contract between authors and editors, in which editors expect an author to be honest and serious. Because he was a scientist and they were not, they relied on him to get the science part of it right. Their second point was that the truth of the science was irrelevant anyway. Theirs is a journal with a specific and consistent ideological bent, and Sokal's paper, in spite of being amateurish philosophically (as might be expected of a physicist) appeared to be consistent with that ideology. In other words, the general gist of what he was saying was true, or at least consistent with their ideology, and the details, including mistaken statements about basic physical laws, were unimportant, especially in a journal that was not aimed at scientists.

The first point that the editors deferred to Sokal because of his scientific credentials is in line with the "Barnum effect" situational theory of gullibility (Forer, 1949; Layne, 1979). Just as undergraduate research subjects believe trite statements about themselves told to them by an experimenter wearing a white lab coat, so too these eminent editors believed a physics professor from New York University spouting convoluted nonsense about physics. The hoax shows that even accomplished intellectuals with doctorates can be taken in when the supposed expert is from a field different from their own. The second point, that the truth of the science content was irrelevant, because the paper supported the journal's ideology, suggests that Sokal was correct in calling attention to this form of scholarship as empty posturing.

The ideological admission also raises another possible explanation for the editors' gullibility, namely that they were so excited to have a real live physicist echo their ideas about science that they were willing to accept anything he said. This is confirmed in a piece by the journal's co-editors, Bruce Robbins and Andrew Ross, in which they noted that they had tried, for space reasons, to get Sokal to cut his lengthy footnotes, but capitulated when he resisted (as we now know, because that was where some of the most outrageous statements were located). In other words, the affective motives, as is often the case with gullible behavior, were so strong as to overwhelm judgment.

There is another aspect to this story, which reminds me somewhat of *The Emperor's New Clothes*. There is a strong possibility that the several members of *Social Text's* editorial committee (which that journal uses in lieu of outside reviewers) were ashamed to admit that they didn't understand what they were reading. They relied on the group process to define what to do, and as the other members also hid their ignorance, everyone assumed the group knew what it was doing (see the discussion of "groupthink" in chap. 4). This is a commentary on the decision to accept the Sokal paper for publication, but it may also be a statement, as Sokal intended, about postmodern scholarship in general, particularly its tendency to "purposely write in tongues for an initiated elite" (Ruth Rosen, cited in Ellen Willis, Editors of *Lingua Franca*, 2000, p. 134).

GULLIBILITY IN THE ART WORLD

Gullibility has room to operate where objective reality is unclear and there are strong social pressures at work. Both of these seem to be present in the art field, as there is no widely accepted definition of art, let alone "good art," and social processes—as in art fads, manias, and the marketplace—are ever-present. The lack of an objective definition of art can be found by perusing *Theories of Art Today*, edited by Noël Carroll (2000). Probably the closest any of the contributors to that book came to devising a workable definition of art was Marcia Muelder Eaton (2000), who produced a definition of "a work of art" that has three components:

1. It is an artifact (i.e., it is made, not just found).
2. It is treated in aesthetically relevant ways (i.e., people "fluent in a culture" find it worthy of attention).
3. When someone has an aesthetic experience with it, he or she "realizes that the cause of the experience is an intrinsic property . . . considered worthy of attention within the culture." In other words, something is considered a work of art if artistically knowledgeable people in a given culture consider it a work of art. Which brings us smack dab into "Emperor's New Clothes" territory.

Although there is room for gullibility in traditional art, there is far more room in the world of modern and contemporary art, just because there is so much more variability in the forms art can take (e.g., a canvas with monochromatic white paint on it, or a drip painting, or a painting with just words in it). I need to point out that much of the art that I own is nonrepresentational, so I hope that what follows is not seen as a Prince Charles-like rant against modernity.

Living in Colorado, nearly 2,000 miles from the New York-based center of the American art world, I have observed a phenomenon in which once famous, but now over-the-hill, artists come to town for a show at one of the local galleries. I think there is a tendency for them to believe that they can put one over on the rubes, by passing off crap knocked off in minutes, or even seconds, as if it were the kind of art (typically taking days or weeks to complete) of which they are, or at least once were, capable. A notable case of this occurred when a sculptor, justly famous for his low wall-like objects, installed two works (considered a bargain at only about $25,000 each) at a Denver gallery. One consisted of several shiny tiles, of the sort one could buy at a tile outlet store for $1 each, laid out in a straight line, whereas the other used the same kinds of tiles, but had them laid out in a the shape of an "L." When I attended the opening, it took all of my will power to avoid telling the somewhat star-struck gallery owner that in my opinion she had been taken for a ride and that the work (which I nearly stepped on) was a joke being played at her expense.

Even Pablo Picasso, arguably the greatest artist of the 20th century, has been accused of playing this kind of trick on an overly credulous and admiring public. In the latter part of his career, much of his art consisted mainly of squiggles, and he churned out dozens of these cartoon-like drawings in a single brief session (there is a documentary film in which he turns out these quickie squiggle drawings on one side of a pane of glass while the camera films from the other side). Picasso's motivation for doing these impressionistic cartoons was obvious: given how much a work by him was valued, he could make a very spectacular living producing *drek* (a Yiddish expression meaning crap) for unsuspecting buyers willing to pay several thousand dollars to be able to hang a "Picasso" on their living room wall.

I think the late Clement Greenberg, one of the greatest recent modern art theorists, would have agreed with me when I argue that a work of art (or at least a good one) should involve more than a few seconds' effort. In his book *Homemade Esthetics: Observations on Art and Taste*, Greenberg (1999) wrote "quality of art appears to be directly proportionate to the density or weight of decision that's gone into its making" (p. 49). In other words, whether it is the emperor's invisible clothes, or several tiles laid out in an L shape, or a squiggle drawing knocked off by Picasso in 20 seconds, only a gullible person would consider it a work of outstanding aesthetic quality.

Perhaps the most notorious (and literal) case of crap being passed off as art involved Italian artist Piero Manzoni, who died in 1963 at the age of 30 years. In 1961, he filled 90 metal cans with his own feces, wrapped them in paper, numbered them, and wrote on the outside, in several languages, "Artist's Shit." In 2001, London's Tate Modern purchased can #004, reportedly for more than $30,000, and displayed it in a room named "Subversive Objects." In the Tate's catalog (access at www.tate.org.uk and enter "shit" in the search box), Sophie Howarth wrote that Manzoni sold one of the cans for 30 grams of 18-carat gold. Howarth wrote that Manzoni's "decision to value his excrement on a par with the price of gold made clear reference to the tradition of the artist as alchemist already forged by Marcel Duchamp and Yves Klein among others." Howarth then quoted Jon Thompson, who goes on even more floridly, writing: "The Merda d'artista, the artist's shit, dried naturally and canned 'with no added preservatives' was the perfect metaphor for the bodied and disembodied nature of artistic labour: the work of art as fully incorporated raw material, and its violent expulsion as commodity." The only thing missing from this (forgive me) pile of shit is an elaboration of the Freudian notion that art is a symbolic extension of what infants do when they play with and smear their feces.

Undoubtedly, Manzoni—a pioneer of conceptual art—was a serious artist making an interesting point. But his point had more to do with the nature of the art market (namely, the gullibility of critics, curators, and buyers) than it had to do with the nature of the creative process. The value of his shit cans thus come more from their place in art history (as much talked about objects) than as works of art.

Art, and aesthetic taste, is a fertile field for gullibility precisely because the value, and perceived quality, of an art object comes from the opinions of others rather than from any clear or objective standard of what constitutes good or great art. In other words, art is considered good if supposed experts think it is good and if potential buyers can be found who are willing to fork over the bucks for it (it is not an accident that they give away wine at art openings). Social pressure, internal state (being a little buzzed), and ignorance can all contribute to a gullible outcome.

Even in the case of Old Masters art, there is often considerable disagreement about whether a work is by a famous artist or his student, and there are many cases of a barely salable piece suddenly going for millions because of a change in attribution. For every artist who makes it big, there are undoubtedly many artists of equal or greater talent whose work goes unrecognized or unrewarded. Although factors such as luck and social competence (kissing the right behinds) undoubtedly play a role here, the determining factor in the success of an artist may lie in the goodness of fit between his or her art and the susceptibility (i.e., gullibility) of the opinion makers.

COLD FUSION AS AN EXAMPLE OF SCIENTIFIC GULLIBILITY

Often, gullibility occurs in people who are relatively unsophisticated, or otherwise vulnerable. Scientists, on the other hand, are well above average in terms of education and intelligence, and are presumed to be rational and cautious in their approach to new ideas and practices. Yet, there is an extensive literature on what Irving Langmuir (1953/1989) termed *pathological science*, which is science that reflects mass delusion rather than reality. There have been many cases of pathological science in the physical and natural sciences, and also in the health and human services. Pathological science usually flourishes in areas that have proved resistant to solution by traditional methods, as is true of the example that follows.

In a wonderful book titled *The Golem*, Harry Collins and Trevor Pinch (1993) detailed several cases of scientific controversy in which the various positions taken, as well as the ultimate identification of the "winner," was determined as much by emotion and prejudice as by reason and actual "truth." *Golem* is a term used in Yiddish folk superstition, and it refers to a human-like figure made of clay and water, that can do wonderful things. But a golem is a clumsy force that, if one is not careful, can destroy its creator(s), as can be seen in the case of Cold Fusion. In March 1989, Stanley Pons and Martin Fleischmann, two electroanalytic chemists at the University of Utah, announced at a press conference that they had achieved a controlled fusion reaction at room temperature, using a simple experimental procedure in which they ran a mild electrical current through heavy water (which has an extra hydrogen molecule), using two cathodes made of palladium. Their theoretical rationale was that palladium absorbs hydrogen, thus creating excess pressure that causes a fusion reaction in the lattices of the palladium. As proof of nuclear fusion, they claimed to have recorded excess heat and neutrons, in addition to other products, particularly tritium and helium.

The announcement set off a firestorm of media and scientific interest around the world, as the discovery, if true, promised to solve the world's need for cheap, abundant, and pollution-free energy. It was met by skepticism from the physics community, however, because few details had been provided about the (not-yet-published or replicated) study, because more established fusion researchers had been unsuccessful at this quest, and because the theoretical rationale was unconvincing and flew in the face of several established principles of physics. Furthermore, if neutrons had actually been produced in the amount claimed, then Pons and Fleischmann should have been dead. Despite general skepticism from the scientific community, many nonscientists, ranging from politicians, to University of Utah administrators (who established a cold fusion research institute and sought commercial patents), to the mass media and the general public, were inclined to believe Pons and Fleischmann.

There were many reasons for what, in hindsight, was widespread gullibility. These included the following:

1. A magical desire to believe in a wonderful scientific breakthrough with tremendous potential public benefits.

2. A wish to see the (mostly Eastern) scientific establishment humbled.

3. Greed (the University of Utah, and the two researchers, stood to gain billions in royalties).

4. An assumption that the researchers, and their university, would not be so foolish as to make such dramatic claims unless they were on solid ground.

5. A lack of competence to independently evaluate the claims made by Pons and Fleischmann.

Within a relatively short period of time, Pons and Fleischmann were completely discredited (the controversy is thoroughly detailed in books by Close, 1991; Collins & Pinch, 1993; and Huizenga, 1992). They were forced to modify several of their claims (particularly regarding the production of helium and neutrons), and several laboratories, using much more sophisticated measurement devices, either failed to replicate the results, or were able to explain them as artifacts of the methods that had been used. Today, cold fusion, which John Huizenga (1992) called the "scientific fiasco of the [20th] century," is cited as an object lesson of what can happen when science is proclaimed through press conferences rather than through the usual peer-reviewed journals and forums. The cold fusion hysteria has been termed (see www.cosmicbaseball.com) an example of "Blondlotisma," named after the French physicist Rene Blondlot who, in 1903, claimed to have discovered "N-Rays," a discovery later found to be illusory.

Of particular relevance to this book is a consideration of why Pons and Fleischmann were so gullible, assuming, as most observers do, that they were sincerely mistaken rather than duplicitous. A clue comes from the frequent description of both of them (particularly Fleischmann, the more eminent of the two) as having a reputation for engaging in high-risk science. Arthur Hyman (2002), a cognitive scientist and prominent skeptic, studied cases where eminent scientists, including Nobel Prize winners, have adopted comically wrong ideas. What he has noted is that eminent scientists, contrary to the popular stereotype of them as coldly analytical, are often highly intuitive risk-takers, who have had success with such risk-taking in the past, and are inclined to sometimes push their luck too far. This is particularly likely to happen when they are invested in a particular outcome, and when they have moved into a field that is outside their area of true expertise.

It is also likely, as in other cases of gullibility, that Pons and Fleischmann were subject to social pressures, particularly from the administrators at their university. It is very likely that the catastrophic decision by Pons and Fleischmann to present their findings prematurely was affected by anxious concerns expressed to them about the need to establish intellectual ownership and protect patent rights. This anxiety resulted in part from the news that a physicist, Steven Jones, at nearby Brigham Young University, was independently pursuing a similar line of research. It should be noted that Dr. Jones dropped his own press conference bombshell in February 2006, when he argued that the destruction of New York's Twin Towers could not have been caused solely by airplanes and had to have been aided by bombs placed inside the buildings.

Interestingly, the cold fusion fiasco was preceded 17 years earlier by a very similar example of what had come to be known as the "Utah effect." The earlier embarrassment also involved a professor of chemistry at the University of Utah: Edward Eyring. In 1972, Eyring announced that his research group had discovered the x-ray laser. Eyring, like Pons and Fleischmann, had been working in isolation from more established researchers engaged with that problem (such isolation—from experts who might have provided corrective feedback—is almost always found in cases of pathological science). That announcement also made a big splash at the time because the quest to develop a laser using x-rays, rather than visible or infrared light, had proved elusive. As with the later case of cold fusion, the announcement was received skeptically by laser scientists, because Eyring lacked relevant credentials and because his theoretical explanations made no sense. The Eyring discovery was later discredited for reasons (failure to control for experimental artifacts) that were eerily prescient of the later Utah debacle.

Had Pons and Fleischmann been more historically knowledgeable, they would also have been aware of another historical precedent, and such awareness might have saved them a lot of grief. In the 1920s, two German chemists, Fritz Paneth and Kurt Peters, attempted to devise an artificial method for manufacturing helium, a gas needed for the German airship industry, but unobtainable because of an embargo on shipments to Germany imposed by the largest source of natural helium, the United States. Knowing that palladium absorbs hydrogen, Paneth and Peters ran hydrogen over hot palladium, and hoped to create a fusion reaction with helium as a by-product. They initially claimed success, but later found they were mistaken. Swedish scientist, John Tandberg, who in 1927 applied unsuccessfully for a patent to produce helium by running a current through water, using palladium cathodes, later took up this work. Tandberg's method differed from that of Pons and Fleischmann only in the use of ordinary (light) water, rather than heavy water. When heavy water (deuterium) was discovered in the 1930s, Tandberg substituted it for light water, and thus predated the Pons and Fleischmann exact experiment by over 50 years. Tandberg had little success with this method, however, and eventually concluded it did not work. If Pons and Fleischmann had been less secretive they might have learned of this precedent and thus saved themselves and their university much grief.

ACADEMIC HIRING DECISIONS

As part of my long-standing fascination with social incompetence, I am interested in organizational leadership (because social competence is a critical leadership trait) and the process by which leaders are selected. In particular, I am interested in the incompetence often displayed by search committees, as shown when they hire executives who turn out to be disasters. In my experience, these disasters could almost always have been avoided, if the search committee or hiring person had been more attuned to clues from the interview as well as from the candidate's employment history. Bad hiring decisions almost always reflect gullibility toward the lies told by candidates, a gullibility fueled largely by affective and self-deception processes in the hirers.

That these clues are ignored is a function of the seduction aspects of the interview process, in which a skilled candidate will manage to make the hirers so smitten that they will gullibly accept his or her version of past problems without checking them out. There is also a significant amount of self-delusion operating, in which the desire to get closure, combined with reliance on group consensus, causes the process to continue moving ahead when it should grind to a screeching halt. Finally, there is a tendency for hirers to overestimate their own ability to judge the veracity of a candidate, without understanding how difficult it is to see through skilled liars and how different the circumstances of an interview are from the circumstances of a work setting (the gullibility of personnel decision makers was first addressed in Stagner, 1959).

The first principle of psychology is that "past behavior is the best predictor of future behavior," but hiring committees routinely ignore that principle, either because of their own smugness or their desperateness to hire an attractive candidate. An acquaintance who serves as a search consultant to school boards told me of an extreme example of this. He had identified an attractive candidate for a high-level fiscal management position in a large urban school district. The board was impressed and was about to hire this candidate. Just before they did so, the search consultant learned of serious legal allegations, involving misuse of district funds, that were pending against the candidate in his current job and that accounted for his desire to leave for another city.

The consultant investigated further and concluded that the allegations were quite credible; he urgently contacted his client school board and advised them strongly to cancel the hire. They went ahead and hired this man anyway, on the basis of his convincing explanations, his attractive personality, and the fact that on paper he was a perfect fit with the qualities (such as race) that they were looking for. The board came to regret this decision, as the man repeated, as might have been expected, his prior misconduct and eventually went to jail for stealing from the new school district.

One of the factors contributing to hiring gullibility is the tendency of the hirers to overvalue a candidate's ability to get along with superiors (i.e., themselves) and undervalue his or her ability to get along with subordinates. Because of a tendency, which I think is universal, to place far more stock on academic credentials than on "people skills," there is even a widespread mistaken tendency to think that a leader's unpopularity with the troops means that he or she is doing a good job. This tendency to hold onto a pre-set idea (i.e., that a tough and confrontational leader is needed to get an organization whipped into shape) contributes to hiring gullibility and untold numbers of hiring mistakes.

An example of this phenomenon occurred when a well-known public university was looking to hire a president. (As in many real-life cases in this book, identifying information has been altered). The university's board settled on a candidate, "Dr Andrews," who had previously been the president of a comparable university in another state. This man was being let go as president, ostensibly because of a well-publicized dispute with his former board over having taken some important actions without seeking their approval. In fact, there were other, even more serious issues, which had not been made public. I know this because an old college friend of mine had served on the board during that time period. She told me that the last straw came when it was discovered that Andrews had forged the signature of the board chairman on a letter supporting his effort to force a rival top administrator to resign.

Interestingly, at the press conference at which the newly hired president was being introduced, the chairman of the hiring board was asked if he had made any effort to talk to anyone at the university that was pushing this man out. The chairman's response, reflecting supreme arrogance, was "Why should I do that? They are just a bunch of yokels and Dr Andrews is too good for them." This turned out to be a huge mistake, as the newly hired president turned out to have an equally stormy tenure and was eventually pushed out of his new presidency under similar circumstances.

GULLIBILITY AMONG PSYCHOTHERAPISTS AND THEIR CLIENTS

Psychotherapists can be gullible in two ways: first by believing everything told to them by their clients and, second, by buying into wacky therapies that lack adequate theoretical rationales or empirical support. The first of these, believing lies or exaggerations told by patients, has actually been the focus of a lively scholarly literature. Under the rubric of "counselor gullibility" (Miller, 1986), it is one of the few areas of psychology where there has been much discussion of gullibility in the research literature. The second of these was addressed in Greenspan (2004).

The impetus for debate over counselor gullibility is the well-known fact that the complaints and accounts that many if not most therapy clients give about significant people and events in their lives are often subject to distortion if not outright fabrication. The debate within the psychotherapy literature is about whether the notion of "unconditional positive regard" requires the therapist to wholeheartedly believe everything that a client tells her or whether one can still maintain unconditional positive regard while harboring doubts about the truth of the client's stories. My own position, which should be obvious to the reader by now, is that competent people always have to keep their "gullibility monitor" running, but there is no reason why one cannot have healthy skepticism and still have respect for the person who may, consciously or unconsciously, be feeding you a line of bull. In fact, it seems to me that the best therapeutic results usually occur when the therapist helps the client to see through his or her web of self-deceptions and distortions.

On the other hand, being overly quick to dismiss the truth of client accounts can be problematic as well. For example, in the early years of psychoanalysis, Sigmund Freud went from believing the stories that his young female patients told of having been sexually molested by their fathers to automatically dismissing all such stories as hysterical fabrications. In his book *The Assault on Truth: Freud's Suppression of the Seduction Theory*, Jeffrey Moussaieff Masson (1984) attacked this reversal as a cowardly and immoral act, which diverted attention away from a serious social problem and led psychoanalysis down a path he considered unproductive.

A more common, if less written about, form of therapist gullibility involves the use of questionable therapeutic interventions. Very few forms of psychotherapy, up to and including classical psychoanalysis (at one time, the gold standard of therapeutic modalities), have been empirically verified and many of them have theoretical rationales that are shaky at best. If this is true of accepted therapeutic methods, there is little to stop the use of therapies on the fringe.

There are several reasons why therapists, including those with doctorates, would uncritically buy into dubious therapies. One situational reason is because colleagues, including mentors, buy into many of these therapies, and group definition as to what is appropriate or inappropriate is a powerful shaper of behavior. Among the cognitive reasons is because many therapy training programs (such as in social work, which is the source of most therapists today) provide a surprisingly nonrigorous education, and many therapists thus lack the theoretical, substantive, or research skills to know when a therapeutic approach may be dubious.

The flip side of counselor gullibility is what might be termed *client gullibility*. One form this takes is a too eager willingness to believe that a therapist knows what he or she is talking about when providing insights into a client's problems or personality style. A relevant phenomenon here from the social psychology experimental literature is what has been termed (Layne, 1979) the *Barnum effect*, named after the showman, P.T. Barnum. A typical Barnum effect study involves a researcher in a lab coat asking a group of subjects (typically college students) to individually fill out a personality questionnaire containing many questions. When the researcher comes back after a while he hands each of the subjects a phony report that supposedly presents the findings from the questionnaire. The subjects do not know that they each have received the identical report, which for the most part consists of trite Horoscope-type generalizations, such as "you are very sensitive" or "sometimes, you are afraid of the unknown." Subjects are asked to comment on this feedback and typically most subjects indicate that they are amazed at the accuracy with which the comments describe them. What these studies suggest is that people can be easily fooled by quasi-therapists saying things that apply to most members of the human race. Even if the researcher is dead wrong on some of these statements, a confirmation bias is operating in which we look for information that confirms the idea that we are unique and that the psychologist really understands us. Applying this to the phenomenon of client gullibility, this suggests that we tend to attribute a special wisdom to therapists, and to believe that they have much to offer us even when that is not necessarily the case.

An aspect of client gullibility that is potentially a serious problem is the tendency to believe the counselor when he or she responds to a termination request (as the counselor almost inevitably does) with words to the effect that "I don't think you are ready to terminate. There are still some things that I think you need to work on." An example of this phenomenon can be found in a September 1, 2005, article in *The New York Times* titled "Goodbye, Therapist. Hello, Anxiety?" The author, Susan Saulny (2005) quoted several therapy patients who indicated that their attempts to terminate were made very difficult by their therapists. Joye Chizek, a 53-year-old Illinois woman who has run across this problem with all three of her former therapists, noted that "it becomes psychologically a worse problem than you came with, . . . You're there to discuss whatever about your father, then you end up worrying about this other thing, getting in and out of relationships with therapists. It totally becomes its own problem." Ms Chizek said "Nobody ever says 'you're well, get out of here.... I was made to feel as if the loose ends that I was leaving were going to become major obstacles to my future development as a useful human being."

Such resistance by a therapist to a patient's expressed desire to terminate is, most likely, sincerely felt in most cases. After all, who doesn't have some things they could continue to work on? However, it should be noted that every therapist who resists termination has created a conflict of interest situation stemming from the fact that he or she stands to gain financially if the client changes his mind about terminating. An additional ethical consideration, briefly touched on in Saulny's article, is that every mental health professional ethics code has an "autonomy" clause stating that the client retains the ultimate right to initiate or terminate treatment. The "You're not ready" response serves to undermine that autonomy, especially given that many therapy patients are insecure people who have difficulty asserting their will, especially in the face of opposition from a respected parent-like figure such as a therapist.

ALTERNATIVE HEALTH PRACTICES

"Sarah" the daughter of a former colleague of mine, was a single mother in her 30s. Several years ago, she developed breast cancer. A believer in alternative medicine, Sarah resisted the advice to have the lump removed surgically, with the possibility that this would need to be followed by radiation therapy. Instead, Sarah relied on herbal treatments prescribed by someone who claimed to have some expertise as a healer. Unfortunately, Sarah's cancer spread to her bones and various organs, and eventually she passed away.

I don't know what other term to use than *profoundly gullible* to describe someone who would be so quick to put his or her life in the hands of an herbal healer (a dubiously credentialed one at that), instead of traditional medicine, when facing a life-threatening illness. Usually, people turn to alternative treatments when traditional medicine has not worked, and when they don't seem to have anything to lose by trying something different. Thus, when comedian Andy Kaufman was dying from advanced lung cancer, he flew to Manila to be treated by a conjurer who pulled chicken parts out of his chest claiming it was the cancer. If Kaufman was gullible in going to such a quack, it was certainly understandable, given that he had exhausted all of the traditional treatments available to him. But Sarah's willingness to believe nonsense told by someone she knew nothing about reflected a level of gullibility that bordered on psychotic. In fact, Sarah was someone with a history of mental instability.

The topic of gullibility toward alternative health practices is huge, and deserves a book of its own. By alternative health practices, I am referring to treatments or disciplines that are outside the mainstream of modern Western medicine. These practices are often derided or discouraged by physicians as either unhelpful or, in some cases, dangerous. An example of an alternative practice that is potentially dangerous is urine therapy (daily consumption of one's own urine). Taken in tiny doses, as was done by a former prime minister of India, it is probably harmless, but the father of a friend of mine consumed very large quantities, in combination with mega doses of table salt, and lost his eyesight as a result. Another example would be the widespread taking of nutritional supplements bought in health food stores, often on the basis of word-of-mouth recommendations. Professional athletes are susceptible to such recommendations, because they always have aches and pains, are looking for a competitive edge, and are in frequent touch with people who claim to have useful information. One athlete, NBA basketball player Tom Gugliotta, suffered a severe seizure reaction to such a supplement (γ-butyrolactone) in January 2000 and nearly lost his life as a result.

Alternative medicine is a very large industry, generating billions of dollars a year in the United States alone. There are several explanations for this appeal:

1. Many people have chronic, and sometimes subtle problems, such as fatigue or joint pain, that do not respond well to usual medical approaches.

2. Given the subtlety and subjective nature of many symptoms, one can perceive improvements after an alternative treatment that may not actually have occurred, or that are a placebo effect, or that might simply reflect short- or long-term improvements that would have occurred anyway.

3. Many alternative practitioners have an authoritative and reassuring manner and have a convincing, even if questionable, bag of tricks (i.e., they are skilled con artists).

4. The idea of alternative medicine appeals to people who are cynical toward establishment medicine, or the establishment generally, and taps into a respect for non-Western (e.g., Asian or Native American) herbal-based healing beliefs held by many counterculture individuals.

5. Alternative medicine takes advantage of the need of many people to believe in magic, magicians, and the arcane arts.

One basis of the appeal of alternative medicine is that there are still things, particularly the relationship between mind and body that are poorly understood by modern medical science and there are subdisciplines (such as nutrition) in which most physicians receive only cursory training. The ability to spew forth an elaborate theory and treatment regime not known by their physicians may meet the needs of some individuals to feel competent and efficacious in combating their symptoms, and to feel that they possess some unique knowledge, even if the knowledge has only the appearance (but not the reality) of being grounded in science. In short, part of the appeal of alternative medicine is that it takes advantage of the tendency of many people, including some with advanced degrees, to think they know more than they really do.

As in some of the other cases, such as political gullibility, addressed in this book, a key to alternative medicine's appeal to practitioners, and also to consumers, is in the use of a theory that may make sense on a superficial level, especially to those with limited knowledge, but that does not make sense (or may lack empirical support) on a more profound level. An example is chiropractic, an alterative medical discipline invented in Davenport, Iowa, in 1895 by D.D. Palmer and his son B.J. Palmer (who is credited with professionalizing the discipline). The senior Palmer was a faith healer who started off as a practitioner of animal magnetism (Mesmerism, which also influenced the ideas of Mary Baker Eddy and Christian Science) but changed his practice to one based on the use of sudden spinal manipulation, which is still the core technique used by chiropractors today (J.S. Moore, 1993). Spinal manipulation is based on the theory of subluxation, namely that minor dislocations in alignment of vertebrae in the spinal column can account for many diseases and symptoms, including some that are not related to one's muscles or skeleton. A problem with this superficially attractive theory is that there is virtually no evidence from many studies (including examination of cadavers) that subluxation of the spine actually can be found with any frequency (Leach, 1994).

The same argument can be applied to homeopathy, an alternative medical discipline, particularly popular in France, which is based on the notion that extremely diluted solutions of highly toxic substances can bring about cures. One highly touted study claimed to find therapeutic effects with a solution that was so dilute that not even a single molecule of the toxic substance could be found, but this unbelievable finding was later shown to be a delusion (Maddox, Randi, & Stewart, 1988). When health practitioners, not to mention patients, are motivated by a strong emotional need to have certain ideas or outcomes confirmed, gullibility has a clear field in which to operate.

RASPUTIN AND FACILITATED COMMUNICATION

As the brother of a man with an autistic spectrum disorder, I know what parents and other family members go through when there is a child in the family who has a severe illness or disability. The term *chronic sorrow* has been used (Olshansky, 1962) to describe the difficulty that many family members have in accepting the loss of their dream of seeing their child or sibling develop into a healthy, independent, and fully competent adult. Parents of children with chronic diseases may have the additional burden of not knowing if their children will live.

The desperate longing of parents for their child to be "normal" increases their gullibility toward false healers, therapies, or ideas. The prototype for the exploitation of desperate parents by phony or self-deluded faith healers is the story of the filthy and wild-eyed Siberian healer and mystic, Grigory Rasputin, whose ministrations to the young hemophiliac heir to the Russian throne gave him great influence with the boy's parents, Tsar Nicholas II and his wife, Tsarina Alexandra. The monk's actual surname was Novykh, but his sexual misconduct in school caused him to be given the nickname "Rasputin," Russian for "debauched one."

Rasputin came to Saint Petersburg in 1903, where he became known in court circles, which reportedly were quite enamored of the mystical and occult. In 1908, he was summoned to the palace during one of the prince's bleeding episodes, and when the boy recovered, Rasputin announced that he had a vision to the effect that no harm would befall the boy as long as his parents relied on him. Thus began a 10-year period where Rasputin's influence over the Tsarina was so great (and the actions that he caused her and the Tsar to take were so disastrous) that it actually may have contributed to the collapse of the country and the overthrow of the monarchy.

The gullibility of the royal couple can best be appreciated when it is noted that report after report was presented to them about Rasputin's improprieties, and the news that virtually everyone at the royal court considered Rasputin to be a charlatan. In all cases, according to Alex DeJonge (1982), in his book *The Life and Times of Grigorii Rasputin*, the reports were dismissed, with assurances that Rasputin was a good man who was misunderstood. The likely explanation for this gullibility, of course, is that as the prince grew older, his health became more precarious, and the royal parents, especially the tsarina (who was becoming increasingly and bizarrely devout), were desperate to keep Rasputin on the case.

A recent wildly popular human service intervention, which some would consider about as plausible as prayer by a dissolute monk, is facilitated communication (FC), which disability ethicist Wolf Wolfensberger (1994) has termed the *cold fusion of the human services*. FC is a technique invented around 1980 by Rosemary Crossley, an Australian special educator, who used it initially with people who have cerebral palsy and later mainly with individuals who have autism. The technique involves a nondisabled adult (the "facilitator"), typically a para-professional who learns the technique in a brief workshop, placing his or her hand over the dominant hand of a client, who then responds to verbal questions by pointing to letters on a computer keyboard or, more typically, a paper keyboard display. In the latter case, the facilitator calls out each letter, and then each word, thus providing a supposed means for previously nonverbal, or expressively limited, individuals to communicate. The purpose of the hand-over-hand support was to provide gentle back pressure (supposedly to correct for "motor apraxia"), as well as positive encouragement. Crossley and other proponents always claimed that the communicating was coming entirely from the person with the disability.

Little was known about FC outside of Australia before a respected professor of special education from Syracuse University, Douglas Biklen, happened to run across it in the mid-1980s while he was in Australia on a sabbatical leave. Biklen, who had previously been known for his advocacy for the "full-inclusion" movement in special education, proceeded on his return to promote FC tirelessly as a miraculous intervention with individuals who have autism. His writings and workshops caught the attention of ABC's *20/20* news magazine, and a highly laudatory piece caused an incredible explosion of interest in FC.

The aspect of FC that attracted the most attention, and controversy, was the supposed demonstration of advanced literacy, and abstract reasoning ability, in many individuals who were considered to have severe mental retardation (in addition to autism) and who had neither received training, nor demonstrated any prior ability, in writing or spelling. What made some people suspicious of the phenomenon was that the messages coming from the clients were not only extremely articulate (sometimes being produced while the client was engaging in self-stimulatory behaviors and not even looking at the keyboard) but often had a quasi-political message, along the lines of "people with disabilities have many talents." This aroused suspicion, not only because these clients had never previously shown any political awareness but also because the leading promoters of FC in the United States were very much caught up in the disability rights movement, and included such content in the training workshops provided for facilitators.

One of the reasons why FC was so appealing to disability rights advocates was because it made it easier to push for fully inclusionary educational and other human service placements from school officials and rehabilitation bureaucrats who previously would have been very resistant to such demands. There were many cases where facilitated high school students went from self-contained nonacademic classrooms to getting As and Bs in regular academic subjects. This increase in achievement was also supposedly accompanied by increased regard within families.

The unraveling of FC was precipitated by charges of sexual abuse directed against fathers by their disabled daughters, and made through facilitators (who are mostly women). These cases resulted in judges in both Australia and the United States ordering controlled experiments to be conducted to determine whether allegedly abused parties should be allowed to testify through facilitation. These tests showed conclusively that the actual communication originated with the facilitator. As is often the case when a core belief is challenged, however, the supporters of FC tended to dismiss nonsupportive evidence as flawed and irrelevant. Their main argument was that FC depended on a degree of trust and comfort between facilitator and client, and that controlled experimentation created an artificial and anxiety-filled situation. They argued for the use of more naturalistic qualitative research methods. A dissertation done under my supervision, later published as a book, by Diane Twachtman-Cullen (1997) titled *A Passion to Believe: Autism and the Facilitated Communication Phenomenon* met these requirements, I believe.

Twachtman-Cullen looked at three established facilitator–client dyads, at a facility known as a center for exemplary training and use of FC. All three of the clients in the study were young adults who were considered to have mental retardation (MR) as well as autism: one of them was considered to have mild MR, a second was considered to have moderate MR, and a third was considered to have profound MR. Twachtman-Cullen took many hours of videotapes of communication, and subjected the messages to intense analysis. In the two dyads involving the most cognitively impaired clients, Twachtman-Cullen (a certified language therapist) found convincing evidence that the facilitator heavily influenced the messages. In the third case, there was some evidence of actual independent communication coming from this client, who was the most mildly impaired. However, with this least impaired client, the messages were very concrete (e.g., "I want lunch"), whereas the two more impaired clients gave very abstract messages. This supported the view, I believe, that FC is a bogus therapy.

The most interesting question concerns not whether facilitators are consciously faking (some think it was unconscious, done in a trance state), but with how so many professionals could have jumped on this dubious bandwagon. Among the factors contributing to gullible acceptance of FC are the following:

1. The phenomenon is difficult to evaluate or measure through the use of one's sense impressions (this is one of Langmuir's six criteria for pathological science.)

2. Autism is a mysterious and complex disorder.

3. Many disability professionals have weak research training, and lack the knowledge base to see through dubious claims.

4. There was a deep affective longing for this to be real.

5. As in *The Emperor's New Clothes*, when other professionals believe in something, it is hard to feel or express doubts.

CHAPTER 7

Gullibility in Vulnerable Populations

Although gullibility can and does affect everyone, there are some populations that are at increased risk of being duped. Various legal and other protections (e.g., guardianship, supported living) have been devised to protect at-risk populations from social exploitation and to limit their social vulnerability. In this chapter, I explore gullibility in relation to age (children, the elderly), in relation to a particular disability (mental retardation, autism, brain damage), and in relation to particular forms of exploitation (coercive interrogation, consumer scams).

FALSE CONFESSIONS OF PEOPLE WITH BRAIN DAMAGE

Although inexperienced young people, such as Peter Reilly (profiled in chapter 5), are vulnerable to being induced to give false confession, this problem is particularly acute among individuals with mild mental retardation (MR, now increasingly referred to as intellectual disabilities). In fact, the prevalence of false confessions in this population was one of the reasons cited in the 2002 decision by the U.S. Supreme Court in *Atkins v. Virginia*, which declared the execution of people with MR to be unconstitutional. Unfortunately, that decision did not cover people with related vulnerabilities, who did not qualify for the MR label.

An example of such an individual is Richard Lapointe who, like Peter Reilly, is another victim of overly zealous interrogation methods used in Connecticut. The Lapointe case (described in Connery, 1996) is particularly meaningful to me, both because of my long-time membership in a group advocating on his behalf and also because his story is what piqued my interest in exploring the topic of gullibility.

At the time of his arrest, in July 1989, Lapointe was a 43-year-old man living in Manchester, Connecticut, with his wife Karen (also someone with disabilities) and their 10-year-old son, Sean. They lived in a small condominium near Karen's family, and Richard worked as a dishwasher. Lapointe had no history of the sort of violence or sexual acting-out of which he was accused. He was born with hydrocephalus, stemming from a congenital brain malformation that was not detected or treated until his teens. He had multiple disabilities, including visual, hearing and motor impairments, significant learning problems (he repeated ninth grade three times before being encouraged to drop out of school), and severe social information-processing deficits common to people with hydrocephalus and right brain damage. Although his IQ was too high for him to qualify for a diagnosis of MR, he came across as someone with MR, even to the police officers who used to frequent the restaurant where he worked.

One Sunday afternoon in 1987, Karen received a phone call from a relative asking them to check on the condition of her 88-year-old grandmother, Bernice Martin, who lived a short distance from their condo. Richard walked his dog over there but was unable to get an answer to the doorbell. After checking with a neighbor, he thought he saw smoke and he went back and found the doorknob hot to the touch. He then returned to the neighbor and called the fire department. The firemen carried an unconscious and semi-naked Bernice Martin out of her apartment. She had been stabbed, strangled with a ligature and sexually assaulted, and the apartment had been set on fire. Mrs. Martin died a short while later.

Two years went by with no progress in the case, and there was public pressure to solve the crime (a condition that is almost always present when false confessions are obtained). Richard had never been a suspect, as his wife provided an alibi (a very short time frame when he was out of the house), there was a complete absence of physical or motivational evidence, and Richard's impairments (such as limited muscle strength) would have made it unlikely that he could have carried out an act (such as throwing a heavy woman onto a bed and tearing ligatures from a bedsheet) that required considerable strength and dexterity. As a result of some personnel changes in the local police department, however, a young detective who was new to the force took it upon himself to set a trap for Lapointe. His interest in Richard was triggered by the fact that Lapointe would constantly ask the police officers who frequented his restaurant if they had any leads, and this detective (who apparently fancied himself a forensic profiler after taking a brief workshop at the FBI academy) felt this was an indication of guilt.

Richard was asked to come to the police station late on the July 4 holiday, to help them solve the crime. He willingly agreed. The walls were covered with charts indicating the existence of DNA and fingerprint evidence, none of it real, and signed "Sergeant Joe Friday" (the fictional detective on the TV show *Dragnet*), a joke indicating the low opinion the officers had of Lapointe's intelligence. He was interrogated for more than 9 hours, and whenever he said he was hungry or needed to go to the bathroom (something that he had to do frequently, as a result of his medical condition), he was told "later." According to Richard, he was told that his wife would be arrested and his child would be taken away from him unless he confessed. Such threats are illegal, but they could not be proved, given that no taperecording of the interview was ever found. However a taped interview was conducted with Karen at her home by the same officer who supposedly made this threat to Richard, and the transcript of that interview showed the making of a similar threat, thus lending some credence to Richard's accusation. To Karen's credit, she refused to change her alibi story, despite the threats.

After several hours, Lapointe's will to resist began to crumble. He claims that it resulted from the threat of having custody of his son taken away. (I have done research on disabled parents, and they all, without exception, live in constant fear of such a very real possibility.) Also he was exhausted and was told he could go home if he confessed (that is exactly what happened, except that he was arrested later). Lapointe signed three statements, one more absurd than the next. The second statement, for example, said "If the evidence shows I was there, and that I killed her, then I killed her. But I don't remember being there." (As in the Peter Reilly case, Lapointe was apparently told that he didn't remember doing the deed because he had blacked out.)

Three detectives interviewed Lapointe, and the statements they obtained were all different, reflecting the officers' different knowledge of the murder and their need to get him to give them an admission that was more specific and incriminating. The third, and most detailed, statement (obtained by the detective new to the force) said that Lapointe raped Bernice with his penis when in fact an object had been used, and that he strangled her with his hands, when in fact she had been strangled with a ligature.

Lapointe is a meek man who has always been easily fooled and who has been described by people who know him as extremely gullible. He waived his Miranda rights when they were read to him out of the naïve belief, held by many people, that innocent people do not need to assert those rights. Lapointe had always considered police officers to be his friends and took some pride in the fact that they had asked him to help them solve the crime. He naïvely believed them when they said they could have his son taken away from him (in fact, a more savvy person would know that is not within the power of police officers). The state sought the death penalty on the basis of such flimsy evidence, but although he was convicted of first-degree murder, he was given a life sentence (ironically, his disability was sufficient to mitigate the sentence but was insufficient to convince the judge or jury to discount the confessions). Since the day that he was arrested, Richard Lapointe has not seen his son.

SOCIAL VULNERABILITY OF YOUNG PEOPLE

Much discipline practice by parents is based on a conscious exploitation of the gullibility of children. An example of this involved a couple who were on vacation with their two daughters, aged 7 and 10 years. One morning they awoke and all agreed that they would go to the zoo, but when they arrived, the zoo was closed. The parents and the older girl decided to go to the beach instead, but the younger daughter, "Kate" (who often on principle staked out a different position from her older sister "Marie," and vice versa) said "I hate the beach" and ordered her parents to drive back to the place where they were staying. When her father indicated that he would not turn back, Kate became increasingly angry and upset.

When Marie and her mother got out of the car, Kate refused to join them. She indicated that she was going to stay put. Kate's father let her sit in the car for a couple of minutes and then said "All right Kate, you win. You don't have to go to the beach. Let's get some ice cream and then we'll go home." Kate calmed down and agreed to her father's suggestion. Her father then said "First, let's go and ask Mommy and Marie what kind of ice cream we should get for them." Kate agreed with that plan and the two of them walked down to the beach to catch up with the others. When Kate saw her sister in the ocean having a great time, she ran up to her and said, with a sheepish grin, "What kind of ice cream do you want, Marie?" After not getting an answer from Marie, Kate ripped off her jacket and ran into the water to join her sister. She spent about 30 minutes splashing around in the surf with her sister. They then all went back to the car and drove to an ice cream place before heading back home. When her father mentioned to Kate that she seemed to have had a good time at the beach, she just smiled.

Kate was demonstrating gullibility in falling for her father's diversionary tactic (offering to go for ice cream). Even after her father added the condition that they both walk on the beach to ask the ice cream preferences of the others, Kate did not understand her father's motives or the fact that she had been tricked into going to the beach against her wishes. Kate was a bright child with good social skills. Her gullibility was characteristic of all children her age.

The gullibility of children is a theme in the writings of the evolutionary biologist Richard Dawkins (2003). He suggested that gullibility has become a common characteristic of human beings because of its role in helping children to survive into adulthood, and to thus surmount the many potential physical dangers (such as drowning, being eaten by wild animals, or getting run over by cars) that they face during the course of growing up. For Dawkins, gullibility has both positive and negative functions for children. The negative function of childish gullibility is, of course, that it makes them more vulnerable to the deceits of predatory persons who would take advantage of their naïve trust. For Dawkins, this is counterbalanced by the positive function of gullibility, namely that that it predisposes children to incorporate social *memes* (a term and concept coined by him). A meme is a culturally transmitted unit of information that can take many forms, from learning one's native language to learning that hot stoves are to be avoided. Children become competent adults, according to Dawkins, because they are meme-absorbing machines who attend constantly to directions and guidance from adults, especially from their parents. It is this blind trust that keeps children from wandering off or from engaging in highly dangerous behaviors. Consequently, children are hardwired, in Dawkins' view, to believe everything they are told by adults. The process of natural selection (the Darwinian mechanism most used by evolutionary psychologists) ensured that gullibility became prevalent, presumably because nongullible children would have been more likely to be killed off.

The tendency of young children to believe everything told to them by their parents can be seen in a mini-experiment I did involving my own two children when they were 7 and 4 years old, respectively. The inspiration for the experiment came when I was watching sports on TV. An ad for the then-new sports network ESPN News involved a series of fake headlines along the lines of "Jack Nicklaus wins professional beach volleyball tournament" and "Boston Marathon to add 200 yards," followed by the line "if you watched ESPN News you would know if these headlines are true or not" (with a laughing voice exclaiming "Captain Gullible").

In my version of these headlines were stories such as "an Olympic bicycle racer is training by racing around a track. She is going so fast that the bike, with the rider on it, begins to rise up, and the rider and the bike glide slowly through the air just like in the movie 'ET'." Another example of such a headline, this time involving a social, rather than a physical, impossibility, went as follows: "Newt Gingrich [who at that time was Speaker of the House] was watching a movie about the British Royal Family and said to himself 'wouldn't it be a neat idea if the United States had a monarchy instead of a presidency?' So Speaker Gingrich issued a proclamation the next day that declared that the next President of the United States would be declared 'King' or 'Queen' rather than 'President.'"

I read aloud each of these, along with a dozen or so other, phony headlines, and a few plausible fillers (e.g., "A woman was staying at a hotel and she leaned out of her fifth-story window to wave to someone walking by in the street below. She leaned over too far and fell out of the window"), to reduce the likelihood of a child developing a response set. In this pilot study, my subjects were my sons: Alex (then 7 years , 6 months) and Eli (then 4 years, 6 months). After I read each headline, I asked them to tell me if they thought the event described "could have happened" or "could not have happened" and to say why. What I found was that the younger child, Eli, said "yes, it could have happened" to virtually every item, whereas the older child, Alex, was much more likely to say "no, it could not have happened." In other words, there appears to be a qualitative shift, between age 4 and age 7 years (the dividing point between Jean Piaget's stages of preoperations and concrete operations), from pervasive gullibility to non- or, more accurately, conditional gullibility.

When I say that the gullibility of 7-year-olds is conditional, I mean that it depends on the degree of content expertise that is needed. In terms of physical realities (such as the bicycle rising into the air), Alex's responses were firmly not gullible, whereas his response to more socially based items, such as the one involving Newt Gingrich declaring the United States a monarchy, were more guarded and uncertain. With respect to that particular item, this obviously reflected the fact that Alex had little knowledge at that point in his life about American history and constitutional law, and thus lacked a basis for knowing that in America the ability of any single individual to implement such a change, regardless of how important he might be, is as much of an impossibility as is a bicycle imitating an airplane.

A particularly interesting and unanticipated finding was the degree to which the younger child's gullibility remained constant even in the face of efforts on my part to signal that he was being tricked. What happened was that after awhile, Eli started to ask "for real?" after he gave each answer. Wanting to know if it would make a difference, I started responding "yes" followed quickly by "no, I was just kidding" after each "for real?" It didn't seem to make Eli (who, like his brother, was bright for his age) any more wary, and he continued to give gullible responses to each subsequent item. This seems to confirm Dawkins' view of young children as having such a strong drive to believe everything said by adults that they will remain gullible even in the face of fairly obvious clues that they are being tricked.

I agree with Dawkins' view that gullibility is a universal tendency of young children. Anyone who doubts that should think back a few years ago to the "Pokemon" trading card craze, a craze based on a Japanese TV cartoon show of the same name. Millions of school-aged children pleaded with their parents to take them to one store after another in the usually futile hope that a new shipment of cards had arrived and had not yet been snapped up. After awhile, schools in North America began to prohibit Pokemon trading on school buses and playgrounds. The official reason given was that it was a distraction, but an equally important reason, I was told, is that too many younger kids were being cheated in unfair trades by less gullible older kids.

That children can be too easily persuaded, because of their gullibility, into entering into foolish transactions is, in fact, the underlying rationale for the universal requirement that children cannot sign a contract or make any legally binding agreement until they reach a less gullible age (typically 18 years).

FRAIL ELDERLY AND PEOPLE WITH ALZHEIMER'S

One of my late mother's best friends was a very sweet woman whom I call "Donna." Upon her husband's retirement, Donna and her husband moved to south Florida, where they lived over 1,000 miles from their two adult children, who visited them on occasion. After her husband died, Donna continued to live alone and used her car mainly to go to the nearby supermarket. One day, as she was leaving the market, Donna was approached by a well-dressed woman who offered to help her transfer her groceries from her cart to the trunk of her car. Donna was a very friendly person and she accepted this help gratefully.

The woman told Donna that her husband was a jewelry appraiser who could save her hundreds of dollars a year on her insurance premiums by reappraising her jewelry. This prospect appealed to Donna, who was somewhat frugal, and (probably unnecessarily) concerned about her financial situation. Donna invited the woman to her home to look at her jewelry, and even allowed the woman to take the jewelry away with her. Needless to say, the woman, and the jewelry, were never seen again. Donna was devastated by the loss of her jewelry, less because of the financial value than by the fact that she had planned to leave the items to her grandchildren. She went into a very deep depression that resisted treatment, she gave up her will to live, and, despite previously good health, died less than a year after the incident.

A second, somewhat similar, case involved the elderly mother of a former secretary of mine, when I lived in Omaha, Nebraska, and worked at the Boys Town Center for the Study of Youth Development. One day, my secretary, "Marcia," asked me if I knew anything about Alzheimer's disease (AD). When I asked her why, Marcia told me that she was concerned about her mother, who was living alone on the family farm, located in the western part of the state. Marcia found out that her mother had been talked by a neighbor into selling the farm, which concerned her both because the price did not seem fair but also because Marcia had been assured by her mother that the farm would always stay in the family.

I told Marcia that I did not know much about AD (this was long before my interest in gullibility in the elderly), but I gave her the name of the best clinic in Omaha that specialized in the disorder. I also made a suggestion (in hindsight, a big mistake) that Marcia tune into a program on AD that was airing on public television that night. When I checked in with Marcia later, she told me that the people depicted in the program (all with end-stage AD) were much more impaired than her mother, and that she and her sister decided, therefore, that her mother did not have AD, and thus there was no point in pursuing my clinic suggestion or contacting a lawyer to see if they could rescind the impending sale of the farm. Sadly, I learned a few years later that Marcia's mother, who had by then died, had eventually been diagnosed as having AD.

Several similar stories have received significant attention in the media, and they all tell a tale that is becoming all too common. These stories range from relatively small-scale (roving bands of home improvement grifters who walk off with a few hundred or thousand dollars for jobs that are unnecessary and poorly carried out) to schemes in which elderly individuals are deprived of their life savings. In the latter category is a case in which an elderly woman in Hartford, Connecticut, became ensnared in a phony sweepstakes scheme in which she spent more than $50,000 on magazine subscriptions. Also in this category is a story that was on national television, in which several lonely old widows spent fortunes on dance lessons and elaborate vacations with dance instructors/gigolos. There have also been numerous cases, such as that of the entertainer Groucho Marx (see Kanfer, 2001) in which prominent people, nearing the end of their lives, are grievously exploited.

I think that one of the underappreciated factors operating in most of these cases is that dementia, whether or not it ever reaches the level of AD, typically has subtle onset, and there are not very good ways of diagnosing it in its very early stages. It is my contention that social vulnerability and gullibility, in people who were generally of average or above-average social competence in their earlier years, may in fact be a better indicator of the early stages of dementia than more purely "cognitive" measures such as memory tests. Preliminary support for the hypothesis that gullibility is a universal feature of elderly adults with AD was obtained in a study in Australia (Pinsker, Stone, Pachana, & Greenspan, 2006).

It is well known that people who are beginning to experience cognitive decrement as a result of neurological disease tend to go to great lengths to cover up the extent of their new limitations. An explanation for elder gullibility, therefore, is that as one begins to lose confidence in the ability to evaluate information or intentions, the easiest way to cover it up is to become very trusting, and to just go along with whatever is asked of you. I believe that these cognitive and personality factors, along with state factors (greed in the case of my mother's late friend Donna and the woman who fell for the sweepstakes swindle; infatuation in the case of the dance ladies) and situational factors (the skill and rapaciousness of con artists and the absence of spouses or other potential protectors, as in the case of my mother's friend) explain why frail elderly people often exhibit such sad and shocking displays of gullibility.

PEOPLE WITH INTELLECTUAL DISABILITY

In a piece that appeared in Denver's *Rocky Mountain News*, reporter Lynn Bartels (2004) told a poignant story about Sherri Bramer, a 52-year-old woman with mild MR, who became lost for several hours at the huge Denver International Airport, when the airplane on which she flew in from Omaha was diverted to a different arrival gate than the one that was posted, and airline personnel mistakenly directed Sherri to the main terminal's baggage carousel area. Worried family members were "taken from bathroom to bathroom and concourse to concourse while ... [Sherri's 81-year-old mother] futilely hollered her daughter's name." What makes this story, which had a happy ending, relevant to the focus of this book was a quote attributed to Sherri's 57-year-old brother, Keith. He said that the first thing that occurred to him and his mother when they realized that Sherri was lost was "we were scared. Sherri's very vulnerable. She'll do whatever you say, go wherever you want her to." In other words, Sherri's family was afraid that she would be exploited in some manner by a bad person who would take advantage of her naïve trust and extreme gullibility.

Victimization because of extreme gullibility is, in fact, an almost universal concern of parents and other caregivers of children and adults who have MR and related developmental disabilities. For example, it has been reported that young women with Williams syndrome—a chromosomal disorder marked by mildly retarded or borderline intellectual deficit, alleged musical talents, ex-treme verbosity and friendliness, and characteristic "elf-like" facial features—have almost all been victims of sexual molestation, most likely because of the "indiscriminate sociability and overfriendliness" (Jones et al., 2001) and extreme empathy (Rosner, 2002) that are found in most people who have this disorder. Additionally, persons with Williams syndrome have the same deficits in social judgment that are found in all persons with MR, although many observers are so taken by their friendliness and verbosity that they come to overestimate their actual social competence.

Social victimization is a primary reason why an integrated placement, such as living on one's own in a community setting, often falls apart for a person with developmental disabilities. This can be seen in a 2002 award-winning documentary, by the filmmaker Alice Elliot, titled *The Collector of Bedford Street*. The film is in some ways a more current version of Ira Wohl's 1979 Oscar-winning documentary, *Best Boy*. The earlier film told the story of 45-year-old Philly (Ira's cousin), and the difficult decision faced by his aging parents regarding whether to move their mildly mentally retarded son from their home into a group home. The *Collector of Bedford Street*, in line with the paradigm shift in MR services that had occurred over the intervening two decades, is the story (filmed by a neighbor) of 61-year-old mildly mentally retarded Larry, and the struggle by his family (only an aging maternal uncle) and friends to figure out how to help Larry to continue to live on his own in a small rent-controlled apartment in New York's Greenwich Village.

The truly amazing thing about Larry's situation is that the initiative to help Larry continue to live among them was taken by Larry's neighbors, all of whom were unrelated to him. Basically, what they did was to raise a significant amount of money for a trust fund to be administered by a community foundation for the purpose of purchasing case management and other support services for Larry, as well as to supplement the meager income that he earned from social security. The esteem that his neighbors felt for Larry stemmed from the fact that he raised thousands of dollars every year (hence the title of the film) for various charities.

Larry's need for support stemmed from his extreme gullibility, and the threat that this posed on numerous occasions to his wellbeing. Specifically, Larry—who lived alone—was very lonely, and he tended to befriend homeless people living on the street. He would give them keys so that they could use his bathroom or sleep in his apartment, would agree to give them money (when he barely had enough to make it through the month), and was even persuaded, until someone intervened, to run off to live under the boardwalk at Coney Island with one of his homeless friends. Aside from the costs to Larry (such as having his meager possessions repeatedly ripped off), the presence of these strangers in the building—many of them with criminal backgrounds or severe mental illness—was very upsetting to Larry's neighbors, who feared both physical damage to the building (e.g., a shower left running in Larry's apartment caused major water damage) and for their own safety. Thus, the decision by Larry's neighbors to create a "circle of friends" was motivated not only out of affection for him but also because they saw it as an alternative to his eviction (which had been considered at one time) and as a way to protect themselves and Larry from his own gullibility, a gullibility that reflected his cognitive limitations as well as his strong social neediness.

GULLIBLE CRIME VICTIMS

Crime victims can sometimes be considered to be gullible because they fail to exercise escape options that are open to them, or because they believe various lies that are told to them by their victimizers. An example of this would be children who are seduced by a molester, and then are kept ensnared in the relationship because they believe the molester's threat to kill the child's parents or pets or because they believe the molester's assurance that the parents would reject the child if they found out about the relationship.

Sometimes victim gullibility (which might better be considered a form of extreme passivity) takes the form of being so paralyzed by fear and confusion that escape becomes impossible. Perhaps the most egregious example of this took place in 1972 in New Haven, Connecticut, when Harold Mead, a 52-year-old former tow-truck driver and ice cream vendor, attacked three mentally retarded residents of the Greater New Haven Regional Center as they went for a walk in a nearby wooded park. Mead, who has been suspected of four other similar killings, used a rock to bash in the skull of the first of his victims while the other two waited passively for their turn to be slaughtered. (Gullibility of therapists comes into play here also, as Mead's good behavior in prison earned him many unescorted furloughs and it appears that he committed one of his signature head-bashing killings in 1992 while on such a leave.)

A notorious killing of a person with cognitive impairments, in which the victim's gullibility played a role, took place in Clairfield, Pennsylvania, in 1998 (Kinney, 1999). The victim was Kimberly Jo Dotts, a socially awkward 15-year-old girl described by her family as having "severe learning disabilities" (a euphemism, in my experience, for mild MR). As with many young people with mild cognitive disabilities, Kimberly had few friends and wanted desperately to be accepted by more popular peers. A group of her classmates suspected that

Kimberly had begun to snitch on their plan to run away *en masse* to Florida, and they concocted a plan to silence her. Kimberly was invited to spend the night at one of the girls' homes, and the next day they all went to a secluded park, where they went into the woods. They then pretended to play a game in which a rope was tossed over a tree branch, and each of the girls took turns putting the other end around their neck. When it was Kimberly's turn, two of the adolescents pulled the rope taut, and strung her up. When Kimberly was let down to the ground, still alive and gasping for breath, one of the girls, 16-year-old Jessica Holtmeyer, finished her off by bashing in her brains with a rock. Seven young people who participated in this lynching went to prison for varying lengths of time, with two of them, Jessica and the other rope-puller, receiving life sentences.

SEXUAL EXPLOITATION OF PEOPLE WITH DISABILITIES

Although relatively competent adults are susceptible to being seduced by skilled pickup artists (see chap. 8), children and adults with cognitive disabilities are especially vulnerable to the attentions of sexual predators. An extremely unsettling example of the social risk posed by the gullibility of adults with even very mild forms of MR, can be found in an infamous incident, known as the "Glen Ridge rape."

This case occurred in an affluent New Jersey suburb of New York City, in 1989. The incident involved 17-year-old high school student, "Leslie Faber," universally known in the small town as someone with mild MR. Leslie was in a park shooting baskets by herself when a carload of young men, some of whom were on the local high school wrestling team, pulled up to the curb. The young men tried to talk Leslie into coming to one of their houses, but she resisted. One of the young men knew that Leslie had a crush on his brother, and he told her that he would arrange a date for her with his brother if she got in the car. Leslie finally agreed to go with them, and when they arrived at the destination, a stage had been set up in the basement. There were 13 youths in the basement, but a number of them were uncomfortable with what was going on and left, although none made a serious effort to intervene on Leslie's behalf.

Leslie was verbally coerced into performing fellatio on one of the boys and masturbating some of the others, and she was then talked into allowing them to insert a pool cue and a miniature baseball bat into her vagina, to the cheers and laughter of the remaining spectators. Leslie was warned that if she told anyone they would no longer be her friends, she would be expelled from school, and her mother would be mad at her. In fact, Leslie did not tell her parents (she still thought of the boys as her friends, and she was hoping to eventually get the date with the ring-leader's brother), but the boys boasted about what they had done over the course of the next couple of weeks, until nearly 30 people, including one or more teachers, had heard about it (it amazes me that when young people commit or plan a heinous act they seem constitutionally incapable of keeping quiet about it).

The police were called only after a friend of the perpetrators, Charles Figueroa, heard about the incident when he was asked to videotape a planned repeat of the performance. Charles, one of the few Black people living in the town, was so upset by what had been done to Leslie that he told an adult who called the police (outrageously, instead of proclaiming Figueroa a hero, the school superintendent, Rose McCaffery, tried to publicly discredit him, for which she and the school district were eventually sued successfully for defamation). A police investigation uncovered what had happened, and a very widely covered criminal trial ensued. This trial is described in detail in a book by the late Bernard Lefkowitz (1997), titled *Our Guys: The Glen Ridge Rape and the Secret Life of the Perfect Suburb.*

CHAPTER 8

Gullibility in Finance and Relationships

The most common forms of gullibility, and certainly the ones most covered in the mass media, are financial gullibility and relationship gullibility. Three examples of financial gullibility covered in this chapter are confidence scams, investment manias, and bad entertainment choices. Among the many examples of relationship gullibility addressed are sexual seduction and cuckolding, blind faith in family members, falling for practical jokes, believing gossip and rumor, and being suckered by journalists.

Interestingly, a multidimensional model of consumer gullibility similar to the one proposed by me in Fig. 1.1, was developed by two marketing psychologists, Jeff Langenderfer and Terrence A. Shimp (2001), in a paper titled "Consumer Vulnerability to Scams, Swindles and Fraud: A New Theory of Visceral Influences on Persuasion." A difference between their model and mine is that they use the term *gullibility* as input (essentially as a cognitive contributor to vulnerability). In line with an opinion that I express throughout this volume, Langenderfer and Shimp view affect as the main factor explaining why smart people make dumb consumer choices.

CHOICE OF ENTERTAINMENT AND VACATION PURCHASES

In most Western countries, there is a long tradition of gulling the public through novel entertainments that are either blatantly phony or else hyped way more than they deserve. The magician and conjuring historian Ricky Jay (2001) described many of these novelty acts in *Jay's Journal of Anomalies: Conjurers,*

Cheats, Hustlers, Pranksters, Jokesters, Imposters, Pretenders, Sideshow Showmen, Armless Calligraphers, Mechanical Marvels, Popular Entertainments and in other books.

An example of such a novelty was the Bonassus, an animal supposedly discovered in America and introduced to the gullible public in London in 1821. It was described in a flyer as "comprising the head and eye of the elephant; the horns of the antelope; a long black beard; the hind parts of the lion; the fore-parts of the bison; is cloven footed; has a flowing mane from the shoulder to the fetlock joint; and chews the cud" (Jay, 2001, p. 17). In fact, the Bonassus was nothing more than a bison, and even people who had earlier seen one were persuaded by the hype that they were seeing something different. It seems the Bonassus craze was a recycling of an identical scam pulled 70 years earlier, when a "Bonasus" was described as follows: "The lower part of his Head resembles that of a Stag; the Forehead that of a Buffalo, He has Bristles on his Back like a Hog, and is broad on his Back like a Deer, The horns are situated contrary to any other animal" (p. 21). There have been many other such phony amalgam animals, including in 1898 the "Bovalapus" (actually a water buffalo), the "Bactaranus" (presented on the same bill as the Bonassus, actually a camel), the 1885 "Cynocephalus" (a baboon in lederhosen), and P.T. Barnum's 1848 "wooly horse" (in this case, actually a rare breed of horse). People from all walks of life, including royalty, lined up to hand over good money to not miss seeing these heavily hyped specimens.

Today, television, movies, and theme parks provide the functional equivalent of the kinds of overly hyped live exhibits promoted in Barnum's day. David Chase, creator of television's *The Soprano's*, was quoted in a newspaper article as saying "in order to make the boring interesting, everything is hyped." Often, people watch very heavily hyped entertainments, such as the Academy Awards or the Super Bowl, less because they find them of interest than because they don't want to be left out of an event about which other people are talking.

The Disney theme parks seem to be an example of this phenomenon. What a waste of time and money! The experience is not without occasional moments of pleasure, but it is for the most part a lot of waiting in line and the rides and exhibits are mostly nothing special. Based on my single visit to the Orlando park, it is not remotely worth the hype it receives and—from the bored looks I saw on faces of other visitors (most of them unsophisticated)—that was a common reaction. For me, the most interesting thing about Disney World is as an illustration of the role of gullibility in determining taste and how we choose to spend our recreation dollars.

Gullibility in entertainment consumption comes into play when a relatively ordinary, or even substandard, event or destination is hyped as something so special that hordes of people line up to experience it. The great showman P.T. Barnum, was of course, one of the early masters of such hype, and his credo "there is a sucker born every minute" sums up nicely the view that people are gullible when it comes to allowing others to determine whether or not an entertainment event or activity is deserving of one's time, interest, and money.

A recent example of this can be found in the competition, started by the ESPN TV network—to decide who deserves the title of greatest athlete of the 20th century. They managed to milk this invented non-event for months, culminating in a showdown between Babe Ruth and Michael Jordan, with Jordan getting the nod. Other sports media outlets got into the act, with *Sports Illustrated* beating ESPN to the finish line by anointing Muhammad Ali its sportsman of the century. Anyone who watches such invented competitions is highly gullible and in need of getting a life.

An early, and hilarious, exploration of this theme is the book by Ring W. Lardner (1925/1965), titled *Gullible's Travels, etc.* The book consists of five linked short stories, all of them about a Chicago couple, Mr and Mrs Gullible. The first, and title, story involves a vacation that the Gullibles take in Palm Beach, Florida. In his preface, Lardner wrote that the story was inspired by a trip he himself took there once, where he saw a rich society lady in a bathing costume that consisted of a floppy black silk hat, black tights, black shoes, and white gloves. Although the newspapers made much of how exclusive Palm Beach was, Lardner noted that "a person with money who can't crash it these days would be blackballed from the rotary club. And for all that, Palm Beach is worth a visit if you are not deaf or blind" (Lardner, 1925/1965, p. xv). In other words, only a highly gullible person would fall for the hype in the newspapers about the wonders and exclusivity of Palm Beach.

The Gullibles are lower middle-class people who made some money in the stock market and who decided (or at least Mrs Gullible decided) that their long-time friends weren't fancy enough for them anymore. Mrs Gullible pestered her husband to take a train trip to Palm Beach, so that they could stay at one of the exclusive hotels where, according to newspaper stories, the rich and famous hang out. She fantasizes that they will become fast friends with these people, and that they will, as a result, be accepted into Chicago society upon their return. Of course, they are ignored by the other guests, end up eating and dancing alone, and have a miserable time. The wife resists her husband's pleas to leave, however, hoping that things will turn around. The final humiliation comes when Mrs Gullible recognizes (from her picture in the papers) a very prominent society lady from Chicago. The woman walks up to Mrs Gullible, who is too startled to say anything. Mistaking her for a servant, the woman asks Mrs Gullible to please bring some more towels up to her room. Devastated, Mrs Gullible agrees to take the next train home, but makes her husband promise that they will tell all of their friends that they had a swell time.

This story was somewhat poignant to me, because I saw a bit of my late mother in Mrs Gullible. My mom used to tell me wistful stories about rich and famous people, one or two of whom she had known slightly before they became rich and famous. The unspoken message she communicated was that other people were living more exciting lives. The portrayal, in the media, of successful and famous people living wonderful and happy lives (whereas, in reality, many of them are pretty miserable) gives many people the feeling that somehow life's possibilities aren't being experienced. I managed to catch this disease, and it was only with the approach of middle age that I was able to overcome the persistent feeling that other people seemed to be having more fun.

INHERITANCE SCAMS

A common Internet scam involves receipt of a letter from a person from a third-world country who claims to be in line to inherit a fortune. Because of some minor hold-up, the message's sender needs some financial help in straightening the problem out. In return for such help, the recipient is promised a huge return. Once a victim responds positively to such a message, he or she starts sliding down a slippery slope as described in a May 15, 2006, *New Yorker* piece titled "The Perfect Mark" by Mitchell Zuckoff about a Massachusetts psychotherapist, John Worley, whose life was ruined by his gullibly falling for such a "419 scam" (the penal code number that covers such frauds in Nigeria, the country where most such scams originate).

A very successful early 20th-century version of this scam involved the estate of the English seafarer, Sir Francis Drake. The Drake scheme succeeded in swindling 100,000 or more Midwesterners, and became a social movement, known as "the Drakers." The main orchestrator of the scam was a former farm boy named Oscar Hartzell, born in rural Illinois in 1876. A brief description of the scheme can be found in *Hustlers and Con Men*, by Jay Robert Nash (1976), and a more detailed description is found in a *New Yorker* piece by Richard Rayner (2002). An equally successful inheritance scam that duped many of the leaders of France's Third Republic, was perpetrated by a skilled con artist named Thérèse Humbert, and is profiled in Hillary Spurling's (2000) book *La Grande Thérèse*.

The basis of the Drake scam was a story, started by business partners of Hartzell's, that after amassing a sizeable fortune from his days as a privateer plundering the Spanish Main, Sir Francis Drake died without any children. However, there was a legal heir who had emigrated to Missouri in the 18th century. The claim was established in an impressive-looking genealogical report, accompanied by phony legal documents giving the scammers power of attorney to untangle the inheritance. They were prepared to sell a limited number of shares to those who would advance money to pay their legal expenses. With compound interest, the estate was said to be worth more than $10 billion, and the scam artists promised returns as high as 1,000 to 1.

After ousting his initial business partners, Hartzell gave the story a new wrinkle, saying that he had been befriended by an English nun, who told him about the existence of a secret Drake will. The nun directed Hartzell to a church belfry, where he found a document that proved that Drake had a son. This established a new Drake lineage and heir, a Colonel Drexel Drake of London, which trumped the earlier claims regarding the Missouri heir. Hartzell claimed to have papers signed by Colonel Drake, signing all of his rights over to him. Why did Drake sign over his rights to Hartzell, a man whom he had just met? Because Drake was in love with his niece, Lady Curzon, whom he was about to marry (presumably she was wealthy enough that he didn't need an extra $10 billion). Hartzell told investors that the will was being authenticated by a "Lord and King's Commission" as well as the "Crown Commission which is the highest in the British Empire and last place that a case of this kind can be finished" (Rayner, 2002, p. 153). In fact, there was no Colonel Drake, the Commissions did not exist, Sir Francis had left a legal and unchallenged will, and England had a 12-year statute of limitations on inheritance claims.

The scheme was helped by the boom economy in America in the 1920s, where several other fraudulent schemes (most notoriously, the Florida land swindles) were bubbling. The stock market crash in 1929 did not hurt the Drake scheme, for two reasons:

1. Naïve Midwestern investors now reasoned that this was a safer and more plausible investment than stocks, which they associated with Eastern big-money interests.

2. Hartzell integrated the stock market crash into his story, and said that it happened because news of the transfer had begun to leak and the ensuing panic caused the crash; Hartzell was also able to use the crash to explain the delay in the settlement, as British and American financial interests had banded together to try to block the Drake settlement, which Hartzell described as being big enough to buy three or four of the Midwestern states entirely.

Hartzell, who started calling himself Baron Buckland, had become a cult figure. His letters from London were circulated at church picnics and gatherings throughout the rural Midwest, among the tens of thousands of investors (now called "Donators," for legal reasons), who considered this their own inside thing. According to Rayner, a U.S. diplomat, "The 'Donators' believe in Hartzell with the fire of the most rabid religious fanatics." Rayner noted that what " had begun as a speculation had turned into a holy cause" (p. 157).

A big part of Hartzell's success was his ability to play on the distrust that Midwesterners felt toward Eastern elites. Any attack on him was reframed as a conspiracy against the common people. This made it difficult to make a legal case against Hartzell, as Drakers still believed in him, even after several years with no proceeds and reports of his high living in London. Finally, he was deported and put on trial in Iowa, in October 1933. The courtroom was besieged by supporters, who raised a huge sum for his defense. The prosecutor, who was manhandled by the crowd, later wrote "it was like the crusades in the Middle Ages. If you did not believe in Oscar Hartzell, you'd better keep your mouth shut" (cited in Rayner, 2002, p. 160). The lobby of the hotel where Hartzell was staying was besieged with Drakers eager to shake his hand after the day's proceedings were finished. One investor, a farmer, was asked on the stand how much he had invested. He was reluctant to give a figure, and then said "you see my wife and I went into this together and I slipped one over on her and put in . . . more than she did" (p. 160).

Hartzell was convicted of mail fraud and sentenced to 10 years in prison. He was released on bail during his appeal, and gave rousing speeches to rallies of his supporters in which he told them to look at items in the newspapers, such as FDR lighting his pipe, or Huey Long using the phrase "every man a king," as these were secret signs that distribution of the Drake estate was about to occur. Amazingly, Hartzell continued to scam believers out of large sums of money while the appeal was pending. In line with cognitive dissonance theory (where one reframes reality to make it more palatable), the Drakers rationalized Hartzell's conviction. One supporter who had lost his farm gave the following statement after Hartzell had lost his appeal and was finally thrown in prison: "I will say our deal is going fine. This last stunt of taking him away is all in the play" (p. 161). The trial was widely viewed as a smokescreen, because the Drake inheritance was too big for the government to handle. Hartzell was believed to be in a safe place, working on the final details of the transfer. A group of Drakers formed into a cult, called the New Order. They held a meeting to plan a luxury community in Iowa, where they would retire together after they received their inheritance. This story demonstrates extreme gullibility, in which naïve people who cannot face a devastating truth convince themselves even more firmly of the existence of a false reality.

TULIPMANIA AND OTHER INVESTMENT BUBBLES

Investment bubbles are a form of mass gullibility in which individuals invest their life savings in dubious schemes on no other basis than the fact that other people are reportedly getting rich off of these schemes. One of the first of these bubbles occurred in the 17th century in Holland during the years 1634 to 1637. Termed "Tulipmania" it started about 75 years after the first tulip bulb showed up in Europe as a gift from a merchant in Turkey. It began to be considered a mark of class to have a garden planted with rare and exotic tulips. In line with Thorstein Veblen's (1889) *Theory of the Leisure Class*, having an unusual tulip plant became a valued symbol of conspicuous consumption among people with disposable wealth. Everyone of standing wanted to have these plants, and the scarcity drove the price up. An unregulated market in tulip bulbs developed, and they were bought and sold at amazing prices. For example, in 1636, there were only two bulbs of the species *Semper Augustus* in Holland, and neither was of the highest quality. A buyer offered a 12-acre building site for the one in Harlem, whereas the one in Amsterdam sold for 4,600 guilders plus a new carriage, two horses, and a harness.

The market in tulip bulbs went from being a form of conspicuous consumption to being a highly speculative form of gambling, with brokers driving the prices up and down as if they were stocks. At some point, doubts set in and buyers began to default. There was great turmoil, as dealers found themselves holding large quantities of bulbs that were worth far less than what they had been worth just 1 or 2 days earlier. The government stepped in and tried to get buyers to honor their contracts, but the courts refused to enforce them on the grounds that they were a form of gambling. Those who became rich from the tulip trade were allowed to keep their profits, whereas many of those who did not sell were ruined. The Dutch economy suffered great harm, from which it took decades to recover.

There have been other examples of investment bubbles, with more recent ones being the Japanese real estate bubble of the 1980s and the American dot.com bubble of the 1990s. Two 18th-century investment bubbles that bore eerie similarities to Tulipmania were the Mississippi Mania in France from 1719 to 1720 and the South Sea Bubble in England, from 1716 to 1720. These, along with Tulipmania, are described in detail in an amazing book by Charles Mackey, published in 1841, titled *Memoirs of Extraordinary Popular Delusions* (republished in 1996 as *Extraordinary Popular Delusions and the Madness of Crowds*).

One of the sure things about an investment bubble is that it will eventually burst, and people who do not get out at the right time run a good chance of seeing their savings greatly diminished. Yet at the time the bubble is still going strong, participants act as if it will never end and nonparticipants are castigated. As Michael Lewis (2001) wrote in his book about the dot.com mania titled *New New Thing*, "In this new world, skepticism was not a sign of intelligence. It was a sin."

Former U.S. Federal Reserve Chairman Alan Greenspan (no relation, for the 10 millionth time), once gave a speech in which he warned that the tremendous boom in the U.S. stock markets in the mid- and late-1990s was a product of "irrational exuberance." This phrase was actually coined earlier by Yale economics professor Robert J. Schiller, who expanded on his ideas in a book, appropriately titled *Irrational Exuberance* (Schiller, 2001). Schiller's basic idea was that investment bubbles can be understood to be the product of the same forces that drive illegal Ponzi schemes, and that they eventually collapse for the same reasons. A Ponzi scheme is a pyramid scheme, in which a seemingly plausible profit-generating idea is used to convince victims to invest their money with the scheme manager. In fact, there is no profit-generating activity, and funds from new investors are used to pay handsome profits to old investors. The early investors who did quite well tell their friends and relatives, which creates a growing list of new investors. For the scheme to keep going, it is essential that the numbers of new investors grow exponentially, for the simple reason that there is no other source of revenue. Eventually, the number of new investors starts to contract, at which point the initiator of the scam will have skipped town if he or she is lucky.

The scheme gets its name from a New Yorker named Charles Ponzi who, within a 7-month period in 1920, attracted 30,000 investors and issued notes totaling $15 million. Ponzi's proposed plan for making money involved buying postal reply coupons in Europe and reselling them in the United States, and taking advantage of the fact that the currency exchange rates reflected in the coupons did not correspond exactly to the official currency exchange rates (this is not dissimilar to the rationale for hedge funds and day trading schemes today). This in theory sounded plausible, but in practice it was extremely difficult to sell these reply coupons. The story was convincing to the greenhorn immigrants who constituted Ponzi's main market, however, in part because postage reply coupons were something that most of them used and knew something about. According to Schiller, however, the fact "that others have made a lot of money appears to many people as the most persuasive evidence in support of the investment story associated with the Ponzi scheme—evidence that outweighs even the most carefully reasoned argument against the story" (p. 66). In other words, the "evidence" for the legitimacy of the scheme was the fact that later investors knew about the large profits made by earlier investors. The original Ponzi scheme collapsed when the New York postmaster issued a statement that there were not enough postal reply coupons in international circulation to have generated the profits claimed by Ponzi. This caused new investments to dry up, which eventually caused the whole scheme to collapse.

Schiller proposed a social psychological theory to explain all speculative bubbles, including Ponzi schemes. He termed it the "feedback loop theory of investor bubbles." Simply stated, the fact that so many people are participating in the scheme makes it appear safe, at the same time that the perception that others are getting rich makes it appear too good to pass up. The fact that sizable returns keep coming establishes a pattern of expectancy in which the gull convinces him or herself that the pattern of profitability will continue indefinitely. Schiller argued that there is an affective side to this feedback also, akin to the recklessness that comes to gamblers when they are ahead and feeling that they are "playing with the house's money." This dependency on the permanency of a boom market makes it difficult for investors to accept the possibility that this boom, like all others that have preceded it, is temporary and could end at any time. Thus, in a boom market such as the dot.com mania in the United States in the 1990s, stocks are driven higher and higher not on any rational calculation of the earnings or actual value of companies, but by the collective behavior of investors who are caught up in the madness.

BELIEVING RUMORS

There is a tendency to believe the worst about others, and also to improve one's own social standing by being the communicator of previously unknown information. Both of these tendencies explain, in part, the popularity of rumors and the tendency to believe them and to pass them on. Unfortunately, in the age of the Internet a rumor can (literally) take on global proportions with amazing speed, a process that can be very harmful, especially if the substance of the rumor turns out to be exaggerated or totally incorrect. The uncritical acceptance of the truth of unfounded rumors is a form of gullibility of which most of us are occasionally guilty.

After "Paul" left his job for a professorship at another university, he had occasion to be speaking to a former associate, who told him of a rumor involving a senior male colleague whom they both mildly disliked. According to this rumor, the man had drunkenly propositioned one of his female doctoral students in his hotel room while they were both at a conference. Supposedly, the student resisted and the professor bit her neck and left a mark. When the student returned home, her husband asked her about the mark. She told him what had happened and the irate husband went to the department chairperson and complained. The chairperson, a friend of the alleged harasser, said he would investigate, but supposedly swept the incident under the rug. Later on, according to this story, the student was bought off with a temporary teaching position. At least that was the rumor. Whether any of it ever happened, Paul had no idea, as he was now living some distance away.

Shortly after he learned about this rumor, Paul happened to be in touch with "Shirley," a former colleague, a woman who was quite alienated from the department. Paul foolishly mentioned the rumor to Shirley, assuming that if he had heard it, then it must be common knowledge. She said she in fact had not heard about the incident, perhaps because she was not around that much. Shortly after that conversation, the department chairperson sent out a memo announcing an upcoming sexual harassment workshop and indicated that attendance was mandatory. Shirley replied by sending her own memo, which she distributed to the entire faculty, saying that she found the memo hypocritical coming from him and she would willingly attend the workshop if the chairperson divulged (a) the facts of what happened in the hotel room and, (b) the details of how the matter was handled. As might have been anticipated, Shirley's memo set off a firestorm of controversy, and a situation that was so stressful that she eventually resigned her position.

Needless to say, Paul felt pretty bad about the whole thing: for the pain that he had inflicted on the, possibly innocent, target of the rumor; for the impact that this had on Shirley's career (even though her impulsive sending of the memo showed unbelievably bad judgment); and for the embarrassment that he suffered in having been publicly exposed as a gossip (Shirley quickly gave him up as the source of the rumor, which taught him another costly lesson about human nature). Being familiar with the literature on professional ethics, Paul knew that disseminating a rumor about a colleague is unprofessional and something to be avoided. Thus, he violated his own principles, which was one reason why he felt so bad. Of course, sexual harassment is also unprofessional, and possibly illegal, but gossip is not the recommended method for dealing with it, especially by one with no direct knowledge of what happened.

The viciousness, and early onset, of sexually oriented gossip is portrayed in *Fast Girls: Teenage Tribes and the Myth of the Slut*, by Emily White (2002). The book deals with a universal, but little-studied phenomenon, namely that in almost every middle or high school in America, and probably in other countries, there is at least one female student who is the target of rumors along the lines of "she gave a blow job to every member of the football team after practice." These rumors, according to White, are rarely true, but they become quickly believed by almost everyone in the school. The so-called "sluts" are subjected to cruel isolation and harassment, and look back on that period of their lives with great pain and sorrow.

White, a Seattle-based journalist who writes about feminist topics, started her research by posting a newspaper ad in which she asked women who had once, whether rightly or wrongly, been labeled a school slut to call her at an 800 number. White was overwhelmed with calls, and most of the respondents gave very similar stories. For the most part, the school slut phenomenon happens in rural or suburban middle-class schools, and the targets tend to be early-developing girls with big breasts who dress or act a little differently. Typically, the victims describe themselves as having been no more (and often less) sexually active than their peers. The rumors almost always portray the slut as sexually servicing, typically orally, a "train" of young men, such as members of a sports team.

White's position is that the slut phenomenon is almost always a myth, fueled by the anxiety that teenage girls have about sexuality, and their tribal need to punish outsiders through word of mouth. The rumor, according to White, is a control mechanism similar to, if more extreme than, the cattiness exhibited through such remarks as "you look a little fat in that bathing suit." For White, the slut rumor falls in the category of a Jungian archetype, namely an idea that is found fairly universally in the collective unconscious of different cultures. White tells a story in which one of her subjects traveled as a teenager to visit her grandmother in Ireland and was cautioned against writing with red ink for fear of being labeled a "whore." Such hysteria can have tragic consequences, as in *The Magdalene Sisters*, a film depicting the true story of how adolescent girls in Ireland believed to be sluts were forcibly imprisoned, often for decades, in church-run laundries.

White credited a book by Tamotsu Shibutani (1966), titled *Improvised News: A Sociological Study of Rumor*, for providing a theoretical framework for under-standing gullibility toward rumors, including ones involving imagined school sluts. Shibutani viewed rumor transmission as a hysterical phenomenon. The tendency toward rumor epidemics among young women is dealt with in Elaine Showalter's (1997) *Hystories: Hysterical Epidemics and Modern Media*.

As with most other gullibility stories told in this book, there is a strong affective component underlying gullibility toward rumors. Specifically, Shibutani noted that "rumors thrive among populations desperately trying to com-prehend their environment" and that they "flourish in periods of sudden crises, sustained tension, impending decisions [and] boredom from monotony" (cited in White, 2002, p. 43). White noted that all of these elements can be found in high schools. She stated that "the stories are vessels that rescue ... [young people] from the sea of confusion" (p. 43).

PEOPLE INTERVIEWED BY JOURNALISTS

The process in which a journalist interviews a subject for an article, TV piece, or book, is analogous in some ways to a seduction dance. Each party attempts to win the other over: the subject, so that the resulting piece will portray him or her in a positive light; the journalist, so that the subject will open up and continue to provide access. It is possible to consider gullible a journalist who is seduced into producing a too-sympathetic piece, just as no better word can be used to describe a subject whose trust in a journalist is betrayed.

The best work on the subject of journalist betrayal of subject gullibility is, undoubtedly, a book by Janet Malcolm (1990), titled *The Journalist and the Murderer*. It is the story of the seduction, years earlier, by writer Joe McGinnis of an army physician, Jeffrey MacDonald, who was on trial for the crime of murdering his wife and two daughters. McGinnis' resulting book, a best-seller titled *Fatal Vision*, portrayed MacDonald in a highly negative light and concluded that MacDonald was guilty of the crime. MacDonald sued for fraud, claiming that McGinnis had received total access to him, including living in a house with the defense legal team during the trial, through a consistent pattern of lies and misrepresentations (all of them foolishly recorded in a series of letters) about being a supporter and friend. These deceptions continued over a period of years up until the book came out, to block MacDonald from cooperating with authors whose competing books might have diminished sales of *Fatal Vision*. The case was complicated by the fact that the two men were business partners, in that McGinnis, hard up for money, had agreed to share a percentage of the book's advance and royalties with MacDonald.

Despite MacDonald's status as a convicted triple killer, his attorney was able to convince five of six jurors to vote in MacDonald's favor (the case was settled before a retrial, and a payment was made to MacDonald). Ironically, Malcolm at the time she wrote the book, was the target of a libel lawsuit (which dragged out over 11 years) by a subject, psychoanalyst Jeffrey Moussaief Masson, who felt that his words had been misstated in a 1983 series of articles that later became *In the Freud Archives* (Malcolm, 1984). Despite having been in McGinnis' shoes, and agreeing with the view that every book has the potential for a subject to feel betrayed, Malcolm came down strongly on MacDonald's side, feeling that McGinnis had crossed way over the boundary between what is appropriate and inappropriate in the gulling of a subject.

Malcolm (1990) noted that

> every journalist ... is a kind of confidence man, preying on people's vanity, igno-rance, or loneliness, gaining their trust and betraying them without remorse. Like the credulous widow who wakes up one day to find the charming young man and all of her savings gone, so the consenting subject of a piece of nonfiction writing learns—when the article or book appears—*his* hard lesson. Journalists justify their treachery in various ways according to their temperaments. The more pompous talk about freedom of speech and "the public's right to know"; the least talented talk about Art; the seemliest murmur about earning a living, (p. 3)

The feeling of betrayal that sometimes leads a subject to sue is

> no simple matter of an unflattering likeness or a misrepresentation of his views; what pains him ... is [having] to face the fact that the journalist—who seemed so friendly and sympathetic, so keen to understand him fully, so remarkably attuned to his vision of things—never had the slightest intention of collaborating with him on his story but always intended to write a story of his own. (p. 3)

Thus, the fury of a gulled subject toward a betraying journalist has some of the passion one typically associates with a jilted lover or spouse.

As in other forms of gullibility, betrayed subjects often have a vague sense of the dangers facing them, but are overwhelmed by affect into proceeding anyway. This theme is stated by Malcolm as follows: "at bottom, no subject is naïve. Every hoodwinked widow, every deceived lover, every betrayed friend, every subject of writing knows on some level what is in store for him, and remains in the relationship anyway, impelled by something stronger than his reason" (p. 8). Malcolm circled repeatedly around this issue, in an effort to figure out what exactly it is that causes subjects to be so gullible. The best answer she came up with is that "something seems to happen to people when they meet a journalist, and what happens is ... childish trust and impetuosity" (p. 32).

Malcolm argued that the relationship of subject to journalist is analogous to the kind of regression that occurs in psychoanalysis, and that "the subject becomes a kind of child of the writer, regarding him as a permissive, all-accepting, all-forgiving mother, ... [while] of course, the book is written by the strict, all-noticing, unforgiving father" (p. 32). What drives the subject, according to Malcolm, is self-absorption, and a need to get his or her story told. This may have a narcissistic side (McGinnis' explanation of MacDonald's desire for publicity) but in the case of a man in MacDonald's desperate cir-cumstances, one can think of more benign explanations of motive. At any rate, there were three very human processes that help to explain MacDonald's victimization by McGinnis:

1. MacDonald's affect- and circumstance-driven need to get his story known;

2. a lack of wariness that was in part from temperament and in part from inexperience; and

3. a tendency, which Malcolm viewed as universal, to believe the lies told by skilled liars.

Malcolm believes that human nature being what it is, "willing [i.e., gullible] subjects will never be in short supply" (p. 144), even if journalists were to issue a warning to subjects before beginning the interview.

Interestingly, Malcolm came to write her book through an initial invitation from McGinnis' lawyer, after the mistrial (and before the settlement); McGinnis' motivation for seeking to interest journalists in his case stemmed from a belief that the case had potentially chilling ramifications for the future of journalism in America. His position essentially was that nonfiction journalism depends on the ability of a journalist to hide his or her true feelings about a subject; holding a journalist accountable for dissembling about his motives would essentially kill off nonfiction journalism, in McGinnis' opinion, by scaring away potential subjects. Malcolm unwittingly tested this hypothesis in an initial interview that she had with McGinnis. Malcolm had hoped that McGinnis would be in the mood for a free-flowing dialogue, but McGinnis became defensive and called off any further cooperation with her. Malcolm believed this was because she came across as too openly skeptical and challenging, and because she neglected to make the initial seduction moves she probably would have used on a more typical subject. Malcolm went ahead with the project anyway, and produced a book highly critical of McGinnis.

The core of Malcolm's criticism of McGinnis goes beyond the fact that he consistently misled MacDonald about the kind of book he was writing (e.g., he sent a letter to MacDonald in jail saying that the jury was mistaken in convicting him at the same time that he was writing in his book that MacDonald was a psychopathic killer); Malcolm also accused McGinnis of what she considered the more serious offense of intellectual dishonesty, by creating a fictionalized MacDonald: making him more evil (by exaggerating a single reported anger episode), inventing a nonproved murder explanation (amphetamine-induced psychosis), and building a case for a debatable psychiatric diagnosis (narcissistic personality disorder), all for the purpose of making MacDonald (in real life, fairly bland) more interesting and the book more saleable.

In Malcolm's view, the seduction of gullible subjects by a nonfiction writer is justifiable only if one maintains a strict commitment to portraying the "truth," even if negative, about a subject. She made an exception only for editing a subject's actual words to make them flow better on the written page, a practice that she claimed is all she was doing when she was sued for libel by Masson. According to Malcolm, distortion of a subject's character and essence is never justifiable, and fidelity to the truth (which often does not make so compelling a story) should always take precedence over the financial or ego needs of an author. Although Malcolm considered it unseemly for McGinnis to have lied so blatantly to MacDonald, unlike the more subtle "Japanese" approach that she prefers, McGinnis' real sin, she seems to be saying, lay in trying to turn his nonfiction book into a novel.

GULLIBILITY IN SEXUAL RELATIONSHIPS

The term *gullible* can certainly be used to characterize the behavior of victims of sexual seductions. All of the factors that explain gullibility in other settings can be found operating in seduction scenarios. Situational factors, such as opportunity (e.g., being on a business trip) and the deliberate use of lies by a determined seducer, contribute to an outcome in which someone may get involved in a sexual relationship that is not in line with his or her desires or interests. Cognitive factors in seductions mainly involve naïveté (lack of experience) in the victim, as in a case where a young woman whom I call "Roberta" failed to recognize qualities (such as extreme narcissism) suggesting that "Henry" was a womanizer, and failed to see through his obvious ploys (e.g., wrapping himself in environmental and conservationist language, knowing that Roberta was very much involved in those causes). Personality factors operate, as Roberta is a highly trusting, positive, and idealistic woman, who tends to trust and believe everyone with whom she comes in contact. Finally, state factors have obvious relevance in seductions, as there are mood variables (e.g., alcohol use, rushes of romantic feeling, periods of unhappiness with one's marriage) that can make someone temporarily vulnerable and receptive to the attentions of a seducer.

In using the term *seduction*, I refer mainly to a somewhat one-sided situation in which the seducer has a conscious game plan that has the sole purpose of getting the target person into the sack (possibly with the goal of an ongoing sexual relationship), and where the motivation is purely sexual (i.e., it is not accompanied by love or a real caring for the target person). Such a seducer will do and say anything, and has no concern for anything other than winning the prize.

The cynical nature of the seduction game can be found in a book titled *The Machiavellian's Guide to Womanizing*, by an author using the pen-name "Nick Casanova" (1999). The basic message in the book is "never tell the truth, but only say things that are likely to win you the prize." In this, Nick Casanova is taking a page out of *The Prince* by his namesake Niccolo Machiavelli (1516/1995), who wrote "Princes who have accomplished great things have had little respect for keeping their word and have known how to confuse men's minds with their cunning. In the end they have overcome those who have preferred honesty" (p. 96). An example in the area of seduction is the following advice:

> If a pretty woman asks your sign, *don't* demonstrate your wisdom by saying "you don't believe in *that* shit, do you?" The best reply is "Guess," which identifies you as a fellow believer. If she has asked you your sign, there's interest on her part; this means she hopes you're compatible, so she'll pick a compatible sign for you.... Feign interest. Once she's started out believing you're compatible, chances are you *will* be compatible, partly because her attitude will create a self-fulfilling prophecy. (Casanova, 1999, p. 31)

Sexual gullibility comes into play in various other ways, in addition to susceptibility to the insincere lies of a seducer. One obvious area of sexual gullibility involves the self-deception processes used by a cuckold (someone whose partner is involved in a long-term affair) to keep from knowing about what is going on. An illustration of this can be found in the case of "Tony" and "Marlene," whose marriage of 5 years ended when Marlene abruptly asked for a divorce. She showed zero interest in trying to save the marriage, something that is often a clue that someone else is in the picture. Tony's gullibility lay in the fact that he had steadfastly ignored signs of Marlene's infidelity, such as long absences, late-night returns, a drop-off in sexual relations, and even an oblique hint from a colleague who knew about the affair. According to Frank Pittman (1989), in his book *Private Lies: Infidelity and the Betrayal of Intimacy*, only about 10% of cuckolds make a conscious decision that they do not want to know about a spouse's infidelity. Most cuckolds show gullibility by engaging in self-deception, whereby assuming that things are fine makes it easier to avoid the painful reality that they are not fine.

FALLING FOR "APRIL FOOL" AND OTHER PRACTICAL JOKES

One of my duties as president of our neighborhood homeowner's association is to put on an annual community Easter Egg hunt in a big field that adjoins our house. One year, this party took place on April 2. The previous evening, I was stuffing Easter eggs when my wife Helen and our youngest son, Eli, came in excitedly and asked if I had seen the sign posted down by the community mailboxes. I answered "no, what did it say?" They told me, with great animation, that there was a petition posted that was signed by 10 neighborhood children, insisting that I, as the egg hunt coordinator, should dress up in a bunny outfit when we hold that event. I became quite agitated and said "That's ridiculous. No way am I going to wear a bunny outfit." Eli asked me if I wanted to drive down to look at the petition. I hurriedly grabbed my car keys and said "sure, let's go." Then everyone broke into a big grin and shouted in unison: "April Fool." It turns out that our neighbor, Carla, put Helen and Eli up to this stunt. I'd been telling Carla about this in-process book on gullibility and she just wanted to see how much progress I had made in my quest to become nongullible. It seems the correct answer is "not much."

The convention of playing practical jokes on April Fool's Day is reputed to have started in France in the late 16th century to make fun of those who refused to accept the Gregorian calendar (which moved the start of the New Year from April 1 to January 1). It became a general holiday (also called "All Fool's Day") in the 17th century in Britain, and crossed the Atlantic to America in the 18th century. Although most people know that they are likely to be tricked on April 1, this knowledge does not prevent many of them from being fooled. The most outrageous of lies, delivered with a minimum degree of skill, are likely to fool most people. In my case, despite possessing generally adequate intelligence, my strong need to believe others and to be helpful (combined with only a vague awareness of what day it is) explained my falling for the joke, even in the face of obvious anomalies, such as the fact that kids do not circulate petitions.

The model of gullible behavior that underlies this book can be considered "contextualist," in that I view a gullible action as the result of a number of personal factors, including one's history with other actors, all interacting around a specific micro-contextual event. In terms of personal history, one reason I fell for the bunny suit joke is that in my long experience with Helen and Eli, I do not recall them ever having pulled such a trick on me before (thanks a lot, Carla).

The affect stirred up in me by the demand that I wear a bunny suit certainly explains a lot to do with my reaction. In fact, one of the things that I have learned during the course of researching and writing this book is that, of all of the factors that explain why people behave gullibly, affect may be the most important of all. When strong emotion is present, we just are not able to think very clearly.

An example of this came during another memorable practical joke played at my expense. One of the major sources of anxiety that any author experiences when writing a book is that after working on it for a long period of time someone will beat them to the punch by publishing a book covering the same topic before theirs can come out. Knowing that I had some concerns in this area, my friend Alan, who chairs a book discussion group at his local public library, showed me a flyer announcing an upcoming discussion at the library about a book on gullibility by an author whom I had never heard of. The flyer contained all kinds of topics and buzzwords that appeared in an early manuscript of the current book, which I had shared with Alan. It should have been obvious from the wording of the flyer (some of it of an outrageous nature) that it was a joke, but I was so upset by this news that I was incapable of figuring out the bogus nature of the flyer. It was only after a flicker of a smile appeared on Alan's face that I knew that I had been snookered once again.

My earliest recollection of being tricked in this way came in the fourth or fifth grade. I was very shy and socially isolated, mainly because my late mother had a germ phobia and kept me away from any contact with other kids out of fear that I might contract polio (this was in the days before the invention of the polio vaccine, and many children, including the extremely germ-phobic Howard Hughes, experienced such polio-driven parental overprotectiveness). One day, one of the more popular kids in my class, someone who had previously shown no interest in me, came over and made a bet that I lacked the courage to go into a neighborhood shop and say to the manager "a cunt is not a bunt." Having no idea what the C-word meant, I took on the dare, only to be chased out the door by the angry shop owner wielding a broom. The kid who dared me, along with his friends, all had a good laugh at my expense. This was my first important lesson to the effect that people appearing to be my friend may have another agenda in mind. The affect that overwhelmed my judgment in this case was my desperate wish to be accepted and liked.

With respect to the bunny outfit suggestion, after calming down, and upon reflection, I decided that it was not such a bad idea after all. Maybe I will wear one the next time we put on a neighborhood Easter egg hunt.

BELIEVING FAMILY MEMBERS

Former NFL wide receiver Rae Carruth went on trial in North Carolina in late 2000 for arranging the shooting death of his pregnant girlfriend Cherica Adams. During and after the trial, Carruth's mother, Theodry Carruth, gave several TV interviews in which she proclaimed her son's innocence. In one of these interviews, Mrs. Carruth said "I know Rae is innocent. You can't fool mama. Mama always knows." Although it is possible that Mrs. Carruth was posturing for the camera, I believe that she was sincere in her belief in the innocence of her son (who was convicted of conspiracy to commit murder, and received a prison sentence of 19 to 24 years). In her mind, the jury's decision reflected prejudice toward a Black male defendant. The jury, which contained several Black members, was unanimous in its view that Carruth participated in all elements of the crime (the conspiracy, rather than murder, conviction reflected a reluctance on the part of several jurors to sentence Carruth to life when he appeared to have been suckered into authorizing the crime by a more violent friend looking for a payday). Yet, to Carruth's mother, there was not a shred of evidence to support her son's conviction.

Such parental gullibility in rejecting evidence of the moral failings of one's child is fairly universal. An even higher profile example of this occurred in the 2004 California trial of Scott Peterson for the 2002 murder of his pregnant wife Laci and their unborn son Connor. Peterson's parents, Lee and Jackie, have consistently maintained the innocence of their son. For example, in a June 20, 2005, letter published by *People* magazine several months after his son's conviction, Lee wrote: "If an innocent man's life were not at stake here, the comments from the police and prosecution who framed my son ... would be laughable."

Blind belief in the innocence of a family member or close acquaintance accused of a serious crime, without any real attempt to accommodate contrary evidence of guilt, is quite common. In the case of Scott Peterson's parents, it may be reflective of a more general tendency, especially on the part of Scott's mother Jackie, to think of her son as a "golden boy" who could do no wrong. In fact, it has been suggested, such as by Scott's estranged half sister Ann Bird (2005), that he became a murderer precisely because he grew up in a family where all of his wishes, no matter how selfish, were accommodated. A similar profound spoiling process seems to have characterized the Carruth household as well.

There is a tendency to want to believe in the goodness and assertions of people to whom we are related. Such "familial gullibility" is probably a good thing, up to a point. But there are times when blindness to the lies, or at least self-deceptions, of a loved one can prove quite harmful. A common example of this is when a family moves every couple of years because of a cyclical process in which one of the parents (typically the father) decides that there is an opportunity in some other part of the country or world that is too good to pass up. Very often, this assertion is accepted passively by the other family members, even though there is a long history of these opportunities failing to pan out. The initiating parent later always finds some external reason for why the new situation was a bust (e.g., someone reneged on a commitment, the new community—which earlier had been idealized—turns out to be corrupt, etc.). The gullibility here is that everyone accepts the myth that the problem lies in the environment rather than in the family member's repeated inability to follow through on anything or to keep his own promises.

The tendency in many families to believe a relative's promise that he or she intends to change some long-established pattern of self-defeating or otherwise problematic behavior can take many forms. Among these types of promises are that an alcoholic will control his or her drinking, that a verbally or physically abusive person will become nonabusing, and that someone who never can stick for very long with school, career, or other long-term plans will somehow be able to carry through with a new plan. As with other forms of gullibility, there are situational, cognitive, and affective contributors. One of the biggest situational contributors is what behaviorist psychologists call "intermittent reinforcement" (i.e., even the most messed up persons among us are not messed up all the time). Thus, an alcoholic may have periods when he or she does give up, or cut back on, drinking for awhile; an abusive person may have periods when he or she is actually quite pleasant to the usual target of abuse; and a person with a history of giving up on projects may have periods when he or she seems to be applying him or herself diligently to his or her new enthusiasm. Such an intermittent appearance of change can be quite powerful in reinforcing one's emotionally driven need to believe someone's promise that "this time, I mean it."

The cognitive contributor to gullibility toward a family member's change resolution stems from the difficulty in evaluating the sincerity of the person making the promise to change. This difficulty reflects the reality that very few people are good lie detectors (although most of us think we do have this ability). Lie detection is complicated, of course, by the fact that the person making the promise to change may very well be sincere at the time the promise is made (this theme of self-deception is discussed briefly in chap. 9). Thus I, at one time a runner who almost never missed a day, have not run, because of various ailments, for almost 20 years. But I still tell myself and others that I intend to take up running again, I carry a bag with running shoes in the back of my car, and there are even times when I believe that one of these days I will actually put them on.

Of course, people can and do sometimes change, and even the most long-deferred resolutions (such as this serious procrastinator promising to actually write this book) do occasionally come true. Even during a year-long period when a partially completed draft sat untouched on a shelf, my wife never stopped believing me when I said I intended to finish it and to see it through to publication. The thing that made her nongullible in this case is that I have a track record of coming through on publications (albeit much shorter pieces), even after long delays, and she knew that I possessed the ability and desire to pull it off. On the other hand, if she were to believe my occasional promises to become neater and better organized, then she probably would be guilty of gullibility, even though I often make the statement that "one of these years I intend to get organized."

The reason why alcoholics, spouse abusers, and habitual quitters should generally not be believed is because after awhile their pattern of failure and regression is so entrenched, and their response to stress so well established, that it is pure fantasy to think that they can change. At some point, in other words, belief and trust equates with foolishness. The affective component, in this as in most other forms of gullibility, is probably the most powerful contributing factor.

CHAPTER 9

Questions About Gullibility

In chapter 1, I presented briefly a theory of gullibility causation that contains four explanatory factors: situation, cognition, personality, and affect and state. In each of the many stories in the preceding seven chapters, one or more (sometimes all four) of these factors have been invoked in explaining the gullible behaviors portrayed. I put off a more in-depth and systematic discussion of these factors until this chapter, now that many concrete examples have been presented. In this chapter, I address a few critical questions about the three within-person (cognition, personality, and affect) contributors to gullibility The fourth (external) factor, "situation" will be addressed mainly in chapter 10. I conclude this chapter with a discussion of ethics, specifically whether being gullible can be considered a moral failing.

IS GULLIBILITY A FORM OF STUPIDITY?

The Stoic philosopher Epictetus wrote "take the time to assiduously study clear thinking and you won't be hoodwinked." He was suggesting that people who are hoodwinked, that is, those who are tricked into believing things that are false, are not thinking straight. Although such people might have low IQs (certainly people with intellectual impairments are probably more likely to be gullible), for most people it is not a matter of having a low IQ as it is a matter of not using their intelligence wisely. Certainly, if this book proves anything, it is that having above-average intelligence is no protection against behaving stupidly (i.e., gullibly). For that reason, I prefer to use the term *cognitive processes* rather than intelligence, because gullibility typically reflects lazy thinking rather than an inability to think.

There are two reasons that help to explain why very smart people can behave stupidly, as when they engage in gullible conduct. The first of these—the short-circuiting of intelligence by personality, state and situational factors—is touched on in various stories in this book. The second reason is that there are aspects of intelligence that are not tapped by one's IQ score. In other words, people who are smart on academic tasks (i.e., have a high IQ) may be lacking in other forms of intelligence (such as "social intelligence"), or may have a cognitive style (such as excessive reliance on intuition) that makes it difficult for them to bring their intellectual capacities to bear in a particular situation.

In recent years, there has been increasing emphasis on the notion of multiple intelligences. Howard Gardner (1983), in his book *Frames of Mind*, has been given credit for originating this notion, but in fact the currently most widely used model was first written about by E.L. Thorndike (1920) more than 85 years ago. That model, which I have used in my own work (Greenspan & Driscoll, 1997) has three components: "academic intelligence" (abstract problem solving, tapped by measures of IQ), "practical intelligence" (ability to understand mechanical and physical processes), and "social intelligence" (ability to understand people and social systems). The latter two ability areas, which are only moderately predicted by one's IQ, have particular relevance to gullibility. For example, someone with low practical intelligence might believe the most dubious of explanations for some phenomenon, whereas someone with low social intelligence might fail to pick up on deception cues or to understand that a particular threat made by an interrogator is beyond his or her ability to carry out. Another type of intelligence written about recently is "emotional intelligence," a variant of social intelligence having to do with understanding and regulating emotional processes in oneself and others. If Peter Reilly (profiled in chap. 5) had possessed better emotional intelligence, he would have known that the theory that he killed his beloved mother in a fit of unremembered rage was a monstrous invention with almost no possibility of being true.

There has been much written abut the styles of lazy thinking used by gullible people, particularly in relation to the ease with which they can be made to believe nonsense. The prominent skeptic Michael Shermer (1997), in his book *Why People Believe Weird Things*, lists 25 cognitive fallacies that contribute to credulity toward wacky ideas. Some of the most important fallacies that Shermer believes contribute to gullibility are as follow:

1. A belief that scientific validity can be established entirely through anecdotes and sense-impressions.

2. A belief that an authoritative style and simplifying "theory of everything" is an indicator of substance.

3. The belief that the burden of proof falls equally on both established and proposed alternative truths.

4. The ad ignorantiam fallacy, which states that failure to prove that something does not exist means that it must exist.

5. The belief that if one does not understand something it cannot be explained rationally.

6. A belief that rigidly holding onto one's beliefs and assumptions in the face of contrary evidence is a good thing (Shermer terms this the "Planck Problem," after the observation attributed to the great physicist Max Planck to the effect that a new idea is accepted in science not because opponents of the idea change their minds but because they eventually get old and die).

7. Hasty generalization (jumping to conclusions before all of the facts are in).

8. Circular reasoning or tautology (e.g., justifying the existence of God because the Bible says so, and then certifying the authenticity of the Bible by attributing its authorship to God).

9. Effort inadequacies (an excessive need for certainty through simplistic explanations).

Similar lists of illogical thinking styles that contribute to gullibility can be found in *Inevitable Illusions: How Mistakes of Reason Rule Our Minds* by Massimo Piattelli-Palmarini (1994) and many others. A point made by Canadian educational psychologist Keith Stanovich (1999) is that gullible behavior is a sign not of low intelligence but of low rationality. Irrationality, as in the case of gullible behavior, happens when one thinks intuitively (i.e., when emotion and impulsivity create an inability to use the problem-solving strategies that one might otherwise be capable of using in less demanding circumstances).

HOW DOES AFFECT CONTRIBUTE TO GULLIBLE BEHAVIOR?

In perhaps the majority of the cases described in this volume, some form of affect, whether positive or negative, played a role in precipitating the gullible action. Affect causes judgment to become impaired and causes one to rush into something prematurely. The likelihood that rushed decisions will be gullible ones is, in fact, recognized in such legislated practices as building a waiting period into the activation of marriage licenses (except in places like Las Vegas) and the 72-hour rescind period that many states build into financing contracts for cars and houses.

There are two implicit reasons why decisions made in a more dispassionate state are less likely to be gullible decisions. The first reason has to do with the fact that "cold cognition" (thinking without the presence of strong emotion, or some judgment-altering substance such as alcohol) is more likely to be rational than is "hot cognition" (thinking with the presence of strong emotion). A cooling-off period provides a person with the opportunity for her emotions to cool and, thus, for the person to more fully bring his or her intelligence to bear on a proposed course of action. The second reason is that many gullible actions are made when one is being unduly influenced by a particular person or group and a cooling-off period allows one to get away from that influence and to seek countervailing advice and support from others.

There is a small but important body of literature that confirms my view that when emotion walks in the door, reason flies out the window. This is not exactly a new idea, as the 17th-century Dutch philosopher Baruch Spinoza (1677/1989) wrote that emotions "make the mind inclined to think one thing rather than another" (cited in Frijda, Manstead, & Bem, 2000, p. 1). Almost 2 millennia earlier, the Greek philosopher Aristotle noted in the *Rhetorica* (I, II.5, cited in Frijda et al., 2000, p. 1) that "the judgments we deliver are not the same when we are influenced by joy or sorrow, love or hate (*Rhetorica* I, II.5). Until recently, however, the emphasis by emotion researchers has been less on the contribution of feelings to thoughts and more on the contribution of thoughts to feelings (as in the work of cognitive psychotherapists such as Albert Ellis (Ellis & Harper, 1966), who believe that all mental illness stems from faulty thinking).

Two recent edited books have redressed the balance somewhat. The first, *Emotions and Beliefs: How Feelings Influence Thoughts*, edited by Frijda, Manstead, and Bem (2000), three Dutch psychologists, deals with thinking broadly defined, whereas a second, *Feeling and Thinking: The Role of Affect in Social Cognition*, edited by Australian psychology professor Joseph P. Forgas (2001), deals more narrowly with thinking about people and social events. Both books provide considerable support for the notion that thinking done under the influence of strong emotion is not only different, but also less adequate, than is thinking done in a nonemotional state.

One of the main ways in which affect contributes to a gullible outcome is by getting someone to engage in self-deception. Many times, there are clues given off by a manipulator or by a situation that should cause an individual to be on guard. However, if a strong affect pulls for a behavior suggested by the manipulator, then we often will talk ourselves into the action by denying or minimizing the reality of the dangers.

DOES LOW ENERGY CONTRIBUTE TO GULLIBILITY?

It is reported that former U.S. President Bill Clinton has said that "every major error I have made in my life I have made when I was tired." The same applies to most other people. Remaining nongullible, or otherwise maintaining one's autonomy, is a matter of asserting one's will when it is under assault. The ability to remain level-headed under such a circumstance takes some stability and energy. It is to encourage impulse buying, for example, that free wine is typically served at art gallery openings. For similar reasons, police or military interrogations usually take place at night and go on for hours, as one's will to resist is much more likely to crumble when one is exhausted or sleep-deprived (Blagrove, 1996).

The leading current personality theorist who has explored the role of energy depletion as a contributor to incompetent or deviant behavior is undoubtedly Roy Baumeister, of Florida State University. In a number of studies, with both children and adults, Baumeister and colleagues (Baumeister, 2001; Munraven & Baumeister, 2000; Munraven, Tice, & Baumeister, 1998) have found a distinct lessening of perseverance and performance occurring on a variety of tasks as one's energy becomes depleted. Even relatively small demands, such as asking someone to resist eating a cookie or to not think about an object for a period of time, can result in what Baumeister termed *self-regulatory depletion*. Baumeister has not specifically addressed the topic of gullibility, but it seems a very small leap to infer from his findings that externally induced exhaustion will cause increased susceptibility toward appeals or pressures that might otherwise be resisted.

As stated by Baumeister (2001), "the exhaustion theory holds that once the self has become depleted, it lacks the resources necessary for further exertion of volition" (p. 310). Baumeister viewed willpower as an important aspect of personality that is very susceptible to exhaustion and self-regulatory depletion (Schleicher & Baumeister, 2004). He stated that "the concept of willpower resembles that of strength or muscle power, which tires after exertion" (p. 305). He has conducted a number of studies that show that stress causes a breakdown in willpower and self-control, whereas these can be replenished and substantially restored through rest (it is not by accident that cults, such as the Moonies, strive to induce sleep deficits during recruiting weekends).

Baumeister and colleagues also found that positive emotions, such as from watching a funny videotape, can help to reverse the effects of ego depletion much faster than can negative emotions.

Baumeister argued that "self-regulation operates by consuming a common, limited resource, . . . [a] resource that would necessarily have to be regarded as one of the self's most important aspects" (p. 307). There is evidence, furthermore, that this resource becomes depleted when a person has to make difficult decisions (as would be involved in most gullibility-inducing situations). Baumeister argued that "the self has a single resource that resembles energy or strength . . . [and it] is used for a broad variety of seemingly quite different operations, including making choices, taking responsibility, exerting self-control, showing initiative, and avoiding passivity. All aspects of self-regulation (including regulating thoughts, controlling emotions, managing performance, and restraining impulses) use this resource" (p. 308).

HOW DOES SELF-DECEPTION AFFECT GULLIBILITY?

In the *Third Olynthiac*, the ancient Greek writer Demosthenes wrote "nothing is easier than self-deceit. For what each man wishes, that he also believes to be true." He was indicating the truth that gullibility is helped along not just by the lies that are told by others but by the lies that we tell ourselves, lies that are motivated by some underlying affective need for them to be true.

The process by which we deceive ourselves is called *self-deception*. Substantial literature exists on the topic of self-deception, and much of it is psychoanalytic in nature. This reflects the fact that perhaps the main task of psychoanalysis is to explore and challenge the use of defense mechanisms, such as denial or projection, to deceive oneself about one's true feelings. A summary of this literature can be found in *Vital Lies, Simple Truths: The Psychology of Self-Deception* (Goleman, 1985).

In their book *Losing Control: How and Why People Fail at Self-Regulation*, Baumeister, Hetherton, and Tice (1994) described "the strange case of self-deception" as "convincing oneself of something that one prefers to believe, presumably something that is not really true" (p. 95). They noted, further

> with self-deception there are two competing processes. On the one hand, the person wants to believe some particular thing. On the other, the person wants to know the truth; after all, it is no good simply to believe something pleasant if it is false. The search for truth, and the search for a particular answer thus operate against each other, and whichever overrides the other will emerge as the winner. In this sense, self-deception is . . . an example of self-regulation. (p. 95)

The conflict comes from the fact that reality is sometimes painful or unpleasant, whereas what the person wants to be true is usually pleasurable and pleasant. Thus, "what the person wants is impossible. Whether to accept miserable truth or pleasant illusion is thus the issue" (p. 95). Successful self-deception is, thus, defined by Baumeister et al. as "a failure of the mind's effort to learn and know the truth" (p. 95).

Philosophers, such as Jean Paul Sartre (1953) in his *The Existential Psychoanalysis*, tend to treat self-deception as an impossibility. This may be a reflection of their reliance on armchair methods, and their assumption that everyone else spends as much time ruminating over their thoughts and feelings as they themselves do. In *By the Grace of Guile: The Role of Deception in Natural History and Human Affairs*, Loyal Rue (1994) summarized the philosophical skeptic view that self-deception is " no less incoherent than the bogus concept of a square circle" (p. 144). In this view, all deception is intentional and the self is seen as incapable of simultaneously believing and disbelieving something. Rue countered by arguing that self-deception is understandable if one recognizes that not all deception is intentional and that people are complex beings. Rue developed a theory of self-deception, with the following factors: (a) other versus self-deception, (b) evasive versus perversive means, and (c) constructive versus deconstructive ends. Evasive means are those that leave the dupe in a state of ignorance on some matter, whereas perversive means are those that leave the dupe in a state of false belief about that matter. Constructive ends are those that enhance one's self-esteem, whereas deconstructive ends are those in which a threat of self-annihilation is diminished or precluded. An example of constructive–evasive self-deception given by Rue is the supposed discovery of N-rays in 1903 by French physicist René Blondlot, just 8 years after German scientist Wilhelm Roentgen discovered x-rays. Although an American scientist, R.W. Wood showed conclusively that N-rays were a fiction, gullible French scientists ignored Wood's paper and continued to pursue this chimera. This was an exercise in collective self-deception motivated by a desire to shore up the prestige of French science (a constructive end) in the face of German advances. The evasive means consisted in the avoidance of any information (i.e., about the true nature of N-rays) that would cause damage to French science.

Constructive–perversive self-deception occurs when individuals engage in, or communicate, fantasies that enhance their sense of self-worth and enable them to convert messy reality to illusory perfection, or when they engage in superstitious rituals (such as a gambler rolling the dice softly when he wants a low number) that convince them that they have some personal control over what are actually chance events.

Deconstructive self-deception enables individuals to cope with sources of anxiety (such as fear of death and concern about one's competence to perform a job) that threaten their ability to carry on in the world. When used evasively, deconstructive self-deception takes the form of defense mechanisms (such as repression and denial), as seen in the poignant cases noted by Rue of Cambodian survivors of unspeakable atrocities who developed psychosomatic blindness. When used perversively, deconstructive self-deception involves blaming others for one's own failings (e.g., going off a diet attributed to a hostess offering ice cream rather than to oneself for accepting it), and for buying into fantastic after-life schemes (such as offered by the Mormon religion) to deal with one's fear of dying.

SHOULD GULLIBLE PEOPLE BE BLAMED FOR BEING GULLIBLE?

Will Rogers was supposed to have said "I would rather be the man who bought the Brooklyn Bridge than the man who sold it." This reflects the general view that those who take advantage of others are to be condemned, whereas those who are taken advantage of are more to be pitied. However, there are some who believe that gullibility can also be condemned on moral grounds, especially when such gullibility reflects intellectual laziness rather than stupidity. This is the stance taken by theology scholar Jacob Neusner (1986), in his book *Reading and Believing: Ancient Judaism and Contemporary Gullibility*. Neusner used the term derisively, to refer to scholars who accept at face value the prevailing wisdom concerning the authorship of various Talmudic sayings, without bothering to critically evaluate the original sources. For Neusner, the word *gullibility* invites moral scorn, as when he says that the authors of shoddy scholarship have engaged in the "sin of gullibility" (p. 115).

A somewhat less harsh moral condemnation of gulls can be found in *Belief's Own Ethics*, by philosopher Jonathan E. Adler (2002). The traditional position in epistemology (the branch of philosophy concerned with knowing the truth) is that the strength of belief should be proportional to the strength of evidence, but that leaves open, according to Adler, the possibility that under certain circumstances it may be acceptable to believe something for which one has little or no evidence. As a "strong evidentialist," Adler's position is that the critical question we should ask (about everyday matters; he is less interested in religious or scientific beliefs) is not "what should we believe?" but "what must we *not* believe." Adler's answer is that we should not believe things for which there is little or no evidence. Gullibility and credulity are, therefore, immoral acts. Thus, unlike other (weaker) evidentialists, Adler does not consider that basing belief on evidence is just one option among many. For Adler, there is no other legitimate justification for believing something than the fact that there is evidence for it. And by evidence, Adler is referring to something like the scientific method, even when applied to everyday beliefs that fall well outside the normal sphere of what we consider science.

Although Adler characterizes belief not backed by evidence as immoral, he is concerned that "occasions on which we recognize that we have been duped or gulled [may] lead to an overreaction in which a general attitude of trust is regarded as naïve." He wrote that "our credulity could not position us to be suckers for false or deceptive testimony without the well-founded expectation of truthfulness and reliability that are ripe for exploitation. The lesson is the importance of knowing *when* not to be trusting" (p. 12). One is justified, in Adler's view, in trusting people or statements that are typically trustworthy, and the fact that such trust may be deceptively exploited on occasion is insufficient justification for becoming a nontrusting person. Adler, who seems more interested in general (and largely hypothetical) cases than in individual differences, implies that trust in others is generally justified by the fact that most people understand that telling the truth is both the correct and the generally useful thing to do. So, for Adler, a person not deserving trust is someone who tells us things that are "grossly unlikely" (he seems not to provide any direction for identifying individuals who reject the norm of truth-telling). Adler's "default rule"—to always trust another except when he or she gives very obvious reason not to trust him or her—ignores the twin realities that (a) untruth and deception are often subtle rather than obvious, and (b) empirical confirmation or disconfirmation may not be easy to come by, especially for those with limited knowledge or truth-verifying skills (this last reality is, in fact, mentioned by Adler as a reason for erring on the side of trusting sources that are generally trustworthy).

Although Adler viewed false belief as a moral flaw, he was fairly forgiving of those who make incorrect judgment calls in situations where it is reasonable to trust someone. For example, he wrote that "in reading *Pride and Prejudice*, we can both recognize that Elizabeth could have done more to check the ward's story before she accepted it, and also think that her judgment was not markedly hasty in the circumstances. There is enormous background support for her proceeding as she does" (Adler, 2002, p. 229). An example of unjustified credulity, on the other hand, would be someone believing the widespread story that former basketball star Jerry Lucas—a noted mnemonicist—had memorized all 1 million names in the Manhattan phone book. Adler considered that to be just too difficult, time-consuming, and meaningless a feat to be believed without more evidence than the fact that some people repeat the rumor and appear to believe it. Rather than repeal the use of the default rule (which is that one is generally safe in believing and trusting people), Adler suggested that it be fine-tuned to take into account certain exceptions, such as one should "not default accept memory reports on events during infancy" (presumably, Adler here was influenced by the widespread discrediting of recovered memories obtained by incompetent and biased therapists of sexual abuse allegedly carried out on patients when they were infants).

Thus, to Adler, although it is immoral to believe things that are in need of empirical verification, it is also immoral to not believe or trust the word of others in situations where obvious indicators of implausibility are lacking. Adler noted that as a result of the default rule, the ratio of belief to nonbelief of others should be overwhelmingly on the side of belief. Adler did not see that as problematic, as he considered deliberate deception to be a minor exception to the rule that people generally tell the truth, and that the problem of truth determination mainly involves the message rather than the messenger.

For example, Adler wrote

> The hold on us of the default rule depends in large part on the fact that the assertions we are offered are dominantly true.... If so, why regularly expend energy to evaluate [these assertions]? Granted, you will sometimes accept what is false, but that will be the unusual case, and you will surely lose more valuable information if you adopt this skeptical attitude generally. Additionally, we cannot well evaluate testimony on our own, particularly where we have limited time and resources. (p. 161)

In asserting that falsehood is a rare and generally benign event, Adler may himself have been demonstrating a certain amount of naïve belief, and it is certainly not a belief for which he had any evidence. Furthermore, although Adler was correct in saying that trust is a better lifestyle choice than blanket distrust, the intellectual laziness he recommended can be a formula for life-altering disaster on those occasions when the source of information is someone looking for a gullible victim on whom to prey.

IS GULLIBILITY A PERSONALITY TRAIT?

Gullibility is often talked about as if it were a personality trait, as when one says about a friend "John is so gullible; he is always being taken advantage of." In this book, I describe gullibility as an outcome behavior, which is affected by the situation (the external pull to gullibility), interacting with three "personal" factors internal to the individual. One of these personal factors is termed *personality*, whereas the other two are termed *cognition* and *affect/state*. Thus, I view personality mainly as an input variable, that is a factor that can contribute to a gullible outcome. This differs from a trait view of gullibility, in that any given individual does not behave gullibly all the time, but only when certain factors are in alignment. Such a view of behavior as a dynamic transaction between person and situation owes much to the thinking of Walter Mischel (2007), as reflected in a recently republished seminal essay.

This transactional view differs from a traditional trait perspective, in that "gullibility" is not a tendency that an individual carries around with him or her and that impels the individual to behave gullibly. Nevertheless, individuals obviously do differ in the ease with which they can be duped, even in situations that most people can resist and even when in a relatively rested and affectively stable state. Such a higher tendency toward social vulnerability can be explained, however, not as stemming from a gullibility trait but rather from some combination of cognitive and other personality factors. The list of personality qualities that can predispose someone to behave gullibly is quite long, and includes high interpersonal trust, a factor mentioned earlier. Two other personality factors, discussed briefly here, are accommodation (also known as agreeableness) and hypnotic suggestibility.

Accommodation/agreeableness refers to one's need to be liked. It is a problem that I have, which has both its up side (people who need to be liked generally behave in a manner that causes them to be liked) and its down side (people who need to be liked often say "yes" when their interests or wishes would be better served by saying "no"). Accommodation is one of the components in the widely used "Big Five" personality model—a refinement of other models with a larger number of factors—which is used by many psychological researchers (a good discussion of the Big Five can be found at http:/www.centacs.com/quickstart.htm). Michael Shermer (2002) used the Big Five to explain a very curious event in the history of science, which was the partial retreat by Alfred Russell Wallace from his great scientific achievement: the co-discovery of evolution by natural selection.

There are those who believe that Wallace deserved greater credit than his much better known (and well-connected) co-discoverer, Charles Darwin, as elements of the theory were published by Wallace in papers that significantly predated Darwin's and Wallace was very generous in sharing early drafts of his ideas with Darwin. Yet, Wallace also was a long-time believer in the pseudoscience of phrenology (reading of head bumps), was a firm proponent of Spiritualism (communicating with the dead), was taken in by a literary hoax involving a poem falsely attributed to Edgar Allen Poe, and even was eventually persuaded to modify aspects of his life's great achievement—the theory of evolution—to accommodate objections from critics with a creationist perspective.

In *The Borderlands of Science: Where Sense Meets Nonsense*, Michael Shermer (2002) used Wallace to illustrate how the Big Five model could explain gullibility toward "pseudo" or "borderland" notions, even in a great scientist. Using a rating version of the Big Five developed and standardized by Cal-Berkeley professor Frank Sulloway, Shermer rated Wallace and several other famous scientists, such as Stephen Jay Gould and Carl Sagan he knew well on the scale (he knew Wallace well as a result of writing a biography of him for his doctoral dissertation). Shermer rated Wallace as very high (77th and 73rd percentiles, respectively) on conscientiousness/consolidation and extroversion; extremely high (99th percentile) on agreeableness/accommodation and openness to experience/originality; and extremely low (6th percentile, which is good given the reversal of items) on neuroticism/need for stability. The key trait in differentiating Wallace from other (much less gullible) great scientists, according to Shermer, is agreeableness/accommodation. All original scientific thinkers, including Wallace, are very high on conscientiousness/consolidation and on openness to experience/originality, in Shermer's opinion. This is as one might expect: Conscientiousness accounts for the scientists' extreme drive and task orientation, whereas openness to experience accounts for their intellectual creativity.

Where Wallace differed markedly from more skeptical scientists, however, was in his extraordinarily high agreeableness. Whereas other scientists, such as Sagan, did not suffer fools gladly (and thus, were rated as low on agreeableness), Wallace was described by many of his contemporaries as someone who was extraordinarily magnanimous and welcoming of input from everyone. This put him at risk, according to Shermer (2002), as he "was simply far too conciliatory towards almost everyone whose ideas were on the fringe. He had a difficult time discriminating between fact and fiction, reality and fantasy, and he was far too eager to please, whereas his more tough-minded colleagues had no qualms about calling a foolish idea foolish" (p. 163). Shermer noted that "good scientists must find that exquisite balance between being open-minded enough to accept radical new ideas, but not so open-minded that all manner of goofiness is embraced" (p. 163). Wallace, because of his overagreeableness, was not able, according to Shermer, to maintain that balance, making him extremely susceptible to dumb ideas, even going so far as to partially renounce his great achievement to accommodate objections by much less-sophisticated acquaintances.

Another personality variable that has been cited as contributing to gullible conduct is hypnotic suggestibility. The leading investigator of individual differences in our responses to hypnotic suggestions—as well as our capacity for self-hypnosis—is Herbert Spiegel, a professor emeritus of psychiatry at Columbia University and the author, with his son David Spiegel (Spiegel & Spiegel 1987/2004) of *Trance and Treatment: Clinical Uses of Hypnosis*. Spiegel's discoveries about hypnotizability have been ably described in Donald Connery's (1982/2003) *The Inner Source: Exploring Hypnosis*. As an advocate for Peter Reilly, whose notorious case of false confession to his mother's murder was profiled in chapter 5, Connery learned of Spiegel's research when he heard the psychiatrist testify as an expert witness for Reilly at a hearing for a new trial.

Spiegel's own psychological test, the Hypnotic Induction Profile, had satisfied him that Reilly, on the low side of the hypnotizability spectrum, was not the type of person who would have "blacked out" his memory in the wake of a terrible event. After protesting his innocence to the police interrogators, the youth had thought himself guilty and confessed falsely only after naïvely accepting their claim that amnesia accounted for his inability to remember the killing that he had not, in fact, committed. Spiegel's testimony, devastating the state's case, opened the door to Reilly's exoneration. His clinical experience with tens of thousands of patients had led Spiegel to the realization that low, mid-range, and high hypnotizability—on a 5-point scale—directly relates not only to low, mid-range, and high "eye rolls" but to distinct and fixed personality types that he called Apollonians, Odysseans, and Dionysians.

Apollonians (0–1 score), whose eyes will scarcely move even if they try to make them roll upwards, are difficult to induce hypnotically. Seldom lapsing into trance, they like to be in control while revealing rational judgment over emotional reactions. At the other extreme, Dionysians (4–5) are easy to induce hypnotically, unless the person is mentally ill, and are prone to shift into altered states of consciousness. Most people are Odysseans (2–3) who occupy the broad middle ground. It is the Dionysians, especially "the 5s," who are particularly fascinating. If asked to "look all the way up while slowly closing your eyelids," their eyes will roll up and reveal complete whiteness. In terms of personality traits, they have a "proneness to accept the reasoning and the directions of other people, especially when, without being aware of it, they [slip] into spontaneous trance states" (Connery, 1982/2003, p. 127). Citing Spiegel, Connery noted

> there was something credulous and guileless about highly hypnotizable individuals. . . . They tended to act on their feelings more often than on logic or analysis. Instead of insisting on facts and figures, as many people do, they relied on their intuition. . . . It seemed to be in their nature to accept the control of others in many instances—rather than to insist on being in charge themselves. They almost seemed to be saying "Tell me what to believe and I'll believe it." (p. 160)

Spiegel described such individuals as having "The Grade 5 Syndrome," the defining features of which are "their high eye rolls, their high-intact profiles and their propensity for spontaneous trance experiences" along with "their way of adopting a 'naïve posture of trust' in relation to many if not all people in their environment" (Connery, 1982/2003, p. 161).

Connery notes that highly hypnotizable people can get into trouble, especially when they are emotionally disturbed or otherwise impaired, because their extreme suggestibility, in combination with "gullibility and a naïve trust in others, can make the highly hypnotizable personality vulnerable to deception" (Connery, 1982/2003, p. 162). Although people in trances cannot be made to do things that violate their moral scruples, a Dionysian can be made to do virtually anything if he is tricked into thinking that he is acting out of a noble motive, such as saving his country from enemies. Thus, Spiegel believes that a scenario such as was found in the (original version of the) film "The Manchurian Candidate," where an American POW was programmed by his North Korean captors to return home and assassinate a presidential candidate, is not out of the question. Presumably, hypnotic susceptibility, in combination with other personality indices of suggestibility, can help to explain a wide range of other gullible behaviors, including the acts carried out by terrorist suicide bombers, who are often under the hypnotic sway of Svengali-like leaders.

IS GULLIBILITY AN ABSENCE OF AUTONOMY?

One way of looking at gullibility is as a loss of autonomy in the face of social pressure that would override one's will. There are those, such as Pope Benedict XVI in a speech during his 2008 visit to the United States, who argue that autonomy is one of the evils of modern civilization, and that bowing to authority (specifically, to church leaders) is a good thing. But I think that the Pope would agree that many of the great figures in his own Catholic tradition are those who possessed the moral intelligence and courage to say "no" to orders that violated their beliefs and values.

In fact, the behavior of most human beings (as well as many nonhuman animals) is driven by a desire to maintain a certain degree of freedom from coercive influence (Deci & Ryan, 2002). Autonomy is not an absolute good however, as when taken too far it can influence a person to respond selfishly and nontrustingly to the legitimate requests of others, or to remain impervious to information about the self-destructiveness of certain actions. In a book titled *The Perversion of Autonomy*, Willard Gaylin and Bruce Jennings (1996) argued that the pendulum toward autonomy as an absolute ethical principle guiding the provision of health decisions has been taken to nonsensical extremes, as in the case they discuss of a mentally ill homeless man who refused the services of an ambulance crew when he was critically ill and was, as a consequence, allowed to die to avoid restricting his autonomy.

I agree with Gaylin and Jennings that there are times when autonomy should be curtailed, as when gullible parents prefer to treat their child's bowel obstruction with prayer rather than taking the child to a physician. In terms of promoting gullibility-resistance, however, the key is to enhance the exercise of autonomy rather than restrict it. Restriction of autonomy is justified when the combination of judgmental incompetence (e.g., one is extraordinarily gullible) and danger to self or others is so strong (e.g., someone is at high risk of dying) as to make respect for autonomy problematic.

But there are too many gullible people and exploitative situations in the world, involving consequences that are not life-threatening and victims whose incompetence is not great enough, to see much role for the state in intervening every time someone's exercise of autonomy threatens to harm him or her. (An obvious exception would be some reparative intervention after the fact, in situations involving fraud or where the victim can be found to have been seriously impaired.) A more logical preventive role for government is to enhance the intelligent exercise of autonomy through educational programs aimed at increasing people's awareness of illogical and coercive practices. A related role for government is to crack down on the predators themselves, by doing a better job of monitoring and regulating coercive practices aimed at misleading and mistreating gullible people.

Although he does not directly address the topic of gullibility, there is much in Lawrence Howarth's (1986) book *Autonomy* that speaks to the notion of gullibility-resistance as involving an ability to remain autonomous in the face of coercive pressures. To Howarth, there are two major factors that contribute to incompetent decision making (of which gullibility can be seen an example): (a) inability to withstand external social pressures, and (b) inability to withstand internal affective pressures. Thus, Howarth noted that "self-rule is not possible if the person's objectives are simply borrowed from others" and "self-rule is not possible if the person's passions and impulses dictate his responses" (p. 43). A nongullible person can be viewed as being able to withstand situational coercive pressures, including the affective responses called forth by those pressures. Being nongullible, therefore, always involves an exercise in maintaining autonomy.

By viewing coercion as an act intended to limit autonomy, there is a tendency to see all forms of coercion as bad. Gaylin and Jennings (1996) argued to the contrary that coercion is morally neutral, in that it generally involves psychological pressure rather than constraint or physical force. Anyone has the right to express his or her own autonomy by applying psychological pressure (e.g., appeals to motives such as guilt, shame, greed, etc.), to another, as long as it does not step over certain boundaries. Psychological pressure can be resisted, as seen in the fact that there are many people who are not moved by such appeals. If I cave in under such pressures, such as when my late grandmother and mother used guilt trips to get me to do things that I didn't want to do, was that their fault or was it a result primarily of my own inability to stand up to them?

Sometimes, coercion can be in the service of facilitating autonomy. Gaylin and Jennings provided the example of a child's willingness to share her toys with other children. Most parents would want a child to share out of her own autonomous generosity, but there are times when a parent must encourage the development of such a trait by pointing out situations in which sharing behavior is expected. So too, Gaylin and Jennings pointed out that although the goal of psychotherapy is to enhance a client's ability to function autonomously, the process of psychotherapy is inherently coercive, in that it involves subtle forms of psychological manipulation, involving "reeducation" of the client's value system, by the therapist.

Rather than condemn all acts of coercion, Gaylin and Jennings—the founder and former director, respectively, of the Hastings (New York) Center on Bio-Ethics—argue that each act of coercion must be evaluated in terms of the specific context, methods, and intentions that are involved. Thus, brain-washing is considered an unacceptable form of coercion because it is a method that overwhelms the autonomy of its targets and is used to mistreat rather than benefit them. Coercion that precipitates a gullible reaction can be acceptable or unacceptable, even when it activates emotional and nonrational processes, depending on whether it undermines the capacity of the individual to make rational decisions in the future. Coercion (such as in a political ad) that appeals to the better nature of people is ethically preferable to coercion that appeals to fear, hatred, or other negative emotions. So too, it is necessary to consider the developmental and competence levels of the person being coerced when deciding whether a gullible outcome stems from an acceptable (i.e., autonomy-respecting) or unacceptable (i.e., autonomy-undermining) exercise of coercive influence.

IS GULLIBILITY PART OF THE LEGAL DEFINITION OF INCOMPETENCE?

Achieving a better understanding of gullibility has implications for developing better methods for defining and determining human competence and incompetence. This is because incompetent outcomes (such as having one's life savings fraudulently wiped out) typically occur in a context in which gullibility is a central factor. Yet, to my knowledge, gullibility is not explicitly discussed in current constitutive (theoretical) or legal definitions and measures of incompetence that are used for purposes such as putting guardianship arrangements in place or for negating commercial or other transactions that take advantage of an individual whose judgment and competence are impaired.

Notions of risk and incompetence tend to focus on nonsocial dimensions, despite the fact that for most people (not living in mountain lion and bear country like I do) the biggest non car-related risks to their safety and wellbeing come from other people, and involve social rather than physical assault. This can be seen in the case of "Priscilla" and "Sam Gregory," a middle-aged brother and sister who became concerned when they found evidence that their stepmother had been getting their severely stroke-damaged elderly father to practice signing his name. Sam and Priscilla (whose mother had died years earlier) knew that their father's second wife had complained frequently about a prenuptial agreement that she had signed that severely limited her inheritance rights, and they were concerned that she might be trying to get her impaired husband to sign a revised agreement or will.

The siblings asked their father's neurologist to arrange to have Mr Gregory evaluated for the purpose of determining his legal competence to sign such a document. The evaluation, carried out by a neuropsychologist, used a standard test battery that tapped academic and abstract skills such as memory, reasoning, and language processing. Based on the test scores obtained, which showed significant brain damage-related cognitive impairments, the neuropsychologist wrote a report indicating that Mr Gregory should be declared incompetent and in need of a conservator (he died before the siblings could take the recommendation to a judge, but also before his wife could get him to change his will). An aspect of this process that was unsettling to Priscilla Gregory (herself also a psychologist, but not a practicing clinician) was the absence of any test items used by the neuropsychologist that spoke to her father's ability to see through and withstand interpersonal pressures of the sort that she had reason to suspect were being used to convince her father to alter his will. Also lacking, from what she could tell, was the absence of any clear test score or other objective criterion that guided the neuropsychologist's recommendation. The recommendation was based on the subjective judgment of the clinician to the effect that Mr Gregory needed a conservator, and it was never actually articulated why he felt that to be the case. Although Sam and Priscilla were pleased that the recommendation was in line with their wishes (which more often than not is the case when one is paying for an assessment), the subjective nature of the decision process meant that it could just have easily have gone the other way.

The need for a fiscal conservator or guardian is typically grounded not in a concern that an impaired individual lacks the arithmetic skills to balance a checkbook (although that may be a consideration) but that he or she lacks the social judgment to see through and fend off those who would coerce the individual to write them a check (or sign a deed, etc.). But a comprehensive review by Jennifer Moye (2003) of forensic measures used in guardianship evaluations shows considerably more emphasis on arithmetic skills than on social skills. Contained in a book edited by the prominent forensic psychologist Thomas Grisso (2003) titled *Evaluating Competencies: Forensic Assessments and Instruments*, Moye's paper reviews the current state of the art, both in terms of measures and concepts used by forensic mental health practitioners and by the courts in determining whether a person is in need of a legal guardian or conservator.

Moye pointed out that states have moved away from relying on diagnoses (mental retardation, dementia, etc.) in determining legal incompetence, but instead have moved toward use of more specific functional standards (whether one can prepare meals, etc.). Presence of an explanatory medical condition is still a consideration in such assessments, but it is now seen as a necessary but not sufficient condition for determining incompetence, on the assumption that not everyone given a particular diagnosis meets the legal criterion of incompetence. (A problem I have with this approach is that there are many people who meet the functional criterion for legal incompetence but who may not have a clear underlying medical basis; they are often left unprotected under such a formula).

Moye noted that there are three components mentioned in various state competence statutes: (a) a mental or physical condition (the necessary but not sufficient provision mentioned above), (b) cognitive or decision-making impairments (e.g., impaired memory or thinking), and (c) certain behavioral outcomes or consequences (e.g., wandering off, not eating adequately, etc.). In line with the preference of psychologists for indirect predictor (e.g., test score) data over direct outcome (e.g., observed behavior) data, the third component is the one that is most often omitted in competence assessments. This is unfortunate from my standpoint, as the frequent actual occurrence of vulnerable behavior (such as being talked into spending thousands of dollars on sweepstakes contests) is a far more important consideration in a competence hearing than one's score on a standardized measure of short-term memory.

Various model statutes have been developed that incorporate the three components noted by Moye. An example of such a statute is the 1997 Uniform

Guardianship and Protective Proceedings Act, also known as Article V of the Uniform Probate Code. It "defines legal incapacity of the person as: 'any person who is impaired by reason of mental illness, mental deficiency, physical illness or disability, chronic use of drugs, chronic intoxication, or other cause (except minority) to the extent of lacking sufficient understanding or capacity to make or communicate reasonable decisions'" (Moye, 2003, p. 315).

Although examiners are now expected to conduct a more ecologically oriented assessment, for example by interviewing family members and others, doing testing and observations on more than one occasion, and seeking a clearer understanding of the specific areas of functional concern, there is still a tendency to specify mental functions (such as attention, information processing, delusions, and affect) with much more detail and specificity than the everyday tasks to which such functions are applied. With respect to assessing geriatric patients (where guardianship determination is most likely to be sought), the tendency has been to borrow from the various measures of "adaptive behavior" that have been developed to aid in the diagnosis of mental retardation.

I have long studied and written about adaptive behavior in mental retardation (Greenspan, 1999) and I can emphatically state that such measures are generally quite inadequate as a guide to determining social incompetence; for example, they contain much emphasis on sociability (amount of socializing) and on socioemotional stability (presence or absence of mental illness) and contain little or no emphasis on social intelligence (shrewdness and with-it-ness in social relationships). Furthermore, with respect to gullibility (the implicit reason why guardians are often sought, particularly in handling one's finances), this domain of vulnerability is simply not mentioned in any adaptive behavior or guardianship assessment protocols with which I am familiar.

For example, when an advisory group to the Department of Veterans Affairs put together a 1997 set of guidelines aimed at helping psychologists and other clinicians when conducting guardianship assessments, they emphasized "a performance based assessment of the specific capacity in question (e.g., writing checks and counting change)" (Moye, 2003, p. 321). In other words, the emphasis in competence assessment is still on arithmetic skills rather than social skills in a domain (fiscal management) where the main source of vulnerability comes not from inability to balance a checkbook as from inability to ward off predators seeking access to one's checkbook.

Because unusual gullibility in the impaired person is the factor that implicitly underlies the desire of family members (such as the Gregory siblings) to seek an incompetence hearing, then it is logical to include some consideration of the person's gullibility in the assessment process. This could be done in a couple of ways. The first would be to set up some simulations where you

CHAPTER 10

Becoming Less Gullible

I was tempted to limit this book to describing the phenomenon of gullibility, saving a discussion of "gullibility proofing" for a future book. This view was based in part on my belief that one could learn a lot about how to avoid being gullible just by reading about the many ways and whys of the duping phenomenon. However, I have come to understand that most readers would appreciate a more explicit discussion of how they can reduce, or protect against, the consequences of gullibility in themselves and others. In this concluding chapter, a number of suggestions are presented concerning how people can help themselves, and in some cases others, to be less gullible. Finally, I conclude with a discussion of the critical need to help children to grow up nongullible, and the need to develop self-protective mechanisms (healthy skepticism) without crossing over into pervasive distrust (cynicism).

MAKE IT A POINT TO AVOID ACTING IMPULSIVELY

In perhaps the majority of the gullibility episodes described in this book, a nongullible outcome would have been obtained if the victim had simply said "I need a day or two to think about this" and then taken the opportunity to talk the situation over with a friend, family member, or advisor. Decisions made when one is rushed, and perhaps affected by emotion, are often bad ones, and there is rarely anything to be lost by buying oneself a little more time. Furthermore, bringing other, more objective, people into the mix, can be very helpful, both in neutralizing the social pressure exerted by the influence agent(s) and in giving yourself the benefit of whatever content expertise and wisdom that they might possess.

Because state factors such as impulsivity and exhaustion often contribute to gullible or otherwise foolish actions, I try and adhere to something that I call "Monfredo's Law," named after Frank Monfredo, an attorney who once got me out of a gullibility-induced jam. The principle can be stated as follows: "Never make any major decision, such as a sizeable purchase, without sleeping on it and giving yourself at least 24 hours to think it over."

ENGINEER SITUATIONS THAT REDUCE THE LIKELIHOOD OF GULLIBLE OUTCOMES

Nancy Cantor (2000), a psychologist who became a university chancellor, developed, with several colleagues, a theory of "social intelligence" that focuses more on "macro" lifestyle strategies (e.g., attaining career goals, such as presumably becoming a university chancellor) than on the more frequently used cognitive processing of here-and-now "micro" social situations or encounters. Although there is a general tendency, among more mechanistically oriented psychologists, to see situation as cause and human behavior as effect, Cantor understands that successful people consciously select situations that are more likely to help them attain their goals and avoid situations that pose obstacles to success.

One example noted by Cantor (2003) that seems particularly relevant to gullibility avoidance is the engineering of situations that can compensate for one's limitations or areas of inexperience. She discussed the case of people who have difficulty being successful with members of the opposite sex and so select settings (such as, presumably, singles groups) that are designed precisely to make it easier for one to overcome such a personal limitation. An opposite example would be an alcoholic avoiding parties where everyone is consuming alcohol, and a problem gambler avoiding going on vacation at a hotel or locale that has a casino.

People with specific gullibility problems would be well advised to avoid situations in which such gullibility pressures are present. For example, someone who is unable (because of guilt) to say "no" to a salesperson in a shoe store or clothing store would be well advised to do their shopping in a place (e.g., a discount department store) where shoes and clothes are on display for self-service, and where salespeople, if there are any, are likely to leave them alone. Another situation-selection strategy would be to never put oneself in a setting that cannot be navigated safely without taking a friend or relative along who is given the job of protecting you from yourself. Some of the heuristics discussed elsewhere in this chapter, such as never engaging a telephone solicitor in conversation (including going so far as to use a "no solicitor" answering message to screen out such calls), may be considered variants of a strategy of avoiding situations that pull for a gullible or overly compliant response.

For people whose social vulnerabilities rise to the level of a "disability," various protective mechanisms can be used to limit exposure to gullibility-inducing situations. On the more extreme end are such formal legal arrangements as conservatorships or guardianships (also discussed elsewhere in this volume) and such highly restrictive settings as group homes or other congregate care facilities. Although such settings are typically described as providing physical protections (e.g., against starvation or malnourishment), they may also be seen as protecting residents from their own vulnerability to various forms of social exploitation. Less restrictive arrangements such as "supported living," in which staff drop in on a daily basis rather than be present on a 24-hour basis, may also be considered as having at least an implicit function of limiting opportunities for exposure by vulnerable people to influence agents.

KNOW ONE'S LIMITATIONS

I've known a few "geniuses" from the sciences and other fields and the one thing that these extremely smart people have in common is a willingness to admit when they don't know something. People who are less intelligent, or less secure about their intelligence, often think they know more than they do or are afraid that saying "I don't know" is an admission of weakness or stupidity. This has obvious relevance to gullibility because a key to being nongullible is to know the limits of one's knowledge, and to be able to defer judgment in situations where one needs more information. This is illustrated in a case involving "Harold," a friend from my college days in Baltimore.

Harold is a successful lawyer, and a man of above-average intelligence. He is very diligent in his work, and is likely to scrutinize any legal situation, such as a contract, with great care to be certain that a client is not being taken advantage of. But Harold goes to a healer who engages in some pretty questionable practices, and Harold trusts this man in ways that I am certain he would never do in his law practice. I asked Harold to tell me what the healer (a chiropractor, who also uses a wide variety of nonmanipulation techniques) does that is so special, and he told me that he has a machine with wires coming out of it, and he hooks the leads up to different parts of your body and it will tell you various amazing things about yourself: traits and preferences, as well as medical problems. For example, the healer got the machine to look at possible infections that Harold might have, and a list was generated. Two of the infections on the list were pneumonia and some horse microorganism that Harold had never heard of. I asked Harold if he had either of these diseases and he said "no, but my mother had died of pneumonia recently and I do have some horses on my property, and I might have been exposed." Harold also told me that his wife had been tested and the machine printed out a list of the kinds of flowers she likes. One of the items on the list was "flowers in country settings." Harold thought that was amazing, because his wife has a phobia about cities and preferred to live in the country. When I suggested that a confirmation bias was operating (a small number of fuzzy "hits" from a larger list, seen as confirming evidence by someone inclined to believe), Harold looked at me like I was crazy.

I asked Harold to tell me how this machine worked. He kept saying "he hooks it up to various parts of your body," until I conveyed that what I was really asking for was information about the underlying mechanism or theory. Harold's answer was to the effect that the machine (which, from what I could tell, did not penetrate the skin) measured the atoms in different parts of one's body and compared the results to atoms in various objects or microorganisms. I asked Harold if there was any scientific literature on this procedure, and he didn't know. I asked him why he thought this explanation of the machine was so convincing and he answered, somewhat defensively, "I took science courses; I know about atoms." When I suggested that taking some science courses decades ago did not qualify him to evaluate this atomic theory explanation (which he could never articulate on a detailed level), Harold, a confident man with a strong ego, assured me that he did possess that ability. When I suggested that such a magical machine would surely be in every doctor's office in the country if it were scientifically valid, Harold replied in the same conspiratorial vein that he often uses when talking about judges, politicians, and corporations, namely that chiropractors and other alternative healers have special knowledge that organized medicine is afraid of and tries to squelch. Harold's affective tendencies (a preference for magical medicine, and a distrust of the establishment), combined with an unwillingness to assess his own limitations, and an apparent affection for this healer, makes him a sitting duck for someone whom I would consider a fraudulent practitioner.

The device that Harold thinks so highly of is, in fact, very similar to some of the "quack machines" described in a book by Bob McCoy (2000), titled *Quack: Tales of Medical Fraud from the Museum of Questionable Medical Practices*. On a visit to this amazing museum, in Minneapolis, my friend Bob Shilkret and I actually had Mr McCoy demonstrate a "psychograph" machine on one of us. The psychograph was invented in 1905 by a Wisconsin man, Henry C. Lavery, who was enamored of the pseudo-science of phrenology (the reading of head bumps), at a time when the great French neuropathologist and anthropologist Paul Broca had already showed convincingly that it was based on a faulty understanding of how the brain works. The psychograph takes readings of head size in different areas of the skull and prints out a score based on ratings (from 1 to 5) on each of 32 mental faculties, with suggestions based on those scores. For example, a score of 3 (average) on "suavity" would come with the following recommendation: "You can be pleasant, polite, and tactful with others, but with many people you achieve more by exercising more diplomacy and courtesy." Good advice, for sure, but advice that applies to most people on planet Earth. Because the psychograph scores are based on size of different head areas (which, in fact, has been found to have no correlation with intelligence or character), a watermelon would receive maximum scores on all of the domains measured by this machine.

Social psychologists have studied something called the "Barnum effect" (Forer, 1949; Layne, 1979), which helps to explain why so many people are taken in by devices such as the psychograph or the atom analyzer used by Harold's healer. In these studies, an experimenter in a white lab coat administers a brief personality measure to research subjects and later hands them all a report (the same for all subjects, although they do not know that) with a long list of statements supposedly generated from the results about their character and behavioral tendencies. Subjects are then asked to comment on the accuracy of the statements and the great majority of subjects express amazement at how accurate and insightful these statements are. The explanation for this effect is that everyone wants to think that they are unique, and there is a general desire to find out something useful about oneself from this kind of procedure. Thus, there is a tendency to focus on the few items that seem particularly on-target (in a long list, one can assume some will be correct randomly), to ignore the items that seem off target, and to naïvely fail to understand that most of the statements apply to everyone.

Gullibility is, in part, a failure to tell when something is not true. Or, to put it another way, gullibility occurs when someone believes something that is not true, whether or not it is an intentional lie. The various cases explored throughout this book fall into two broad categories: gullibility in an interpersonal context (such as when being conned or fooled by a particular person) and gullibility—or credulity—in a more general sense, as when believing some dubious theory, such as "trickle down economics," that one hears about from a more indirect source (such as a TV ad or news article). These two topics overlap to some extent, but the main focus in this book has been on the first type of gullibility.

One of the major contributors to gullibility, in both individual and mass forms, is that the truth is often ambiguous and inaccessible. This position is confirmed by the philosopher Edo Pivcevic (1997), whose book *What is Truth?* addresses some of the major issues and theoretical positions in epistemology, the field concerned with knowing the truth of things. A key to nongullibility is understanding when you do not possess the ability to know the truth or false-ness of a persuasive communication. I studied political science, economics, and history for several years, obtaining a master's in the latter subject. Yet when I hear two political candidates going on about their plan for reforming Social Security or Medicaid, or about the economic benefits of their respective trade reform packages, I lack the detailed knowledge to know which candi-date is telling the truth. At least I am aware of my limitations, know where to go for more information, and possess some basis for recognizing when a claim seems dubious. What is someone with no training in government or economics, and no idea of how to obtain unbiased information, to do when faced with widely varying claims? The answer is that he or she will likely rely on intuition or emotion, a reliance that, as we have seen, is often a formula for gullibility. In the immediate interpersonal sphere, truth detection isn't much better, as the literature on the inadequacy of humans as lie detectors makes abundantly clear. Thus, one of the keys to being nongullible is to be aware of the limitations of one's ability to know the truth and of the need to defer action or judgment in potentially misleading or socially dangerous situations.

SEEK TO BECOME MORE SOCIALLY INTELLIGENT

For most of us, changing our personality is difficult if not impossible. But all of us can continue to acquire new information and learn new concepts, even up to the end of our days. Although personality, motivational, and affective factors play a major role in gullibility, being gullible is, ultimately, a failure of social intelligence. If one were able to recognize the faulty logic, wrong information, or coercive tactics that are being brought to bear on us, then we would be much less likely to be influenced to change our behavior in a way that does not meet our true interests or desires. Thus, the best way to become less gullible is to become more socially "with it."

There are a growing number of socioemotional curricula available to schools, but—in line with the general ignoring of the gullibility construct—little or no emphasis on gullibility is contained in these curricula. The major impetus for the growth of socioemotional learning has been the problem of school violence, and the view, promoted by such scholars as psychologists Roger Weissberg and Mark Greenberg (1998) that teaching self-regulatory and other "emotional intelligence" skills can be a means for helping young people to adopt nonviolent methods for dealing with interpersonal conflict. These interventions are based on the idea that violence occurs when one becomes "hijacked" by emotion, and that techniques aimed at helping young people to stop and consider better social problem-solving methods can be effective at replacing hot responses with cooler and more deliberate ones.

As numerous examples in this book make clear, the problem of social incompetence—in both children and adults—manifests itself in many ways other than violence. Exploitation of one's gullibility may be considered a form of psychological aggression, and gullible individuals should be given tools for recognizing and warding off such aggression whenever it occurs. One way is to become better at "reading" social cues indicating that someone may be a predator in disguise (i.e., an exploiter posing as a friend). Another would be to acquire some content-relevant knowledge, such as by learning some of the ploys used by influence agents and the ways in which they distort reality. A third way would be to acquire some defensive verbal ploys to use in various influence situations.

Social intelligence, which has to do with one's ability to think about and make sense of interpersonal situations and phenomena, enters into the gullibility equation in that it helps one to label a situation as exploitative and to recognize an exploiter as "not the friend he pretends to be." The ability to read nonverbal cues, such as facial expression or voice tone, can contribute to an awareness that someone might be lying. Insight into the manipulation games that individuals who coerce others use can also help one recognize when one is being manipulated. Knowledge about social institutions (such as the legal system) can also enable one to know when one is being told a lie (such as when Richard Lapointe was told that failure to cooperate would result in loss of his child).

The relationship between gullibility and social intelligence has been explored most fully by Toshio Yamagishi, a professor of social psychology at Japan's Hokkaido University. Yamagishi (2001; Yamagishi, Kikuchi, & Kosugi, 1999) and colleagues explored the widespread belief among Japanese people "that distrusters are smarter, less gullible, more successful, and more likely to be of the elite than are generalized trusters" (Yamagishi, 2001, p. 121). The results of experimental studies have shown, to the contrary, however "that high trusters are shrewder in potentially risky social interactions than distrusters" (p. 121). Yamagishi attributed this finding to the fact that people low in trust, because of their fear of betrayal, avoid many interactions, thus limiting both their opportunity to learn as well as their opportunity to succeed.

The mistaken common assumption that individuals high in trust are more gullible than those low in trust fails to take into account the fact that people become low in trust because they lack the social intelligence to discriminate who and when to distrust. People with adequate social intelligence are more able to pick up on cues indicating when to distrust someone (as when the other person cheats at a game), and thus are more likely to base their withdrawal of trust on evidence rather than on a global overgeneralization that nobody is to be trusted. People with low social intelligence lack the ability to know when to distrust someone, so they wind up distrusting everyone. This is a vicious circle, in that people who do not trust others deprive themselves of the opportunity to become more socially intelligent as well as the opportunity to engage in potentially beneficial interactions, Furthermore when a person with low social intelligence and low trust does decide to trust someone, he or she is still just as likely as before to demonstrate gullibility, according to Yamagishi. Thus, "socially oblivious and gullible people—those who do not pay proper attention to signs of untrustworthinesss—come to regard everyone as a thief because they often become victims of the 'thieves'" (p. 124). Furthermore, "distrust breeds further distrust because social isolation prevents distrusters from improving their social intelligence and skills in detecting risks in social interactions. There is a mutually reinforcing relationship between generalized distrust and gullibility or lack of social intelligence" (p. 125).

Although gullible people with low social intelligence are more likely to not trust others, Yamagishi (2001) cautioned that people high in social intelligence are not necessarily likely to be very high in trust. This is because socially intelligent people are more confident in their ability to escape nongullibly from high-risk encounters and therefore are more likely to enter into such risky encounters. Because they have a higher frequency of socially risky encounters, they are likely to get burned on occasion, for the simple reason that all human beings have the potential to be victimized by others. Thus, "it is not as certain as in the case of distrust that experiences breed further trust" (pp. 125–126).

Socially intelligent people, those who according to Yamagishi make a conscious effort to learn how to keep from behaving gullibly while still opening themselves up to social opportunities

> need to learn, first, not to be discouraged by isolated incidents of victimization; they need to learn to focus on the gains of successful interactions rather than on a few negative experiences. Distrust breeds on its own, but generalized trust is available only to those who make a conscious effort to develop such a cognitive style as well as the social intelligence to detect risks in social interactions. (p. 126)

This is a message, based on empirical research, that is attractive for a number of reasons. First, it is attractive on moral grounds, in that people who adopt a paranoid and cynical stance to other people are, to me, far less appealing as human beings than those who continue to be open to others even after they are victimized. Second, it is attractive on logical grounds, in that the experience of being victimized only entitles you to draw conclusions about that specific victimizer and not about anyone else. Third, it is attractive on practical grounds, in that the message of Yamagishi's research is that the way to become less gullible is to keep on interacting socially with others, and to look at such encounters not as something to fear but as something to learn from.

DEVELOP A REPERTOIRE OF DISENGAGEMENT TACTICS

A friend of mine, "Joan," mentioned that she wanted to have some psychotherapy and asked for the name of a female therapist. I asked a colleague, who chaired my university's graduate program in counseling psychology, and I passed on the name of the person she recommended. After a couple of months, Joan told me that she felt she had accomplished her goals and wanted to terminate the therapy, but her therapist kept telling her that she wasn't ready and that she still had some issues that she needed to work on. Joan asked for my advice and I suggested she tell her therapist the following:

> It seems as if you have some countertransference issues [where a therapist develops feelings for a client] that you need to work on, but that is your problem, not mine. I shouldn't have to pay for therapy sessions that are more for your benefit than for mine. So I suggest two alternatives. Alternative 1 is that we meet, but you pay me. Alternative 2 is that we meet for a drink sometime and talk over your issues as friends. At any rate, I have gotten what I want out of this therapy and today is the last day that I will be here in a paying capacity.

Joan told me that she followed this script and that the therapist declined (as I expected) either of those alternatives and dropped any further effort to pressure her into staying in therapy.

The applicability of this story to the topic of preventing gullibility is that one very important key to being nongullible is to short-circuit the influence techniques that a victimizer may be using on you by throwing a heuristic (simple verbal tactic) at him or her that serves to disengage you from his or her clutches. The important thing is to frame your communication in a manner that indicates that you have made a firm decision and have no interest in discussing the matter any further. Robert Cialdini (1984) stressed the importance of getting in touch with your own feelings about the exploiter and his or her tactics (by doing a gut-check, so to speak) and then practicing some words that will extract you quickly and easily from a situation you find coercive or unsatisfying.

Although the use of heuristics, instead of formal logic, is a common source of error (and gullibility) in addressing ambiguous cognitive problems, there are times when a heuristic can have the opposite effect. In their book *Simple Heuristics that Make us Smart*, Gigerenzer, Todd and the Adaptive Behavior and Cognition Research Group (1999) of Berlin's Max Planck Institute for Human Development discussed ways in which reliance on heuristics can serve to create the impression and outcome of "smartness" in situations where one might otherwise be confused and in danger of failing. They did not specifically include a discussion of verbal disengagement procedures, but I believe that such disengagement tactics are a good example of a simple heuristic that makes individuals smart in side-stepping any interpersonal ploy that has the intent of sucking them into a relationship or commitment that they wish to avoid. People who have a repertoire of such verbal heuristic tactics are more likely to deal assertively and effectively with a wide range of potential victimizers, whether it is a therapist, a phone solicitor, a scam artist, or a recruiter for the Moonies.

A key to remaining nongullible in dealing with an influence agent, according to Cialdini (1984), is to side-step the victimizer's spider web of coercive ploys before getting ensnared in it. Thus, when a telephone solicitor gets you on the phone (assuming one doesn't use the heuristic of a no-call list or "no soliciting" answering message), a very important heuristic to use is to never answer their opening question: "How are you today, Mrs Jones?" (Research shows that people who answer that question, or who exchange other pleasantries with the solicitor, are much more likely to buy his product.) Instead, put the solicitor on the defensive by asking what he or she is selling, and then interrupt (before he or she can get into his canned speech) with "Thank you for calling, but I'm not interested," followed by a quick hang-up of the phone. Impolite? Perhaps, but then the fact that this person is intruding in your home with an unwanted phone call (often, by intention, around dinner-time) is an act intended to exploit, rather than befriend, and the best way to keep from being exploited is to escape as quickly as possible from the snare.

The most common ploy used by an influence agent is to ask a question ("Wouldn't you like to save hundreds of dollars a year on your insurance bill, Mrs Jones?") and the best heuristic to use is to never respond to such a question.

A very effective way of putting an influence agent on the defensive (and to get you out of a spot where you feel pressured and uncomfortable) is to respond to his or her question not with an answer but with a question of your own. Thus, in response to the question about insurance savings, one might reply "Didn't you know that I'm on my state's no-call list? Didn't you know that ignoring such a list is a punishable offense? Is it the policy of your company to break the law?" If only Richard Lapointe had possessed an escape heuristic (such as "I need to talk to a lawyer") for side-stepping a police interrogation, he would still be a free man, but then I would not have been inspired to write this book.

HELP YOUNG PEOPLE TO BE LESS GULLIBLE

Stuart Vyse (1997), author of a book about magical thinking, suggested that one way to reduce gullibility (in his case, involving paranormal and dubious beliefs) is to expose individuals—for him, college students, but one could see it extended downward to younger ages—to the elements of critical thinking. Although Vyse acknowledged that such instruction may not have dramatic effects, it is likely that a few individuals exposed to such a curriculum would become aware of their need to examine more rigorously the nature of their belief processes. Vyse suggested the use of a modified version of a belief typology first proposed by the great American "pragmatist" philosopher Charles Sanders Peirce. Peirce argued that there are four ways of "fixing knowledge":

1. Tenacity: believing something because one believes it and refuses to give it up.
2. Authority: believing something because someone you respect tells you to believe it.
3. Intuition (termed *a priori* by Peirce): believing something because it feels right in your gut
4. The scientific method: believing something because it passes the test of evidence and reason.

Because there is no single scientific method, and because it usually involves some combination of the following two elements, Vyse divided the scientific method into two categories: empiricism (seeing whether an idea has evidence to support it) and logic (seeing whether an idea makes sense in terms of theory and formal reasoning).

Vyse had obvious preference for the last two methods—empiricism and logic—although he noted that some reliance on authority is unavoidable because most of us lack the scientific credentials to conduct our own experiments, or to understand the reigning theories, in all areas of knowledge. We are, thus, dependent on authority for some of our beliefs, for example that cigarettes cause cancer or that an electrical current is made up of moving electrons. When relying on authority, therefore, the key is to learn how to tell the difference between an authority who is trustworthy and one who is not. People who believe (as more than 90% of college students do) that cigarette smoking increases one's risk of cancer are lucky in that particular choice of authority. However, those who believe (as a small but significant percentage of the population does) that the most effective treatment for cancer is prayer or folk healing, rather than medicine, are showing what most would consider excessive trust on dubious authority and unfortunate faith in their own intuition. Vyse teaches students that there is nothing wrong with relying on authority or intuition in areas that are not subject to empirical testing (such as belief in God), but it is important to learn that (a) such belief is not the same thing as a proved reality; and (b) blind faith, where verification of a belief is possible, can get one in serious trouble.

Considerable research evidence (e.g., Baumrind, 1967) shows that socially competent children are more likely to have been exposed to parental discipline styles that encourage both good behavior and the ability to function autonomously. In particular, competent parents always allow for the child's expression of independent feelings and thoughts, even when setting limits on inappropriate behaviors (Ginott, 1965/2003; Greenspan, 1978).

Religion-based childrearing "experts," such as James Dobson (1982) and John Rosemond (1991) espouse an obedience-centered brand of discipline advice, supposedly derived from scripture, that emphasizes the single domain of parental control. This style of discipline is essentially coercive, and typically results in either rebellion (chaotic coercion is the most common discipline style in families of delinquents) or else in abject abandonment of autonomy. Given the value placed on influencing children to buy into their fundamentalist religious views, it is not a concern to the religious right if a child's need for autonomy is undermined. The downside of such an outcome, however, is that autonomy is necessary for the development of adult social competence in general and for gullibility resistance in particular. The increased gullibility of children whose autonomy is undermined helps to explain, of course, why most of the children of fundamentalists come to hold religious beliefs identical to those held by their parents.

CULTIVATE SKEPTICISM, BUT NOT CYNICISM

I mentioned once to Harold, the friend mentioned earlier who falls constantly for quack medical remedies and diagnostic methods, that the scientific method is based on a demand for evidence and that he should think about being a little more scientific (i.e., skeptical) about unverified claims. Harold replied that "the scientific method is what is wrong with the world and with people like you." I suppose what he was saying is that by being skeptical I am cutting myself off from various mystical and creative aspects of the human experience. That is certainly a possibility, but I think that Harold may have been overreacting to the word "skepticism" (and to my implicit criticism of him) and assuming that I meant something other than what I actually meant.

I believe that Harold is confusing skepticism with cynicism and thinks that I am saying that one should never believe in anyone or anything. In fact, Harold is probably much more cynical than I am (he sees the evil hand of conspirators everywhere). His cynicism, ironically, contributes to his gullibility, in that he champions alternative medicine in part as a way of saying "screw you" to the more mainstream medical establishment. To my mind, a knee-jerk reaction of "no" (the cynical stance) is no more justified than a knee-jerk reaction of "yes" (the gullible stance) and the essence of skepticism is nothing more than saying "I will maintain an open mind but I want to get a better understanding of the truth of the matter before I commit myself." However, the evidence is often ambiguous and incomplete, and the skeptic is someone who holds out for a higher and more rigorous standard of proof (and of one's own understanding) than the fact that you like someone or want what he says to be true.

Perhaps what Harold was really saying is "I pity people who do not believe in magic." Skeptics are people who believe that the laws of nature and probability underlie all phenomena, and are dubious about claims that there are realms of functioning that are immune from such laws. Harold definitely believes in magic (the real, not the conjuring, kind) and his evidence for this belief is likely to take such a form as "I was thinking about an old friend and the next thing I knew I got a phone call from her." Harold is not likely to be persuaded by the argument that "you thought of 500 other things or people during the same day without such a congruence, but you are focusing on a single congruence that confirms your belief in magic and then holding it up as proof that it couldn't have been a coincidence."

Belief in magic is an intellectually lazy stance to take, as one can absolve oneself of any obligation to master complex reality by passing it off to forces that are unknowable. Belief in magic contributes to gullibility as one can be too easily influenced by misleading external realities or superficial explanations. Just as Harold pities me for not being more intuitive, I pity him for not being more rational. People who eschew skepticism are people at the mercy of charlatans, bogus experts, and false claims. Although I generally admire and like people who are trusting more than people who are distrusting, I think trust needs to be tempered with an understanding that it can be misplaced. Blind trust can be a formula for disaster, as countless stories in this book illustrate. One needs to be alert to warning signs of untruth, whether or not it emanates from conscious deception. To refuse to heed those signs, and to refuse to ask for proof when proof is needed, may be to put oneself in harm's way.

An example of how cynicism is compatible with gullibility can be found in the life of Joseph Stalin, the ruthless dictator who ruled the Soviet Union through periodic murder sprees for several decades. In a review of Simon Sebag Montefiore's (2005) *Stalin: The Court of the Red Tsar*, Ian Buruma (2004) described Stalin, and the equally murderous ruler of China, Mao Zedong, as extraordinarily cynical, that is motivated by power rather than Communist ideology, and generally distrusting of everyone, including family members. There was one area, however, in which both Stalin and Mao were overly trusting, and that had to do with agriculture policy. Driven by an emotional commitment to the notion that Marxism–Leninism had made possible a "creative Darwinism," both men "appear to have been completely taken in by the crackpot science of Trofim Lysenko" (p. 5). Lysenko's experiments in high-yield wheat proved to be a complete disaster in both countries, "but these failures were blamed on 'saboteurs' and 'bourgeois scientists', many of whom were killed, even as people were dying of hunger in far greater numbers than ever. Such things might not have happened if Stalin and Mao had been complete skeptics. But they were gullible as well as cynical, and that is why millions had to die" (Buruma, 2004, p. 6).

GULLIBILITY CAN DECREASE AS ONE BECOMES OLDER AND WISER

The field of psychology, reflecting its early clinical emphasis, has tended to focus on human deficits, symptoms, and illnesses. There have, however, been periodic calls, such as by Abraham Maslow (1954), for the development of a psychology that looks at more positive aspects of human functioning. These calls finally seem to have borne fruit in a burgeoning movement known either as "positive psychology" (Snyder & Lopez, 2002) or "the psychology of human strengths" (Aspinwall & Staudinger, 2003). The emphasis within positive psychology has been on the generation of lists of positive human traits, such as the tentative list proposed by Seligman and Csikszentmihalyi (2000). Psychologists writing about human strengths have also fallen into the list-generation trap, but they seem to have made more of an effort to develop general action models for understanding how people can maintain strength in the face of environmental forces pulling for weakness.

Although gullibility is a human weakness, its investigation has obvious implications for the field of positive psychology. That is because the ability to resist deceptive social predators would appear to be an important human strength, one with important implications for personal survival and happiness. One will look in vain on the lists of positive psychologists, however, for any mention of this strength (under a rubric such as "gullibility resistance" or "healthy skepticism"), although Seligman and Csikszentmihalyi (2000) did include such relevant contributory skills as "personal intelligence" and "courage." Although gullibility resistance has not yet made it into the positive psychology shopping lists, there has been some discussion of personality processes that could, with minor modification, be used to understand why some people are better able than others to resist gullibility-induction ploys.

Mischel and Mendoza-Denton (2003) noted that the positive psychology movement is a useful departure from the view of persons as prisoners of their biology or as solely "pushed by impulses and conflicts from within (as in Freudian theory) or as pulled by rewards and incentives from external sources that control behavior (as in classic behaviorism)" (p. 246). They raised the alarm, however, that positive psychology needs "to move beyond a rosy emphasis on the positive, which risks becoming a 'spin' more than a deep and useful perspective on human nature. The challenge will be to illuminate those psychological processes that enable positive functioning, strength, and well-being" (p. 253). Mischel and Mendoza-Denton argued that "people can transform external stimulus conditions and, by changing the ways they represent those stimuli cognitively, overcome their power to activate automatic, reflexive reactions" (p. 246).

Mischel and Mendoza-Denton recognized that willpower in an immediate appetitive temptation situation (such as resisting an offer of a piece of chocolate) is a far simpler matter than "the pursuit of long-term goals requiring sustained self-regulatory effort" (p. 253), but they stated their belief that "the ability to encode setbacks and successes in relation to the contexts in which they unfold can serve as a buffer against overly emotional, hot reactions, potentially preventing people from becoming derailed and helping them achieve their goals" (p. 253).

The problem of gullibility resistance has some formal similarities to the self-regulatory illustrations used by Mischel and Mendoza-Denton. In a gullibility scenario, the temptation is posed by a deceptive manipulator and by the ideas or actions that he or she attempts to promote, and successful adaptation depends on the ability to convert the affective (hot) schemas activated by the stimuli to the cognitive (cold) schemas necessary for seeing through the deception and coming to the correct conclusion to resist that temptation. A complicating aspect of the gullibility problem, as mentioned earlier, is that the truth of the situation may not as easy to discern as the truth, for example, that "eating too many chocolates is bad for you."

One positive psychology trait that has obvious implications for the development of gullibility resistance is "wisdom." An elusive construct (because it has proved difficult to define adequately), wisdom has been much studied by psychologists in recent years, especially by researchers interested in aging and adult development. This is because wisdom is one aspect of human functioning where older people are supposedly better off than younger people, and where one is believed to continue to improve throughout much of the end-of-life period.

Wisdom has been defined by Paul B. Baltes and Alexandra M. Freund (2003) of Germany's Max Planck Institute for Human Development as the possession of "knowledge of fundamental pragmatics of life and implementation of that knowledge through the life management strategies of selection, optimization and compensation" (p. 23). The term *pragmatics of life* refers to aspects of functioning in the everyday world. *Selection* refers to the process of focusing on a particular goal, *optimization* refers to the efficient marshalling of resources needed to attain that goal, and *compensation* refers to the use of alternative means when preferred or habitual means are no longer available. Wisdom, in Baltes and Freund's view, involves "general knowledge about means-end relationships, or which means best serves to achieve a given goal in a specific person-context constellation" (p. 31). Because wisdom, in practice, mainly touches on an understanding of means–end relationships in interpersonal contexts, I would amend Baltes' definition to read: "the possession of insights about human relationships and social institutions, acquired through experience, that contribute to choosing the best course of action in tricky interpersonal situations."

An aspect of wisdom that is not part of Baltes and Freund's formal definition (although they mention it in passing in their discussion of optimization), is that wisdom almost always involves seeing the hidden dangers in a situation. When someone gives us "wise counsel," it is usually along the lines of "I think you should pass on that risky opportunity" or "I don't think that sending that angry letter is such a good idea." Thus, when dealing with a very angry person, in almost all cases, a wise person would counsel walking away (no matter how in-the-right one might feel) rather than saying something that might escalate or maintain the conflict.

This ability of a wise person to substitute cool for hot courses of action is similar to the self-regulatory model proposed by Mischel and Mendoza-Denton (2003) and has obvious implications for gullibility resistance, in that a wise person is likely to counsel against getting involved in a dubious course of action. Part of wisdom is, thus, the ability to keep things in perspective and to see the pitfalls lurking behind temptations. Thus, if late President Kennedy had possessed as much wisdom as he did intelligence, he would have said "this is a bad idea" to his advisers, and the United States would have avoided the twin fiascos of the Bay of Pigs and the Vietnam War. Ditto for George W. Bush and Iraq.

Because gullibility resistance increases as a function of wisdom acquired in the course of human experience, I am optimistic about my own, and others', ability to become less gullible. As one accumulates experience with people, their schemes, and their foibles, one can acquire the ability to recognize some idea or proposed action as possibly unwise. The ability to hold off being influenced by someone selling a false notion is an ability that can, I think, increase with age and experience. Obviously, that will not always be the case, especially where there is cognitive impairment or where the social pressure is too great or where a scheme calls forth a strong emotion (such as greed) or where the victim has a personality in which dysfunctional schemas are too entrenched and where there is, consequently, an inability to learn from past mistakes.

Duping is a part of human nature as is gullibility, but one lesson from the study of gullibility is that many people can learn, if they are truly motivated, to function in the world with a healthy balance of trust and skepticism. Thus becoming less gullible can be seen as part of a broader acquisition of interpersonal wisdom.

References

Abbott, J.H. (1981). *In the belly of the beast: Letters from prison*. New York: Random House.

Adler, J.E. (2002). *Belief's own ethics*. Cambridge, MA: MIT/ Bradford.

Aspinwall, L.G., & Staudinger, U.M. (Eds.). (2003). *A psychology of human strengths: Fundamental questions and future directions for a positive psychology*. Washington, DC: American Psychological Association.

Aylseworth, J. (2001). *The tale of tricky fox*. New York: Scholastic Press.

Baldwin, N. (2001). *Henry Ford and the Jews: The mass production of hate*. New York: Public Affairs.

Baltes, P.B.., & Freund, A.M. (2003). Human strengths as the orchestration of wisdom and selective optimization with compensation. In L. G. Aspinwall & U. M. Staudinger (Eds.), *A psychology of human strengths.: Fundamental questions and future directions for a positive psychology* (pp. 23–35). Washington, DC: American Psychological Association.

Bartels, L. (2004, January 3). Disabled woman lost at DIA for hours: Flight info changed, family grew frantic. *Rocky Mountain News*. (p. B-7)

Barthel, J.A. (1977). *A death in Canaan*. New York: Dutton.

Baumeister, R.F. (2001). Ego depletion, the executive function, and self-control: An energy model of the self in personality. In B.R. Roberts & R. Hogan (Eds.), *Personality psychology in the workplace* (pp. 299–316). Washington, DC: American Psychological Association.

Baumeister, R.F., Hetherton, T.F., &., & Tice, D.M. (1994). *Losing control: How and why people fail at self-regulation*. San Diego: Academic Press.

Baumrind, D. (1967). Child care practices anteceding three patterns of preschool behavior. *Genetic Psychology Monographs, 75*, 43–88.

Becker, E. (1973). *The denial of death*. New York: Simon & Schuster.

Bird, A. (2005). *Blood brother: 33 reasons my brother Scott Peterson is guilty*. New York: HarperCollins.

Bird, S. E. (1992). *For Enquiring minds: A cultural study of supermarket tabloids*. Knoxville: University of Tennessee press.

Bjorklund, D.F. (Ed.). (2002). *False-memory creation in children and adults: Theory, research, and implications*. Mahwah, NJ: Erlbaum.

Blagrove, M. (1996). Effects of sleep deprivation on interrogative suggestibility. *Journal of Experimental Psychology, 2* (1), 48–59.

Boyle, F. (2000). *Swift as nemesis: Modernity and its satirist*. Stanford, CA: Stanford University Press.

Brodie, R. (1996). *Virus of the mind: The new science of the meme*. Seattle: Integral Press.

Bronner, S.E. (2000). *A rumor about the Jews: Reflections on antisemitism and the Protocols of the Learned Elders of Zion*. New York: St. Martin's Press.

Brown, F., & McDonald, J. (2000). *The serpent handlers: Three families and their faith*. Winston-Salem, NC: J.F. Blair.

Buckley, W.F., Jr. (1985). *Right reason: A collection*. New York: Doubleday & Co.

Buruma, I. (2004, May 13). Master of fear. *New York Review of Books*, pp. 4–6.

Byrne, R., & Whiten, R. (1987). *Machiavellian intelligence: Social expertise and evolution of intellect in monkeys, apes and humans*. Oxford, UK: Oxford University Press.

Cantor, N. (2000). Life task problem-solving: Situational affordances personality needs. In E.T. Higgins & A.W. Kruglanski (Eds.), *Motivational science: Social and personality perspectives* (pp. 100–110). Philadelphia: Psychology Press.

Cantor, N. (2003). Constructive cognition, personal goals and the social embedding of personality. In L.G. Aspinwall & U.M. Staudinger (Eds.), *A psychology of human strengths: Fundamental questions and future directions for a positive psychology* (pp. 49–60). Washington, DC: American Psychological Association.

Carroll, N. (Ed.). (2000). *Theories of art today*. Madison: University of Wisconsin Press.

Casanova, N. (1999). *The Machiavellian's guide to womanizing*. New York: Castle Books.

Cather, W., & Milmine, G. (1993). *The life of Mary Baker G. Eddy and the history of Christian Science*. Lincoln: University of Nebraska Press. (Original work published 1909)

Ceci, S.J., & Bruck, M. (1995). *Jeopardy in the courtroom: A scientific analysis of children's testimony*. Washington, DC: American Psychological Association.

Ceci, S.J., Toglia, M.P., & Ross, D.F. (1987). *Children's eyewitness memory*. New York: Springer-Verlag.

Cialdini, R.B. (1984). *Influence: The psychology of persuasion*. New York: William Morrow.

Close, F. (1991). *Too hot to handle: The race for cold fusion*. Princeton, NJ: Princeton University Press.

Cole, J. (Ed.). (1983). *Best-loved folktales of the world*. New York: Anchor Books.

Collins, H., & Pinch, T. (1993). *The golem: What you should know about science*. New York: Cambridge University Press.

Collodi, C. (1968). *Pinocchio* (J. Walker, Trans., W. Dempster, Illustr.). Santa Rosa, CA: Classic Press. (Original work published 1881)

Connery, D.S. (1977). *Guilty until proven innocent.* New York: Putnam.

Connery, D.S. (1996). *Convicting the innocent: The story of a murder, a false confession, and the struggle to free a "wrong man."* Cambridge, MA: Brookline Books.

Connery, D.S. (2003). *The inner source: Exploring hypnosis.* New York: Allworth Communications. (Original work published 1982)

Cremin, L.A. (1970). *American education: The colonial period, 1607–1783.* New York: Harper & Row.

Dallek, R. (2003). *An Unfinished Life: John F. Kennedy, 1917–1963.* Boston: Little Brown.

Davidson, K. (2004, March 17). Lack of weapons of mass destruction comes back to haunt Bush. *San Francisco Chronicle.* (p. A-1)

Dawkins, R. (2003). *A devil's chaplain: Reflections on hope, lies, science and love.* New York: Houghton Mifflin.

Deci, E., & Ryan, R.M. (2002). *Handbook of self-determination research.* Rochester, NY: University of Rochester Press.

DeJonge, A. (1982). *The life and times of Grigorii Rasputin.* New York: Putnam.

Demi. (2000). *The emperor's new clothes: A tale set in China told by Demi.* New York: Simon & Schuster.

Dershowitz, A. M. (2000). *The genesis of justice: Ten stories of biblical injustice that led to the Ten Commandments and modern law.* New York: Warner Books.

Dethridge, L. (2003). *Writing your screenplay.* Crows Nest, Australia: Allen & Unwin.

Dixon, N. (1976). *On the psychology of military incompetence.* London: Jonathan Cape.

Dobson, J. (1982). *Dare to discipline.* New York: Bantam Books.

Donovan, P. (2004). *No way of knowing: Crime, urban legends, and the Internet.* New York: Routledge.

Ducat, S. (1988). *Taken in: America gullibility and the Reagan mythos.* Tacoma, WA: Life Sciences Press.

Dundes, A. (Ed.). (1991). *The blood libel legend: A casebook in anti-Semitic folklore.* Madison: University of Wisconsin Press.

Eaton, M.M. (2000). Sustainable definition of "art." In N. Carroll (Ed.), *Theories of art today* (pp. 141–159). Madison: University of Wisconsin Press.

Eberle, P., & Eberle, S. (1993). *The abuse of innocence: The McMartin preschool trial.* Buffalo, NY: Prometheus Books.

Editors of *Lingua Franca.* (2000). *The Sokal Hoax: The sham that shook the academy.* Lincoln: University of Nebraska Press.

Editors of *The New York Times.* (2004, March 26). *The Times and Iraq.* (editorial available at www. mtholyoke.edu/acad/intrel/iraq/times.htm).

Ekman, P. (2001). *Telling lies: Clues to deceit in the marketplace, politics and marriage.* New York: W.W. Norton.

Ellis, A. & Harper, R.A. (1966). *A guide to rational living.* Chatsworth, CA: Wilshire Book Co.

Ferris, T. (1997, April 14). The wrong stuff. *The New Yorker,* p. 31.

Festinger, L., Riecken, H.W., & Schacter, S. (1956). *When prophecy fails.* Minneapolis: University of Minnesota Press.

Forer, B. R. (1949). The fallacy of personal validation: A classroom demonstration of gullibility. *Journal of Abnormal and Social Psychology, 44*, 118–123.

Frankel, M. (2004, February 29). Reading Alger Hiss's mind: A legal scholar attempts to fathom a truly impenetrable lie. *New York Times Book Review*, p. 23.

Forgas, J.P. (Ed.). (2001). *Feeling and thinking: The role of affect in social cognition.* Cambridge, UK: Cambridge University Press.

Frijda, N., Manstead, A.S.R., & Bem, S. (2000). *Emotions and beliefs: How feelings influence thoughts.* Cambridge, UK: Cambridge University Press.

Furedi, F. (2002a). *Culture of fear: Risk-taking and the morality of low expectation* (rev. ed.). London: Continuum.

Furedi, F. (2002b). *Paranoid parenting: Why ignoring the experts may be best for your child.* Chicago: Chicago Review Press.

Gardner, H. (1983). *Frames of mind.* New York: Basic Books.

Gardner, M. (1993). *The healing revelations of Mary Baker Eddy: The rise and fall of Christian Science.* Buffalo: Prometheus Books.

Gaylin, W. (1982). *The killing of Bonnie Garland.* New York: Penguin.

Gaylin, W. (2003). *Hatred: The psychological descent into violence.* New York: Public Affairs.

Gaylin, W., & Jennings, B. (1996). *The perversion of autonomy: Coercion and constraints in a liberal society.* New York: The Free Press.

Gigerenzer, G., Todd, P.M., and the ABC Research Group. (1999). *Simple heuristics that make us smart.* New York: Oxford University Press.

Ginott, H.G. (2003). *Between parent and child: The bestselling classic that revolutionized parent–child communication* (revised and updated by A. Ginott & W. Goddard). New York: Three Rivers Press. (Original work published 1965)

Glassner, B. (1999). *The culture of fear: Why Americans are afraid of the wrong things.* New York: Basic Books.

Goleman, D. (1985). *Vital lies, simple truths: The psychology of self-deception.* New York: Simon & Schuster.

Goleman, D. (1995). *Emotional intelligence: Why it can matter more than IQ.* NY: Bantam Books.

Greenberg, C. (1999). *Homemade esthetics: Observations on art and taste.* New York: Oxford University Press.

Greenspan, S. (1978). Maternal affect-allowance and limit-setting appropriateness as predictors of social adjustment. *Genetic Psychology Monographs, 98*, 83–111.

Greenspan, S. (1999). A contextualist perspective on adaptive behavior. In R. Schalock (Ed.), *Adaptive behavior: Conceptual basis, measurement and use* (pp. 61–80). Washington, DC: American Association on Mental Retardation.

Greenspan, S. (2004). Credulity and gullibility among service providers: An attempt to understand why snake oil sells. In J. Jacobson, R.M. Foxx, & J.A. Mulick (Eds.), *Controversial therapies for developmental disabilities: Fads, fashion, and science in professional practice* (pp. 129–138). Mahwah, NJ: Erlbaum.

Greenspan, S. (2009). Foolish action in adults with intellectual disabilities: The forgotten problem of risk-unawareness. In L.M. Glidden (Ed.), *International review of Research in Mental Retardation*, vol. 36 (pp. 145–194). New York: Elsevier.

Greenspan, S., & Driscoll, J. (1997). The role of intelligence in a broad model of personal competence. In D.P. Flanagan, J.L. Genshaft, & P.L. Harrison (Eds.), *Contemporary intellectual assessment: Theories, tests and issues*. New York: Guilford.

Greenspan, S., Loughlin, G., & Black, R.S. (2001). Credulity and gullibility in people with developmental disorders: A framework for future research. In L.M. Glidden (Ed.), *International review of research in mental retardation* (Vol. 24, pp. 101–135). New York: Academic Press.

Grisso, T. (Ed.). (2003). *Evaluating competencies: Forensic assessments and instruments*. New York: Kluwer Academic/Plenum Publishers.

Gudjonsson, G. (1992). *The psychology of interrogations, confessions and testimony*. London: Wiley.

Harrison, B.G. (1978). *Visions of glory: A history and a memory of Jehovah's Witnesses*. New York: Simon & Schuster.

Hersh, S. M. (1998). *The dark side of Camelot*. Boston: Little Brown.

Hesketh, R. (2002). *Fortitude: The D-Day deception campaign*. New York: Overlook Press.

Hollander, P. (1981). *Political pilgrims: Travels of Western intellectuals to the Soviet Union*. Oxford, UK: Oxford University Press.

Hook, S., Bukovsky, B.K., & Hollander, P. (1987). *Soviet hypocrisy and Western gullibility*. Lanham, MD: University Press of America.

Howarth, L. (1986). *Autonomy: A study in philosophical psychology and ethics*. New Haven, CT: Yale University Press.

Huizenga, J. R. (1992). *Cold fusion: The scientific fiasco of the century*. Rochester, NY: University of Rochester Press.

Hunt, I. (1986). *Across five Aprils*. Saddle River, NJ: Prentice-Hall. (Original work published 1965)

Hunter, J.P. (2003). *Gulliver's Travels* and the later writings. In C. Fox (Ed.), *The Cambridge companion to Jonathan Swift* (pp. 216–240). Cambridge, UK: Cambridge University Press.

Hyman, R. (2002). Why and when are smart people stupid? In R.J. Sternberg (Ed.), *Why smart people can be so stupid* (pp. 1–23). New Haven, CT: Yale University Press.

Inbau, F.E., Reid, J.E., & Buckley, J.P. (1986). *Criminal interrogation and confessions*. Baltimore: Williams & Wilkins.

Janis, I.L. (1980). *Groupthink: Psychological studies of policy decisions and fiascos* (2nd ed.). New York: Houghton Mifflin.

Jay, R. (2001). *Jay's journal of anomalies: Conjurers, cheats, hustlers, pranksters, jokesters, imposters, pretenders, sideshow showmen, armless calligraphers, mechanical marvels, popular entertainments*. New York: Farrar, Straus & Giroux.

Johnston, J. (1974). *Gullibles travels: Writings*. New York: Links Books.

Jones, W., Bellugi, U., Lai, Z., et al. (2001). Hypersociability: The social and affective phenotype of Williams syndrome. In U. Bellugi & M. St. George (Eds.), *Journey from cognition to brain to gene: Perspectives from Williams syndrome* (pp. 43–71): Cambridge, MA: MIT Press.

Joseph, A., Jr. (1995). *We get confessions*. Rochester, NY: A. J. Book.

Kallman, M. (1981). Monoideism in psychiatry: Theoretical and clinical implications. *American Journal of* Psychiatry 35, 235–243.

Kanfer, S. (2001). *Groucho: The life and times of Julius Henry Marx*. New York: Random House.

Kinney, D. (1999, January 18). Two charged for hanging, torturing girl for snitching. *Laredo Morning Times*, p. 7.

Kosko, B. (1993). *Fuzzy thinking: The new science of fuzzy logic*. New York: Hyperion Books.

Kressel, N.J., & Kressel, D.F. (2002). *Stack and sway: The new science of jury consulting*. Boulder, CO: Westview.

Lakoff, G. (2002). *Moral politics: How liberals and conservatives think*. Chicago: The University of Chicago Press.

Langenderfer, J., & Shimp, T.A. (2001). Consumer vulnerability to scams, swindles and fraud: A new theory of visceral influences on persuasion. *Psychology and Marketing, 18*, 763–783.

Langmuir, I. (1989). Pathological Science (lecture presented at the Knolls Atomic Power laboratory of General Electric). *Physics Today*. (Original work published 1953)

Lardner, R.W. (1965). *Gullible's Travels, etc.* Chicago: University of Chicago Press. (Original work published 1925)

Latimer, J. (2001). *Deception in war: The art of the bluff, the value of deceit, and the most thrilling episodes of cunning in military history, from the Trojan horse to the Gulf War*. New York: The Overlook Press.

Layne, C. (1979). The Barnum effect: Rationality versus gullibility? *Journal of Consulting and Clinical Psychology, 47*, 219–221.

Leach, R. A. (1994). *The chiropractic theories: Principles and clinical applications* (3rd ed.). Baltimore: Williams & Wilkins.

Lefkowitz, B. (1997). *Our guys: The Glen Ridge rape and the secret life of the perfect suburb*. New York: Vintage.

Lewis, M. (2001). *New new thing: A Silicon Valley story*. New York: Penguin Group.

Lobe, J. (2004, May 12). *Chickenhawk Groupthink? Inter Press Service* (http://www.commondreams.org/headlines04/0512-02.htm).

Louis, F.D. (1981). *Swift's anatomy of misunderstanding: A study of Swift's epistemological imagination in A Tale of a Tub and Gulliver's Travels*. Totowa, NJ: Barnes & Noble Books.

Lykken, D.T. (1981). *A tremor in the blood: Uses and abuses of the lie detector*. New York: McGraw-Hill.

Maccoby, H. (1992). *Judas Iscariot and the myth of Jewish evil*. New York: The Free Press.

Machiavelli, N. (1995). *The prince and other political writings* (S. J. Milner, Trans.). London: J. M. Dent. (Original work published 1516)

Mackay, C. (1996). *Extraordinary popular delusions and the madness of crowds* (M.S. Fridson, Ed.). New York: Wiley. (Original work published 1841)

Maddox, J., Randi, J., & Stewart, W.W. (1988). "High-dilution" experiments a delusion. *Nature, 334*(6180), 287–290.

Malcolm, J. (1984). *In the Freud archives*. New York: Knopf.

Malcolm, J. (1990). *The journalist and the murderer*. New York: Knopf

Malcolm, J. (1999). *The crime of Sheila McGough*. New York: Knopf.

Mann, R. (2001). *A grand delusion: America's descent into Vietnam*. New York: Basic Books.

Maslow, A. (1954). *Motivation and personality*. New York: Harpers.

Masson, J.M. (1984). *The assault on truth: Freud's suppression of the seduction theory*. New York: Farrar, Straus & Giroux.

McCoy, R. (2000). *Quack: Tales of medical fraud from the museum of questionable medical practices*. Santa Monica, CA: Santa Monica Press.

McDonald, P. (1993). *Make 'em talk: Principles of military interrogation*. Boulder, CO: Paladin Press.

Miller, M.J. (1986). Counselor gullibility. *Counselor Education and Supervision, 26*, 103–107.

Mischel, W. (2007). Toward a cognitive social learning theory reconceptualization of personality. In Y. Shoda, D. Cervone, & G. Downey (Eds.), *Persons in context: Building a science of the individual* (pp. 278–326). New York: Guilford.

Mischel, W., & Mendoza-Denton, R. (2003). Harnessing willpower and socioemotional intelligence to enhance human agency and potential. In L.G. Aspinwall & U.M. Staudinger (Eds.), *A psychology of human strengths.: Fundamental questions and future directions for a positive psychology* (pp. 245–256). Washington, DC: American Psychological Association.

Montefiore, S.S. (2005). *Stalin: The Court of the Red Tsar*. New York: Knopf.

Moore, J.S. (1993). *Chiropractic in America: The history of a medical alternative*. Baltimore: Johns Hopkins University Press.

Moore, J.W. (2002). *The internet weather: Balancing continuous change and constant truths*. New York: Wiley.

Moye, J. (2003). Guardianship and conservatorship. In T. Grisso (Ed.), *Evaluating competencies: Forensic assessments and instruments* (pp. 309–389). New York: Kluwer Academic/ Plenum Publishers.

Munraven, M.R., & Baumeister, R.F. (2000). Self-regulation and depletion of limited resources: Does self-control resemble a muscle? *Psychological Bulletin, 126*, 247–259.

Munraven, M.R., Tice, D.M., & Baumeister, R.F. (1998). Self-control as limited resource: Regulatory depletion patterns. *Journal of Personality and Social Psychology, 74*, 774–789.

Nash, J. R. (1976). *Hustlers and con men: An anecdotal history of the confidence man and his games*. New York: M. Evans.

Neusner, J. (1986). *Reading and believing: Ancient Judaism and contemporary gullibility* (Brown Judaic Studies, no. 113). Atlanta: Scholars Press.

Nuttall, A.D. (1995). Gulliver among the horses. In C. Rawson (Ed.), *Jonathan Swift: A collection of critical essays* (pp. 264–279). Englewood Cliffs, NJ: Prentice-Hall.

O'Grady, J. (1989). *The prince of darkness: The devil in history, religion and the human psyche.* New York: Barnes & Noble Books.

Olshansky, S. (1962). Chronic sorrow: A response to having a mentally defective child. *Social Casework, 43*, 190–193.

Pagels, E. (1995). *The origin of Satan.* New York: Random House.

Paladin Press. (1991). *Interrogation: Techniques and tricks to secure evidence.* Boulder, CO: Author.

Patey, D.L. (1995). Swift's satire on "science" and the structure of *Gulliver's Travels.* In C. Rawson (Ed.), *Jonathan Swift: A collection of critical essays* (pp. 216–240). Englewood Cliffs, NJ: Prentice-Hall.

Peters, C. (2003). *Gullible's travels: The adventures of a bad taste tourist.* Guilford, CT: The Globe Pequot Press.

Piaget, J. (1969). *The child's conception of the world.* Totowa, NJ: Littlefield Adams. (Original work published 1926)

Piattelli-Parmarini, M. (1994). *Inevitable illusions: How mistakes of reason rule our Minds.* New York: Wiley.

Pinsker, D.M., Stone, V., Pachana, N., & Greenspan, S. (2006). Social vulnerability scale for older adults: Validation study. *Clinical Psychology, 10*(3), 117–127.

Pittman, F. (1989). *Private lies: Infidelity and the betrayal of intimacy.* New York: Norton.

Pivcevic, E. (1997). *What is truth?* Aldershot, UK: Ashgate.

Pollan, M. (2001). *The botany of desire: A plant's-eye view of the world.* New York: Random House.

Prados, J. (2004). *Hoodwinked: The documents that reveal how Bush sold us a war.* New York: The New Press.

Press, B. (2001). *Spin this: All the ways we don't tell the truth.* New York: Pocket Books.

Rayner, R. (2002, April 22 & 29). The admiral and the con man. *The New Yorker,* pp. 150–161.

Ricks, T.E. (2006). *Fiasco: The American military adventure in Iraq.* New York: Penguin.

Rix, B. (Ed.). (1996). *Gullible's travails.* London: Andre Deutsch.

Rosemond, J. (1991). *Parent power: A common-sense approach to parenting in the '90s and beyond.* Kansas City: Andrews McNeel Publishing.

Rosner, B. (2002). Empathy and personal distress in young people with Williams syndrome. *Dissertation Abstracts International, 62*, 5390.

Rotter, J. B. (1980). Interpersonal trust, trustworthiness and gullibility. *American Psychologist, 35*, 1–7.

Rourke, B.P. (1989). *Nonverbal learning disabilities: The syndrome and the model.* New York: Guilford Press.

Rourke, B.P., Young, C. & Leenars, A.A. (1989). A childhood learning disability that predisposes those afflicted to adolescent and adult depression and suicide. *Journal of Learning Disabilities, 22*, 169–174.

Rue, L. (1994). *By the grace of guile: The role of deception in natural history and human affairs*. New York: Oxford University Press.

Sartre, J.P. (1953). *The existential psychoanalysis* (H.E. Barnes, Trans.). New York: Philosophical Library.

Saulny, S. (2005, September 1). Goodbye therapist, hello anxiety? *New York Times*.

Schiller, R.J. (2001). *Irrational exuberance*. New York: Broadway Books.

Schleicher, B.J., & Baumeister, R.F. (2004). Self-regulatory strength. In R.F. Baumeister & K.D. Vohs (Eds.), *Handbook of self-regulation: Research, theory and applications* (pp. 84–98). New York: Guilford.

Schumaker, J. F. (1990). *Wings of illusion: The origins, nature and future of paranormal belief*. Buffalo, NY: Prometheus Books.

Schutze, J. (1997). *Bully: Does anyone deserve to die? A true story of high school revenge*. New York: William Morrow.

Seidel, M. (2004, May 14, 2004). Personal communication. New York: Columbia University.

Seligman, M.E.P., & Csikszentmihalyi, M. (2000). Positive psychology: An introduction. *American Psychologist, 55*, 5–14.

Shermer, M. (1997). *Why people believe weird things: Pseudoscience, superstition, and other confusions of our time*. New York: W.H. Freeman.

Shermer, M. (2001). *How we believe: The search for God in an age of science*. New York: W.H. Freeman.

Shermer, M. (2002). *The borderlands of science: Where sense meets nonsense*. New York: Oxford University Press.

Shibutani, T. (1966). *Improvised news: A sociological study of rumor*. Indianapolis: Irvington Publishers.

Showalter, E. (1997). *Hystories: Hysterical epidemics and modern media*. New York: Columbia University Press.

Shuy, R.W. (1998). *The language of confession, interrogation, and deception*. Thousand Oaks, CA: Sage.

Silverman, K. (1996). *Houdini !!! :The career of Ehrich Weiss*. New York: HarperCollins.

Sloan, B. (2001). *I watched a wild hog eat my baby: A colorful history of tabloids and their cultural impact*. Amherst, NY: Prometheus Books.

Smith, E. (1968). *Brief against death*. New York: Knopf.

Snyder, C.R., & Lopez, S.J. (Eds.). (2002). *Handbook of positive psychology*. New York: Oxford University Press.

Spiegel H., Spiegel D. (1978/2004). *Trance and Treatment: Clinical Uses of Hypnosis*. New York; Basic Books,

Spurling, H. (2000). *La grande Therese: The greatest scandal of the century*. New York: HarperCollins.

Stagner, R. (1959). The gullibility of personnel managers. *Personnel Management, 41*, 226–230.

Stanovich, K.E. (1999). *Who is rational? Studies of individual differences in reasoning*. Mahwah, NJ: Erlbaum.

Stowe, S. (2004, January, 23). Police decline to open file on exonerated defendant. *New York Times*.

Thorndike, E. L. (1920). Intelligence and its uses. *Harper's Magazine, 140*, 227–235.

Tuchman, B. (1984). *The march of folly: From Troy to Vietnam*. New York: Knopf.

Twachtman-Cullen, D. (1997). *A passion to believe: Autism and the facilitated communication phenomenon*. Boulder, CO: Westview Press.

Twain, M. (1907). *Christian Science*. New York: Harper.

Veblen, T. (1889). *The theory of the leisure class*. New York: Macmillan.

Vyse, S.A. (1997). *Believing in magic: The psychology of superstition*. New York: Oxford University Press.

Warner, G. (2000). Personal communication. Littleton, Colorado.

Weisberg, B. (2004). *Talking to the dead: Kate and Maggie Fox and the rise of spiritualism*. New York: HarperCollins.

Weissberg, R.P., & Greenberg, M.T. (1998). School and community competence-enhancement and prevention programs. In I.E. Sigel & A. Renninger (Eds.), *Handbook of child psychology (5th ed.). Vol. 4: Child psychology in practice* (pp. 878–954). New York: Wiley.

White, E. (2002). *Fast girls: Teenage tribes and the myth of the slut*. New York: Scribner.

Wills, G. (1987). *Reagan's America: Innocents at home*. New York: Doubleday

Wistrich, R.S. (1991). *Antisemitism: The longest hatred*. New York: Pantheon.

Wolfensberger, W.W. (1994). The "facilitated communication" craze as an instance of pathological science: The cold fusion of human services. In H.C. Shane (Ed.), *Facilitated communication: The clinical and social phenomenon* (pp. 57–122). San Diego: Singular Publishing.

Yamagishi, T. (2001). Trust as a form of social intelligence. In K.S. Cook (Ed.), *Trust in Society* (pp. 121–147). New York: Russell Sage Foundation.

Yamagishi, T., Kikuchi, M., & Kosugi, M. (1999). Trust, gullibility and social intelligence. *Asian Journal of Social Psychology, 2*, 145–161.

Zipes, J. (Ed.). (1992). *The complete fairy tales of the brothers Grimm*. New York: Bantam Books.

Zuckoff, M. (2006, May 15). The perfect mark: How a Massachusetts psychotherapist fell for a Nigerian e-mail scam. *New Yorker*, p. 6.

Zwerger, L. (Ed.). (1991). *Hans Christian Andersen's fairy tales*. New York: North-South Books.

Index

About the Author

STEPHEN GREENSPAN has a BA degree in political science from Johns Hopkins, an MA in history from Northwestern, a PhD in developmental psychology from the University of Rochester, and a postdoctoral certificate in developmental disabilities from UCLA. He has been a policy analyst for the U.S. Department of Commerce and for the Rochester (New York) Center for Governmental Research, a researcher and clinician for at-risk youth at Father Flanagan's Boys Town, a professor of developmental psychology at Vanderbilt and the University of Nebraska, and a forensic consultant in criminal cases. Dr. Greenspan retired from the University of Connecticut as emeritus professor of educational psychology. All of these diverse experiences were needed to write so wide-ranging a book as this.

For more than 30 years, Dr. Greenspan has studied the phenomenon of social incompetence—particularly low social intelligence—in children and adults. For the last 10 years, his interest has focused increasingly on a specific type of social intelligence failure: gullibility. Dr. Greenspan has nearly 100 scientific publications, and his several papers on gullibility have been very influential in bringing about a greater awareness among psychologists and other scholars of the importance of this relatively overlooked topic. Dr. Greenspan resides with his wife and two children in Colorado, where he is clinical professor of psychiatry at the University of Colorado. (Contact information at www.stephen-greenspan.com)